Unfinished
Business

By the same author

The Great Richmond Terminal (1970)
Edward Porter Alexander (1971)
A History of the Louisville and Nashville Railroad (1972)
Prisoners of Progress: American Industrial Cities,
    1850–1920 (1976)
The Life and Legend of Jay Gould (1986)
Union Pacific: The Birth, 1862–1893 (1987)
Union Pacific: The Rebirth, 1894–1969 (1990)

Unfinished Business

The Railroad in American Life

Maury Klein

University of Rhode Island

Published by University Press of New England
Hanover and London

University of Rhode Island
Published by University Press of New England,
   Hanover, NH 03755
© 1994 by Maury Klein
All rights reserved
Printed in the United States of America   5 4 3 2 1

UNIVERSITY PRESS OF NEW ENGLAND
publishes books under its own imprint and is the publisher for Brandeis University Press, Brown University Press, University of Connecticut, Dartmouth College, Middlebury College Press, University of New Hampshire, University of Rhode Island, Tufts University, University of Vermont, and Wesleyan University Press.

   Library of Congress Cataloging-in-Publication Data
Klein, Maury, 1939–
   Unfinished business : the railroad in American life
/ Maury Klein.
     p.   cm.
   Includes bibliographical references and index.
   ISBN 0–87451–657–9.
   1. Railroads—United States—History.   I. Title.
TF23.K54   1993
385'.0973—dc20   93–8112
∞

All photographs courtesy of the Union Pacific Railroad Museum, Omaha, Nebraska.

This book is dedicated to the three men who did more than anyone else to develop my love and respect for history:
Professor John L. Stipp of Knox College
Professor Bell I. Wiley of Emory University
Professor James Harvey Young of Emory University

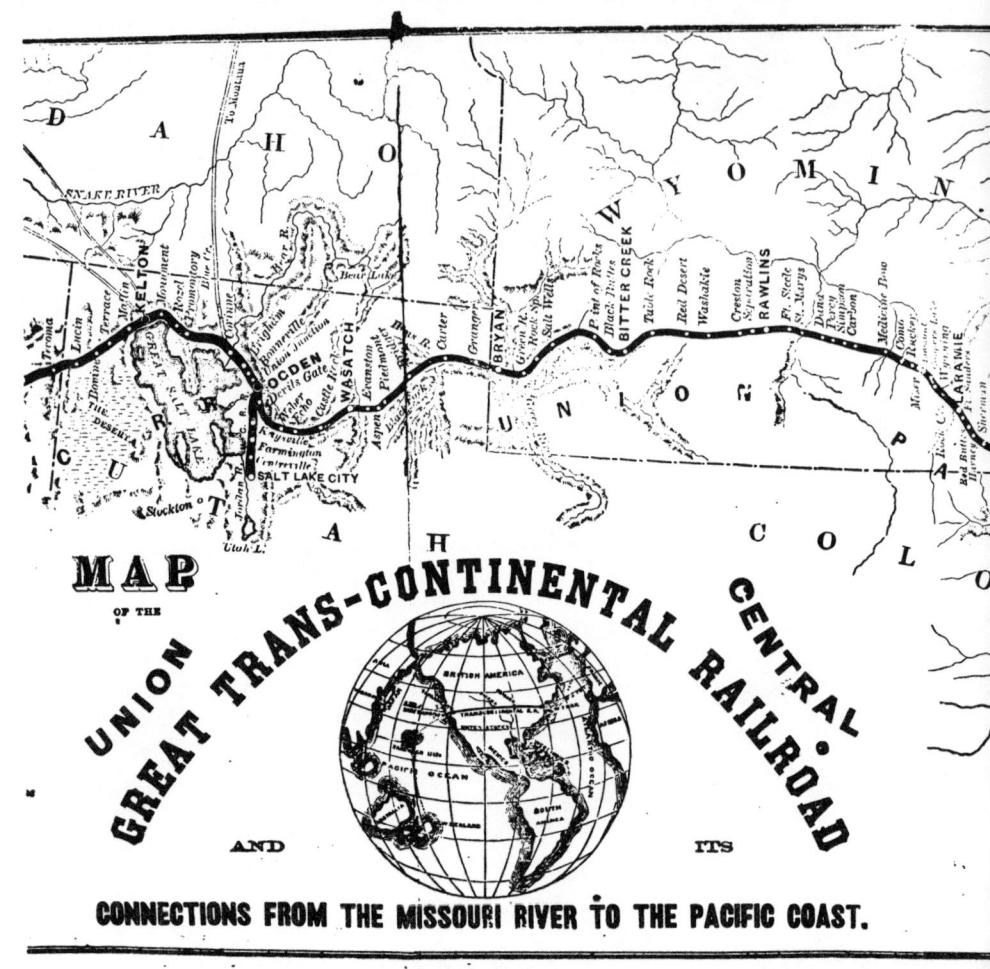

Contents

A Memoir by Way of Introduction;
or, How I Got Here from There   1

Patterns of Early American
Railroad Development   8

The Rise of the
Iron Horse   18

The Strategy of
Southern Railroads   31

Southern Railroad Leaders, 1865–1893:
Identities and Ideologies   48

The Overland Route:
First Impressions   68

In Search of
Jay Gould   83

The Man Who Saved
the Railroads   110

Competition and Regulation:
The Railroad Model   122

The Turning Point in
American Railroad History   135

Replacement Technology:
The Diesel as a Case Study   143

Contents

High-Speed Trains:
America's Lost Opportunity   155

The Unfinished Business of
American Railroad History   166

Notes   187

Bibliography of Articles and Papers   217

Index   219

Illustrations follow page 82

A Memoir by Way of Introduction; or, How I Got Here from There

This collection of essays and articles represents work done over a period of twenty-five years.[1] It includes scholarly articles, papers, pieces done for popular magazines or public occasions, and one new essay. What they all have at their center is a fascination with the role played by the railroad in American life. Together with some of my books, this work has branded me as a specialist in railroad history among historians and others interested in railroads. While flattering in its way, this was not a reputation I had ever sought or intended. Like many people, I found myself with a career I had never coveted or even known existed.

Life has a peculiar way of luring people through unmarked doors, drawing them ever inward and then locking the door behind them. Railroads had never been anything special in my life when I was young. They were something on which I traveled during a childhood that took me all over the United States before the age of fifteen. Even then we moved mostly by automobile, and trains had for me none of that mystical lure and haunting call to faraway places captured so eloquently by Thomas (not Tom) Wolfe and other writers. The romance of the rails was as unknown to me then as romance of any other kind.

Railroads entered my professional life not even through a side door but rather a trapdoor. I went to graduate school at Emory University hoping to become a professor so that I could support myself while I wrote—which is what I really wanted to do but didn't know how to go about earning a living at it. At Emory I fell under the tutelage of Bell I. Wiley, whose kindness and enthusiasm kindled my already keen interest in the Civil War. While groping about for a thesis topic, and trying to conceal how empty my mind was of suitable subjects, I remembered a board game I had played that replicated the battle of Gettysburg.

Talk about educational toys: the cardboard game pieces, representing individual army units, had taught me the names of the commanding officers on both sides. One name stuck in my head, reinforced by reading I had done in Wiley's course. Edward Porter Alexander seemed to me a fascinating character, an artillerist as eccentric as he was brilliant. Best of all, no one had done much work on his life. With Wiley's warm support I decided to do his biography as my dissertation.

By this cold, calculating, scientific process I came to a fateful decision on my professional future. It proved a happy choice. The Alexander family had bequeathed a rich lode of papers dating back to the late eighteenth century. Moreover, Alexander himself had left behind a detailed personal memoir in addition to his published *Military Memoir of a Confederate* (1907), a well-researched and objective study that said surprisingly little about his own role. I plunged happily into the thesis, convinced that the biography would become my first book as well.

What has all this to do with railroads? Simply this: Alexander lived a long and productive life. After the war, wasting no time mourning the Lost Cause, he drifted into railroading and became an officer in several southern roads. This obliged me to learn something about the railroads of the South as well as the particular lines Alexander served. To understand any of it, I had to acquire some grasp of the larger postwar southern economy and the role played by railroads in it. This seemed simple enough; how could I possibly have recognized the sound of a door opening?

In 1964 I got a position at the University of Rhode Island, and finished my thesis there that winter. During my second year, while I struggled to shape a very long thesis into a very short book, the history department brought to campus as a speaker Professor Arthur M. Johnson of the Harvard Business School. At lunch I found myself across the table from Arthur, and amid the chitchat mentioned how the Alexander biography had aroused my interest in southern railroads. He asked if I knew about the Newcomen Fellowship offered by the Business School. When I shook my head, he urged me to apply for it even though the deadline was only two or three weeks away. I rushed my materials to the Business School with little expectation of anything coming from it. To my astonishment, I got the fellowship.

Although I did not know it at the time, the year spent at the Harvard Business School had the effect of locking the door behind me. My office lay deep in the bowels of Baker Library, surrounded by a treasure trove of research materials on railroad history in which I was free to roam daily. I shared the office with Kozo Yamamura, a bright and affable economist then at San Diego State, who did much to reduce my innocence of economics and statistics. Arthur Johnson and another faculty member, James P. Baughman, opened my eyes not only to business history but to a wide array of research possibilities of which I had known nothing. By the year's end Kozo and I had written an article that later won a prize, and I completed most of the research on a history of the Richmond Terminal, my first foray into the world of railroads.

The Richmond Terminal was an early holding company that swept together a motley assortment of southern railroads, including those managed by Alexander. In studying his career I had become intrigued not only by the complexity of this strange company but also by the cast of characters that inhabited it. Biography appealed to me because character study has always been a passion of mine, and the Terminal offered a wonderful gallery of contrasting types. While at the Harvard Business School, I decided not only to learn the southern railroad scene but also to attempt a different kind of book on the Terminal—one that illuminated the human dimension of decision making. Two major articles flowed from this effort in addition to the one coauthored with Kozo; both are reprinted here.

In this convoluted way I came to a basic understanding of what mattered to me in history. I had originally majored in the subject for a very practical if simplistic reason: it seemed to me that you could talk about almost anything in a history course, which made it hard to get bored with your subject. My nomadic childhood had taken me to nearly every region of the United States and left me with an insatiable desire to understand what lay at the heart of so diverse and complex a culture. Unlike most people I had no roots in the usual sense, no particular state or place to call home; I was a citizen in transit, and that gave me a different perspective on American history.

Through a fluke of production schedules, the book on the Richmond Terminal was the second one written but the first one published. While puzzling over what to do next, I received a call from Thomas B. Brewer inviting me to discuss the possibility of doing a book for a new series on American railroads to be published by Macmillan. Shortly afterward I met with Tom and Richard C. Overton in New York and agreed to write a history of the Louisville & Nashville for the series. The project made sense to me in a strange sort of way. After all, I had two vague connections with the L & N: my mother's family came from just outside of Louisville and I had spent part of my childhood there. Moreover, Alexander had served a stint as vice president of the road.

These projects overlapped and fed each other in important ways. The Richmond Terminal book appeared in 1970, the Alexander biography in 1971, and the Louisville & Nashville history in 1972. Suddenly I found myself at age 33 categorized as a specialist in railroad history: invited to review books on railroads and give papers on railroad history, consulted by other scholars working in the field, and solicited by rail buffs for information on subjects that utterly mystified me. Only then did two fundamental truths dawn on me: the historical profession was as unrelenting as medicine or law in pigeonholing its practitioners as specialists, and the particular specialty of railroad historian exposed its practitioners to two very different constituencies, the history buff and the rail fan.

This was not at all what I had in mind. My interest in railroads began as (and remains) a fascination with their role in the business and social development of the nation. I was interested in them as organizations, not as machines. Never did I acquire the rail mystique, that rapture for smoke and engines relished by those a colleague once called the "hoot, toot, and whistle boys." While I appreciated and admired the enthusiasm of friends who joyously snapped pictures of passing trains and earnestly debated the merits of this locomotive versus that one, I never caught the fever. They stroked and fondled dormant engines lovingly like giant pets; I admired their power and performance but regarded them as ugly, dirty, smelly beasts on whose smoke I gagged. Here was a cultural rift that, needless to say, I was careful to keep to myself when in the company of the faithful.

A Memoir by Way of Introduction

To me railroads were engines of social, technological, and economic change. They remade the landscape of America in every sense of the word, just as the automobile did in this century. More important, they were for me a window into the broader role of business in American life. My passion was to learn about American life and culture; since business lay at the heart of that culture, it seemed crucial to know as much about business as possible. Railroads provided many instructive lessons in that regard, and my interest in them was always a means to that end.

But these notions did not fit easily into the pigeonholes that define our professional lives. Somehow I had managed to acquire not one but two mistaken identities: as devoted historian of railroads and as rail enthusiast. Nothing seemed to shake this impression. I did a book on urbanization and industrialization, *Prisoners of Progress: American Industrial Cities, 1850–1920* (coauthored by Harvey A. Kantor, 1976), that remains one of my favorite if least appreciated pieces of work. My biography of Jay Gould, *The Life and Legend of Jay Gould* (1986), received widespread attention but changed nothing because so much of Gould's career had revolved around railroads that the book seemed like a natural extension of my "expertise" in railroads.

I completed the draft of the Gould biography in 1982. Finally it was finished, I thought, this tie to railroads, this false identity. Surely now I could get on with my other interests. Then the phone rang again.

This time the call came from people at the Union Pacific Corporation, who were interested in having a history of their railroad written. This was an opportunity difficult to ignore; after all, what railroad has had more impact on American life than the Union Pacific? After some of the most pleasant negotiations in my experience I made them an offer I thought they would refuse—but they did not. As a result I devoted most of the 1980s to researching and writing a study of the Union Pacific that was published in two volumes (1987 and 1990). The experience was a wonderful one and the people involved could not have been more cooperative. I was grateful for the chance to have done the project, but it deepened more than ever the imprint of both of my mistaken identities.

The Union Pacific project also awakened in me an interest in E. H. Harriman, whose biography I have recently completed. This work too kept me in the world of railroads, as did a succession of papers I was invited to give here and in Europe. These papers are reprinted in this volume and have not appeared before in this country. Neither has the final essay, which was written especially for this volume.

This tale is in no way meant to be a complaint. The study of railroads has been good to me and for me, and I hope I have been good for it. Rather it is an explanation of what my work was about, and an apology to those who expected something more or something different from it. Those colleagues who believed ardently that no railroad history was complete without a roster of the company's power and/or rolling stock should now understand why I did not share their world view. Rail enthusiasts, whom I regard as a remarkable breed for their depth of knowledge, should now realize why my eyes glazed over when they invoked certain topics of which I was staggeringly ignorant.

It should also be clear that I regard this collection of essays as a sort of valediction to railroad history. The time is long past due for me to get on with a variety of other projects centered on American life and culture. There remains on my list only one piece of unfinished railroad business: a broad interpretive history of the American railroad experience. I hope to take up that project in earnest one of these days, and when it is done I will bid a fond but final farewell to railroad history. Really. I mean it this time.

The essays in this volume are arranged not in chronological but in rough topical order. The first is perhaps the broadest overview and therefore serves as a convenient introduction to more specialized pieces on regional lines and on my two favorite rail entrepreneurs, Jay Gould and E. H. Harriman. The final four essays all attempt broad interpretations of key aspects of railroad history. In each case I tried to emphasize elements of that history that seemed to be ignored or neglected by scholars.

There is a simple explanation for the large gaps in the chronology of output of these pieces. During most of the 1970s and 1980s I was simply too busy doing books to write articles. Unlike many scholars, I never took the time to extract articles from works in progress—although I have done my share of recycling in other ways. I have always regarded papers and popular articles as forums for exploring ideas that intrigued me. This belief made me less concerned with the scholarly impedimenta attached to the papers than with developing the line of thought. Since papers are meant to be read, the lack of documentation seemed less important than it might when they appear in print.

One final word of explanation on the essays seems necessary. The republication of past work offers an opportunity to update it in the light of more recent scholarship. I have resisted this temptation for several reasons. If these pieces offer a retrospective on my accidental career in railroad history, they ought to remain in their original form to reflect my thinking at the time they were written. Some errors that crept into them were corrected in later work. As to consistency, I prefer to let the reader see firsthand how a historian changes his mind about a subject on further study rather than pretend that I had it right all along.

Artists have long been in the habit of revising old work, often several times, until they got it in a form that satisfied them. But in music, for example, whichever version of a work ultimately wins the public favor, serious listeners and students want to hear each version unto itself and often prefer earlier versions to later ones. So it should be with scholars. It is in the nature of what we do to rethink our work and our views on any subject, but the better way to show these changed perspectives is through new work that is separate and distinct from its forebears. As a friend of mine once said, we owe at least that much to our biographers.

Narragansett, Rhode Island M.K.
January 28, 1993

Patterns of Early American Railroad Development

> This paper was given at an interdisciplinary conference on the impact of railroads held at the Zentralinstitut, Erlangen, Germany in 1992. As with most papers, it was necessary to condense large ideas into a small space. I used the occasion to put down in skeletal form my outline of how American railroad history developed. In the spring of 1993 the paper was published with the other proceedings of the conference in Germany.

One concept is crucial to understanding the American railroad experience: it has not one but two distinct pioneering eras of development, each with its own context and its own effects on the economic and social environment. In this brief essay I want to sketch these two contexts and compare their impact on the spaces they influenced.

The first era ran from 1830 to 1860 and involved the region between the Atlantic seaboard and the Mississippi River, a distance by rail of nearly 1,056 miles. The second extended from 1865 to 1890 and embraced the region from the Mississippi River to the Pacific coast, a distance by rail of 2,263 miles.

The differences in time and circumstances between these two phases are decisive in explaining their effects on every aspect of development. What separates them is the American Civil War, the outcome of which radically altered the economic and political landscape.

Patterns of Early American Railroad Development

The first phase took place in regions that were already settled and clustered around sea and river ports. The extensive river system in the eastern United States enabled settlers to move upland but not penetrate the interior. The Mississippi River provided a main interior artery for north-south settlement and commerce, but no major river breached the Appalachian Mountain barrier running from New England to Georgia. While the Erie Canal helped draw some east-west traffic over the Great Lakes and down the Hudson River, geography directed the early commerce of the United States along north-south lines via river and coastal shipping.

But ambition sent hardy pioneers streaming westward to transform unclaimed lands into new farms, villages, towns, and states. As the Old Northwest grew, it helped create thriving but remote and isolated centers of agricultural and business activity. During this first era the nation possessed a local economy dominated by merchant capitalists eager to build up the commerce of their city or town at the expense of rivals. The obvious way to do this was to capture the trade of the expanding hinterland.

Thus it was that most early railroads in the United States, like the canals and turnpikes before them, were built to serve local needs and snatch traffic from rival towns. The Boston & Worcester Railroad, for example, sought to divert trade that went to Providence via the Blackstone Canal. Most were built with local capital to provide local transportation for merchants and farmers and were therefore short lines between already established towns. These roads tended to be well built and emphasized passenger traffic over freight. Most of the larger, more grandiose projects of this era fell victim to high costs, inadequate support, and a technology too primitive to serve these more ambitious visions.

The railroads proved a potent weapon in the race for commercial supremacy and shifted the balance of power among rival seaboard cities. Those with large hinterlands that could be tapped by laying rails, like New York, Baltimore, and Boston, prospered; those lacking such outlets, like the island city of Newport, Rhode Island, saw their commercial importance dwindle. When representatives of the fledgling Pennsylvania Railroad asked the city of Philadelphia to invest in the project in 1846, they stressed exactly this point in language that would echo through the century:

No one can shut his eyes to the fact that the enterprise involves . . . the future prospects of Philadelphia. The trade of this city, already retarded by improvements on the North and South, will be so curtailed by the Baltimore and Ohio Railroad at Pittsburgh, and the completion of the railway from New York to Lake Erie, as to . . . impoverish the city and state. . . . On the other hand, we have the means, by furnishing the nearest and best route to and from the West, of securing an unexampled prosperity to this city.[1]

By the 1850s these aspirations had moved beyond local emphasis on short-haul transportation to more ambitious projects seeking to tap distant markets. The larger these ambitions grew, the more they overwhelmed private sources of capital. Several states provided subsidies in forms ranging from bonds to tax relief to land grants to purchases of stock in the enterprise. These and other concessions were often embedded in special charters granted the railroads, which as the largest enterprises of their age required a favorable legal and political environment in which to thrive. By the 1850s, too, rail technology had improved greatly and the telegraph had emerged as a prime instrument of communication for the railroad and the larger society.

The result was an explosion of railroad expansion and integration as new lines stretched deeper into the seemingly endless American hinterland. Boston, New York, and even Portland, Maine, sought to position themselves as the key outlets for great through routes to the West, as did Philadelphia, Baltimore, and Wilmington farther south. The Pennsylvania Railroad breached the Allegheny Mountains to reach Pittsburgh and forge the most profitable rail line in the nation. In New York, Erastus Corning negotiated the merger of fourteen local lines into one through route between Albany and Buffalo which took the name New York Central. At the same time (1853) two other companies built connecting lines from Buffalo to a once remote trading outpost destined to become the rail capital of the nation, Chicago.[2]

Chicago's sudden emergence mirrored the effects of rail expansion. In 1850 Chicago had but one railroad extending from it; a decade later it had fifteen with over a hundred daily trains. By 1860 it had also become the greatest wheat depot in the world. The north-south journey from Chicago to Springfield (the state capital) had been shortened from a three-day ordeal by stagecoach to twelve hours by train.

Chicago flourished because in the Old Northwest the railroad mania took the form of a virulent fever. Total trackage jumped from 1,300 miles in 1850 to 11,000 miles in 1860. The federal government extended its first land grant to help construct the Illinois Central, a rare north-south line that paralleled the Mississippi River for the entire length of the state of Illinois. Completed in 1856, the 705-mile road was the longest in the world.

The success of the Illinois Central illuminated one striking effect of the growing rail system: instead of merely serving as connectors between navigable bodies of water as originally conceived, railroads were replacing them as the preferred form of transport. In 1856 the first railroad bridge was thrown across the Mississippi River—a harbinger of expansion to come. St. Louis, the most important steamboat city on that river, emerged as a rail center second only to Chicago.

By 1860 the United States possessed 30,626 miles of track, an increase of 239 percent in one decade. As the nation stood on the brink of a crisis that would culminate in civil war, it was clear that the railroad had wrought some spectacular effects in only thirty years. It had emerged not only as the preferred form of transportation but also as the chief weapon of commercial rivalry. This belief in the railroad as the source of riches or ruin gave cities and towns a parochial view that prevented any integration of the rail network. Different lines entering the same city were rarely allowed to connect, forcing freight to break bulk and passengers to change terminals to continue their journey. None of the six roads entering Richmond, Virginia, for example, connected with each other. Nor could lines easily make physical connection because they employed different gauges. Of the 351 railroad companies in the United States and Canada in 1861, only 210 or 53 percent utilized what later became standard gauge. The rest used six other gauge sizes.

Obviously the railroad had a decisive effect on regions where space and distance were the greatest obstacles to overcome. Distant markets were connected to seaboard outlets, spurring the growth of new towns and creating major cities such as Atlanta where none had existed. Railroads also stimulated economic growth as the largest consumers of iron, lumber, and other products, thereby spurring industries to which they gave an additional boost of lower transportation costs. Railroads were pivotal in the energy revolution of the nineteenth century. They provided access to remote coal-mining regions and then spread the use of coal by carrying it in quantity at cheap rates. As Albro Martin has said, "coal made railroads necessary, and the railroads made the use of coal possible."[3]

The pattern of rail development during this early period had a momentous if unintentional political effect. Since most American roads ran east to west, the bonds of trade and commerce were increasingly forged in that direction. During the 1850s the flow of trade in the interior began shifting from its traditional north-south river route to new east-west rail routes reaching eastern seaboard outlets. As one astute political observer noted in 1854:

> Time is working a phenomenon on the Mississippi River. . . .There is a West growing with a rapidity that has no parallel [and] the railroads that are being constructed . . . are to take the corn, pork, beef, &c, &c, to a northern instead of southern markets.[4]

Nor was this all. Railroads enabled the Old Northwest to grow with a rapidity that by 1860 made it the decisive weight in the delicate political balance between the northern free states and the southern slave states. The slavery issue had been a growing political cancer since 1820, and the sectional conflict it spawned reached fruition in 1860 when, for the first time, a western man was elected president on a platform dedicated to keeping slavery out of the western territories that were not yet states.

Seen in this light, the American Civil War may be viewed as an accidental byproduct of the development fostered by the pattern of railroad construction along lines that forged closer social and economic bonds between the North and Northwest than between either of them and the South. Similarly, the lack of efficient transportation links between North and South aggravated their mutual sense of isolation and separateness. Two radically different civilizations had evolved and come into conflict, thanks in part to an isolation that deprived them of much firsthand experience with each other and allowed them to hold crude stereotypes of each other's character and institutions.

Northern victory in the Civil War ushered in a second and more spectacular pioneering era of American railroads that would not have been possible under the social and political conditions existing in 1860. The war rid the country of the curse of slavery and with it the explosive political issue that had done so much to block development of the West beyond the Mississippi River. The secession of the southern states in 1861 left Congress for the first time in the control of a political party (the Republicans) devoted to commercial and industrial expansion as well as rapid settlement. In short order Congress responded with acts to aid construction of a Pacific railroad, a Homestead Act, a National Banking act, and a new tariff act.

Put simply, the North's victory opened the West to conquest and exploitation, and the railroad emerged as the primary instrument of development to a far greater degree than it had during the first pioneer era. The scale of construction and number of lines dwarfed the earlier period. Most of the capital was obtained from distant rather than local sources—much of it from Europe. Western railroads were built largely ahead of demand with the avowed purpose of creating settlement and development where none existed. They were more flimsy of construction because the object was to get a road operating quickly and improve it later when enough business developed to warrant it.

Where the first era constructed local lines and then combined them into longer routes, the later period built trunk lines first and added feeder systems for development later. Western roads covered much longer distances over much harsher terrain and obstacles ranging from Indian attacks to fierce weather. Yet so well did they succeed at this task that by 1890 the American rail network totaled 166,703 miles compared to 30,626 miles in 1860, an increase of 544 percent.

To appreciate the effect of the railroad on this region, consider what the West was prior to 1865. Since the 1820s it had been known as the Great American Desert: a vast, desolate terrain lacking those twin pillars of eastern settlement, plentiful water and timber. Settlers found it so hostile that they trudged hundreds of miles past it to settle Oregon and California rather than try their luck on the Great Plains. Large tracts of the land were given to eastern Indian tribes uprooted by war on the assumption that white men would never want to live there. Nor was it easy to move goods. In 1860 it required 12,000 men, 8,000 mules, 68,000 oxen and 6,900 wagons to haul 18,000 tons of freight across the Great American Desert.[5]

Consider also the vast distances involved. The overland stage route from St. Louis on the Mississippi River to San Francisco required a trek of 2,189 miles and took thirty days to cross a plain so vast it seemed like an inland sea, two formidable mountain ranges, and at least one desert. The trip by sea via the malaria-infested Isthmus route took 35 days to cover 5,250 miles. To eyes that had seen it and imaginations that had not, the West seemed as remote as the moon. Indeed, the building of the first transcontinental railroad was to that generation what the moon project was to ours—the planting of a first tentative foot in unknown space.

Except for the Indians and the isolated Mormon colony in Utah, there was no economy. The only white men who inhabited this country were some hunters, trappers, and a few miners who could do nothing on a large scale without heavy equipment and access to markets. It is little exaggeration to say that the railroad itself *was* the first economy of the West, and no exaggeration to say that the railroad created and shaped the early economy of the West.

The key to this transformation was the construction of the transcontinental railroad. The first of these roads, the combined Union Pacific–Central Pacific, offers a striking example of the forces described earlier. Since 1840 there had been agitation to build a railroad across the continent linking the isolated Pacific coast states with the other states. Surveys undertaken by the federal government during the 1850s outlined five feasible routes between the Missouri River and the Pacific coast, but the issue got caught up in the sectional struggle. Both the North and the South wanted the first road built on its soil, and every bill to charter such a road was blocked in Congress. Once the South seceded, however, the Pacific railroad bill sailed through Congress.

Despite incredible physical obstacles, the first transcontinental road was completed in 1869. Twenty years later there were six transcontinental roads, with several more on the way. These first transcontinental roads literally created a new world. They penetrated a wondrous terra incognita and forged a corridor of civilization along which, to the minds of most Americans, the engines of progress and development would work their wonders. To sketch that world even briefly is to catch a glimpse of the decisive effects wrought by the railroad on this huge space that became the American heartland. In one generation the Great American Desert became one of the great bread baskets of the world.

Most obviously the Pacific railroads insured the defeat of the Indians and the conquest of their lands. As tracks for each project were laid, new towns and settlements arose in their wake, triggering real estate speculation and development in many forms. Telegraph wires paralleled the tracks, connecting the once isolated West to the rest of the nation. The major new industries that arose—cattle, farming, extractive mining, lumber—owed their existence on a large scale to the access railroads gave them to distant markets. The rise of the cattle kingdom illustrates this pattern clearly. The railroad enabled more cattle to spread across marginal lands, and large shipments of cattle eastward by rail fostered the rise of giant packing complexes in cities like Chicago and Kansas City. Every new transcontinental road had this same effect of opening vast new stretches of land to development and connecting its products to distant markets.

The result was an economic revolution with four major characteristics. Most obviously there occurred a dramatic rise in output of goods. With this increase in productivity came a steady decline in prices of all goods; the period 1865–1897 remains the longest unbroken era of deflation in American history. Third, national markets were created where none had existed before and on a scale never before imagined. Finally, there was an irresistible tendency toward economic specialization on an unprecedented scale.

Agriculture no less than industry underwent this process. The rise of large-scale staple crop farming on the Great Plains, for example, forced eastern farmers to shift away from these commodities to other crops. Chicago emerged as the meat-packing capital of the nation, Minneapolis as its milling center. Whole trains of fruits and vegetables crossed the continent from California along with endless carloads of lumber from the Northwest, ores from the Rocky Mountains and Montana, cattle from the Southwest, wheat from the plains states.

None of this could have happened without the railroads. Their presence or absence literally defined the map of the West. Cities flourished and towns rose where tracks went, withered away or were stillborn where they didn't go. Large cities like Birmingham, Alabama, sprang up from nothing by the accident of being located at strategic points or atop deposits of valuable raw materials. Not only cities but towns of all sizes developed specialized economies. Specialized towns existed elsewhere before the railroad, but never in such number over such distances as integral parts of one national economy. As Albro Martin observed, "The railroads made small-town America."[6]

The presence of the railroad in these towns made it a potent force in the local economy. For many Americans, working for the railroad was a status so desirable that sons eagerly followed their fathers into the trade. On a broader scale the American iron and steel industry owed its vigorous growth to the railroad's demand for its products. Foundries, machinery, and other industries also thrived. The western roads opened new sources of coal and made it available at low cost, a vital factor in the economy of a region starved for timber. Even that staple crop of the Old South, cotton, experienced a revival as the railroad transformed its delivery to market and the marketing of textiles to distant cities and towns.

The railroad brought to shops and stores across the continent a variety of goods never before possible at low prices. It also made possible the rise of the mail order business pioneered by Montgomery Ward and

Sears, Roebuck, which revolutionized rural merchandising. Just as Sears made severe inroads on the business of local stores, so did a host of other processors and manufacturers utilize the railroad to capture markets on a grand scale. The advent of the refrigerator car enabled giant packing complexes like those of Swift and Armour to undercut local butchers. The brand-name revolution, with products ranging from Quaker Oats to Ivory Soap, was made possible by the ability to distribute these goods over the breadth of the country.

All these changes took place in a political and legal environment that was remarkably encouraging and free of restraints. Indeed, the United States in the late nineteenth century may have been the ideal hothouse for the rapid flowering of a private economy. Government did a little to help and, more important, even less to hinder this explosion of entrepreneurial energy.

The American system was the most open one in the world in terms of maximizing individual decision making. The one constant, observed J. Willard Hurst, "was the theme of resort to law to enlarge the options open to private individual and group energy."[7] This approach resulted in the rise of large corporations, a business form which the railroads of necessity employed to a greater degree than any other industry. During the period 1865–1890 railroads were synonymous with large corporations and all the abuses that attended their rise to a dominant position in American business. They became pioneers not only in the forms and techniques of big business but also in profoundly reshaping the political and legal environment to fit an economic system dominated by large corporations.

The need of railroads for special charters and other legislation led to their deep involvement in politics, and politicians were not slow to involve themselves in railroads. In many state legislatures railroad interests became the most potent force seeking favorable laws or, more often, killing hostile ones. In time the public reacted to this political domination with movements to regulate railroads, curb the powers of large corporations, and check corruption. It was no accident that railroads were the first industry subjected to federal regulation and thus became the model for a practice that would not become widespread until the twentieth century.

The railroads also forced a radical redefinition and updating of American law, both state and federal. A new and highly paid creature, the corporation lawyer, sprang into existence during these years to protect the railroad from the vagaries of a legal system grounded in a world that was fast becoming obsolete. The presence of large corporations and the struggle for national markets forced a rethinking of the laws governing restraint of trade, corporate charters, contracts, damages, bankruptcy, and property rights among others. The Supreme Court, bewildered by the dilemma of how to define the corporation legally, finally declared it to be a person under the Fourteenth Amendment and therefore entitled to the same privileges and protections. The efforts of the states and then the federal government to regulate railroad rates created a legal labyrinth of maddening complexity that endured well into this century.

This second pioneering era of American railroads left a deep and enduring imprint. It defined the nature of relations between government and the transport industries for a century to come. It provided models that would later be utilized by other industries in such keys areas as capital mobilization, corporate organization, accounting, and labor relations.

Perhaps more important, it bound together a huge, sprawling nation into a national market that in time would grow more homogeneous through the spread of standardized products, reading matter, cultural activities, and ease of travel. This fostering of economic and social homogeneity may be its single most important byproduct, for it helped nourish a sense of nationality that had surprisingly weak roots prior to the Civil War. In that sense the one supreme effect of the railroads may have been their role in literally making the United States a nation.

The Rise of the Iron Horse

> This piece, written for the popular history magazine *American History Illustrated* in 1975, gave me an early opportunity to summarize the influence of the railroad on American life. At the time I thought it was something of a farewell to a subject on which, it turned out, I had barely scratched the surface.

Sooner or later every age finds a symbol which best expresses the essence of its character to later generations. For Medieval Europe it was the great cathedrals, for modern times the harnessing of atomic energy. Henry Adams, thunderstruck by his visit to the great Paris Exposition of 1900, saw the spirit of his age mirrored in the dynamo. "Among the thousand symbols of ultimate energy, the dynamo was not so human as some," he wrote, "but it was the most expressive." With his usual keen perception Adams was looking toward the new century, not backward at the one just closed. Those earlier generations, the builders of industrial America, already had a potent symbol for their times: the locomotive.

To 19th-century Americans the locomotive was a wondrous machine, one which fired the loftiest visions of their private and national destinies. Its raw power enchanted starry-eyed dreamers and hard-nosed businessmen alike. Daniel Webster declared flatly in 1847 that the railroad "towers above all other inventions of this or the preceding age." In a more poetic vein Walt Whitman celebrated this new force in his "Passage to India" (1868):

The Rise of the Iron Horse

> I see over my own continent the Pacific railroad
>   surmounting every barrier,
> I see continual trains of cars winding along the
>   Platte carrying freight and passengers,
> I hear the locomotives rushing and roaring, and the
>   shrill steam-whistle,
> I hear the echoes reverberate through the grandest
>   scenery in the world. . . .

From its first appearance the locomotive captured the imaginations of Americans from every walk of life. Other mechanical marvels impressed, even inspired them, but none touched them more deeply. The steam engine revolutionized the process of manufacturing, but its appearance in the factory lacked the dramatic thrust of its presence upon bands of steel that spanned a vast continent. To a people overwhelmed by the sheer spaciousness of their realm, the railroad opened new opportunities which even dreamers of an earlier age could not have conceived. The steamboat had conquered the waters of America but could not penetrate the great landlocked interior. The telegraph, too, bridged enormous distances, but its frail wire moved only information, not goods and people.

The coming of the railroad swept all rival forms of land transportation from its path. Trains routinized the shipment of goods, materials, and people. On regular schedules they hauled larger volumes of more kinds of items at greater speeds than any other method of transport. By lowering the cost of inland transportation they rendered distant markets not only physically accessible but economically feasible. Within half a century the rail system became the lifeline of an industrial society, a network of steel tentacles pushing into every corner of the Republic.

But the railroads were more than just reliable transportation. They became a prime market for other major industries, notably iron and steel, coal, lumber, and heavy machinery. A host of related industries owed their growth to the railroads' constant need for equipment and supplies. And they were the nation's first big business. Railroad corporations pioneered in new methods of finance and new forms of organization. Their complex, far-flung operations required elaborate administrative structures, professional managers, more sophisticated accounting, and other business techniques. In these and other areas the railroads provided blueprints for corporate operation that other industries drew upon as they, too, expanded.

Modern patterns of labor relations developed first on the railroads with their large and sprawling labor forces. The railroads were the first major industry to be unionized and the first to be regulated by government. As the first giant corporations they introduced Americans to the whole panoply of problems wrought by unrestrained big business. They became the model upon which giant corporate enterprise in America was fashioned. In the process they rearranged the nation's economic geography, trained several generations of businessmen and financiers, and laid the foundation for many of the 19th century's great fortunes.

No account of the railroad's impact writ large can convey its force as a symbol of industrial progress for individual Americans. It opened new markets for merchants, new farmlands for settlers, new sources of profit for financiers, new jobs for everyone from managers to day laborers, and new enterprises for those who grasped the railroad's need for goods and services of many kinds.

To cities and towns the presence of the iron horse was a harbinger of their commercial success or failure. Great cities like Atlanta and Birmingham literally rose from the wilderness while others stagnated or died aborning from neglect. Everywhere local bankers, merchants, promoters, and civic groups believed that the presence of the railroad could transform the sleepiest hamlet into a thriving metropolis. This passion to convert wilderness into wealth led men everywhere to share the enthusiasm of Colonel Sellers in Mark Twain's and Charles Dudley Warner's *The Gilded Age* (1873)—that "The whole country is opening up, all we want is capital to develop it. Slap down the rails and bring the land into market."

For rural folk the clang of the locomotive's bell evoked images of distant places to which the train might someday carry them. It was not only the excitement of strange cities that stirred them; it was the urge to seek new prospects, better lives than those at home. To many an ambitious farmboy the locomotive whistle wailing across the endless prairie was a call of destiny. It promised freedom, adventure, and new possibilities.

Not all Americans saw the locomotive as a benign symbol. Some took a darker view, interpreting the engine of progress as an engine of destruction that disrupted what sense of order there was in American life and warped social values by infecting men everywhere with a peculiarly virulent strain of restlessness and materialistic ambition. To these critics the locomotive became a metaphor for the price of industrial progress. Novelist Frank Norris gave this negative image vivid form in *The Octopus* (1901) when he described a speeding locomotive as "filling the air with the reek of hot oil, vomiting smoke and sparks; its enormous eye, cyclopean, red, throwing a glare far in advance; shooting by in a sudden crash of confused thunder; filling the night with the terrific clamor of its iron hoofs."

Where others saw power and majesty in the locomotive's awesome passage, Norris saw a brutal, inhuman force capable of wanton destruction. In hurtling towards its destination the locomotive smashes into a flock of sheep that have strayed onto the tracks. His description of the scene is graphic and unsparing:

It was a slaughter, a massacre of innocents. The iron monster has charged full into the midst, merciless, inexorable. To the right and left, all the width of the right of way, the little bodies had been flung; backs were snapped against the fence posts; brains knocked out. Caught in the barbs of the wire, wedged in, the bodies hung suspended. Underfoot it was terrible. The black blood, winking in the starlight, seeped down into the clinkers between the ties with a prolonged sucking murmur.

Whether a harbinger of progress or destruction, the locomotive dominated the American imagination between the Civil War and World War I. During those decades Americans built their rail system into the largest inland transportation network in the world. It was a prodigious feat of construction. In 1860 the United States possessed 30,626 miles of railway; that figure soared to 193,346 by 1900 and reached 252,845 in 1920.

Prior to the Civil War the nation had already constructed an impressive rail network east of the Mississippi River. On July 4, 1828, Charles Carroll, at 90 years old the last surviving signer of the Declaration of Independence, broke ground for America's first railroad, the Baltimore & Ohio. Within a few years new rail projects sprouted everywhere. Most prewar lines were built by local interests either to connect centers of trade (like the Boston & Albany) or to drain the commerce of an interior region into a port city (like the Central of Georgia or the Louisville & Nashville). The frenetic construction of the 1850's inaugurated a major shift in regional traffic flow from the north-south axis of the Ohio-Mississippi river system to the east-west axis of newly opened rail lines.

Geography helped dictate where the railroads went. Since America's primary river systems flowed north-south while the continental land mass ran east-west, the vast majority of railroads west of the Appalachian Mountains followed the latter axis. One striking exception, the Illinois Central, boldly paralleled the Mississippi River from Chicago and Dunleith to Cairo, Illinois, its two branches meeting in Centralia. Completed in 1856, the 700-mile line was the longest railroad in the world. The South had its own version in the Mobile & Ohio, which ran 483 miles from Columbus, Kentucky to Mobile, Alabama.

But the future lay to the west. The vision of spanning the continent with a connected rail line haunted Americans during the 1850's. Five different routes were surveyed between 1853 and 1855, but the project fell victim to the rancor of sectional politics. Even so the nation's rail system in 1860 traversed thirty-one states, including several beyond the Mississippi River. No less than eleven lines reached Chicago, while Ohio, Indiana, and Michigan alone constructed almost 4,800 miles of new track during the 1850's.

Impressive as this achievement was, it was but prelude to the expansion that followed the Civil War. During the half century after Appomattox new trackage seemed to explode across the national landscape like a prairie wildfire. This era of turbulent growth can be divided into three distinct, if overlapping, phases. First the railroads were constructed; then they were physically integrated; finally they were consolidated and regulated to curb excesses and abuses that arose during the first two phases. In curious fashion these three phases came together during the 1880's, a decade which marked a crucial turning point in the evolution of the American rail network.

The orgy of railroad construction after 1865, interrupted only by periodic panics and depressions, infected every region of the country. In the broad tier of industrializing states between New York and Illinois four dominant roads, the so-called "Trunk Lines," emerged: the Pennsylvania, New York Central, Erie, and Baltimore & Ohio. In their fight for supremacy the Trunk Lines confronted not only one another but a host of smaller lines on every flank, as well as new projects designed to parallel all or part of the giants in hopes of compelling them to buy the interlopers off at an inflated price. Savage rate wars, the steady stream of new lines, and rapidly changing economic conditions all inspired a vicious competition for the region's lucrative traffic.

In the South expansion had to await rehabilitation. The region's railroads, exhausted and ruined by wartime overuse and destruction, had first to be rebuilt. Determined local interests accomplished this task in an amazingly short time, while the turmoil of Reconstruction politics spurred ambitious new rail projects in every state. By the 1880's Southern railroad mileage was increasing at a faster rate than that of the North. There too the expansion of old lines and appearance of new ones spawned a bitter competition for the region's relatively sparse traffic.

West of the Mississippi a similar pattern prevailed. The long-awaited transcontinental link finally materialized in 1869 when the Union Pacific and Central Pacific, the first built largely by gangs of Irishmen and the latter by imported Chinese labor, linked tracks at Promontory Point, Utah amidst jubilant celebrations. The 1,780-mile line was a remarkable achievement, though one rocked by scandal, corruption, and several years of reconstruction on the hastily contrived original roadway. Yet within a single generation after the Civil War four more roads crossed the continent to reach the Pacific coast: the Northern Pacific and Great Northern to the north of the Union Pacific, and the Atchison, Topeka & Santa Fe and Southern Pacific to the south.

From the first the transcontinental roads found themselves locked in competitive struggles with each other and with a proliferation of smaller local roads. To this fray were added the powerful "Granger" roads which served the north central grain states: the Chicago, Burlington & Quincy; Chicago, Milwaukee & St. Paul; Chicago & North Western; and Chicago, Rock Island & Pacific. These four roads, each with its eastern terminal in Chicago, vied savagely for the grain traffic. Eventually competition and expansion brought them into conflict with the growing systems to the south and west.

The frenzy of construction and expansion reached its peak during the 1880's when more than 70,000 miles of new track were built. As major lines expanded and legions of smaller new roads appeared, the competitive struggle grew steadily worse in every section. Once isolated roads found their territory invaded on every flank and retaliated by building new lines or buying existing ones in adjacent territories. The result was to enlarge the battlefield and intensify the combat. Even the best managed roads were plunged into turmoil by the struggle, while poorer or less efficient lines grasped at every straw to capture business.

Growth alone could not create an efficient national rail system. The pre–Civil War rail network was not in any meaningful sense a "system" at all. The hodgepodge of gauges used in constructing early railroads (gauge meaning the width between the two rails) often prevented direct flow of traffic from one line to another. According to the *American Railway Times* of May 11, 1861, only about 53 percent of railroad mileage in the United States and Canada utilized the "standard" 4 foot 8½ inch gauge; the remainder used gauges ranging up to six feet.

In many cases early railroad promoters deliberately chose a different gauge than that used on neighboring lines. Having conceived of the railroad as a means for bringing trade and commerce to their town, they wanted traffic to stop there rather than pass through to another city. The fondest commercial hope of every town was to become a major terminus; the greatest fear was that it might become only a way station. Differences in gauge forced railroads to "break bulk" at the terminal town; it encouraged the flow of local traffic and hampered the flow of through traffic. For the same reasons a city might be reached by several different railroads, none of which physically connected with each other. Richmond affords a classic example. Six railroads entered the city in 1861, five of them built with standard gauge, yet none connected directly with the others.

The gauge differential was the most glaring obstacle to creating an integrated rail system, but there were other problems as well. Neither the Mississippi nor the Ohio rivers had been bridged, which meant that traffic stopped on one side and had to be hauled across by boat. The large number of railroad companies, each with its own running schedule, made coordination of trains and exchange of traffic an exercise that would have taxed the most skilled diplomat.

Rolling stock seldom operated beyond a company's own tracks because no system of car exchange existed and because local self-interest usually discouraged such practices. Nor had the techniques and technology of train control advanced far enough to expedite the flow of traffic over long distances. Even the clock worked against integration of service.

Most railroads operated on local or "sun" time, which varied from city to city. As John F. Stover has noted, "When it was noon in Chicago, it was 11:27 A.M. in Omaha, 11:50 in St. Louis, 12:09 P.M. in Louisville, 12:17 in Toledo, and 12:31 in Pittsburgh. In fact, in Pittsburgh there were six different times for the departure and arrival of trains."

Between 1860 and 1890 railroad companies shed their parochial attitudes and shifted their emphasis from maintaining isolated local lines to fashioning regional, even national systems. In the process they found means of overcoming every obstacle to the integration of American rail lines. During the 1870's the major rivers were bridged and cooperative "fast freight" lines organized to speed the flow of through traffic across the tracks of several companies. Most roads outside the South gradually adopted standard gauge, and in 1886 representatives of all the major Southern broad-gauge roads agreed to convert their tracks to standard width. In a colorful and dramatic effort, often attended by large crowds and capped by festivities, work gangs made the great conversion on May 31 and June 1. On the latter date the United States possessed for the first time what could be called a physically integrated rail network.

New switching, signaling, and other train control devices, the invention of the air brake and automatic coupler, the creation of elaborate car exchange systems, improved methods for handling through freight and traffic exchange, and a host of other innovations also appeared during the 1870's and 1880's. Even the crazy quilt of local times fell victim to progress in 1883 when the railroads adopted the standard time system which divided the nation into four time zones separated by the 75th, 90th, 105th and 120th meridians. Despite the grumbling of some who preferred to operate on "God's time—not Vanderbilt's," the new system won widespread public approval. In 1918 Congress officially adopted it for the nation.

The quest for integration went beyond physical and technological improvements. At the corporate level it was reflected in the tendency of strong railroads to swallow weaker ones until by 1906 seven major interest groups controlled nearly two-thirds of the country's railroad mileage. These groups and their principal roads are listed below along with the mileage controlled by each:

(1) Harriman roads (25,000 miles)—Union Pacific, Southern Pacific, and Illinois Central systems.

(2) Vanderbilt roads (22,000 miles)—New York Central and Chicago & North Western systems.
(3) Hill roads (21,000 miles)—Great Northern; Northern Pacific; and Chicago, Burlington & Quincy systems.
(4) Pennsylvania group (20,000 miles)—Pennsylvania, Baltimore & Ohio; Chesapeake & Ohio systems.
(5) Morgan roads (18,000 miles)—Erie and Southern Railway Company systems.
(6) Gould roads (17,000 miles)—Missouri Pacific and other southwestern systems.
(7) Rock Island group (15,000 miles)—Chicago, Rock Island & Pacific systems.

The trend toward consolidation arose largely in response to the bitter competition for business that characterized railroad activities everywhere. Burdened by overcapitalization (usually a legacy of financial buccaneering by those who built and ran the roads), plagued by depressions and business slumps, and threatened equally by rival roads and fast-changing economic conditions, railroad operators struggled desperately to impose order upon the chaos that was a way of life in their business. At first they tried to minimize competition through such cooperative agreements as pools, which apportioned traffic among competing roads. The more ambitious pools were large, formal organizations, some of which made their agreements public and some of which operated in secrecy. They achieved some success but lacked any standing in law and so could not enforce their rules satisfactorily. Ultimately they failed because the system, based upon gentlemen's agreements, was operated not by gentlemen but by ambitious (or desperate) corporations.

Eventually the stronger companies resorted to the simple premise that the most effective way to eliminate competition was to eliminate competitors. Through new construction, leases, and outright purchases they absorbed rival roads and enlarged their own into great interregional systems. The depression of 1893–97 plunged many important systems into bankruptcy and enabled more solvent interests to gain control over them. By this process the patchwork of small independent roads gave way to a handful of giant integrated systems. In the South one holding company, the Richmond Terminal, gained control of more than sixty separate railroad companies and nearly 8,900 miles of track, which made it the second largest system in the nation. But the Terminal soon collapsed from financial mismanagement, and its jumbled holdings were reorganized by J. P. Morgan into one new giant company, the Southern Railway Company.

Through these decades of frenzied growth, cutthroat competition, technological innovation, and consolidation the railroads incurred a legacy of public resentment which made them a central target of social and political reform. In fairness it could probably not have been otherwise even under the best of circumstances. The railroads were not only the most powerful corporations of the late 19th century, they were also the most visible agents of change. Because their impact upon American life was so far-reaching, they became natural targets for discontent among all classes of people.

This discontent sprang from deeper roots—the painful transition from an agrarian to an industrial society. In this transition it is easy to see why men funneled their resentments and frustrations into the railroads. The farmer could blame the railroad for his steadily declining fortunes. He was utterly dependent upon it for access to market and felt helpless to influence its behavior. He could (and did) attribute his economic distress to the railroad's high, fluctuating rates, classification policies, and other sinister practices. Merchants and businessmen, shippers of every calling, could likewise blame the road for their problems, especially when rebates, drawbacks, and other discriminatory practices gave one firm or group a competitive advantage over another.

Whole communities could hold the railroad responsible for their economic well-being, convinced that the structure of freight rates ultimately determined which towns would flourish as trade centers. If a community prospered, its success could be attributed to a strategic location, good transportation, energetic businessmen, wise civic leadership, and lots of "get up and go." But if a town declined or stagnated or never rose above the level of backwater whistlestop, city fathers were wont to place the blame squarely upon the railroad's discriminatory practices and conspiratorial policies. Shippers complained about high rates, consumers about high prices, and railroad workers about low wages and poor working conditions.

Another bill of complaint charged the railroads and their officers with venality, monopoly, and corrupt political influence. Here critics were on surer ground, for during the decades after Appomattox the railroads left a trail tainted with fraud, inflated construction costs, stock manipulations, rate discriminations, bribery, and political jobbery, to say nothing of incompetent management in some cases. Few roads escaped the tarbrush of unsavory practices which gave the Gilded Age its name.

The most notorious episodes were but the brightest stars in a crowded galaxy of abuses. In the South the scandals produced by Reconstruction politics checkered railway development in virtually every state. Northern entrepreneurs favored the false-front construction company device through which the promoters of a railroad milked their own companies for extra profits. Transcontinental lines seemed especially prone to this technique. The "Big Four" who built the Central Pacific— Collis P. Huntington, Leland Stanford, Charles Crocker, and Mark Hopkins—made themselves rich through their Contract and Finance Company. The Union Pacific produced the most infamous scandal of all, the Credit Mobilier, which tarnished the reputation of the nation's Vice President, a future President, and several prominent congressmen. Not until modern times did the stench of corruption again reach so high into the offices of national government.

Wall Street teemed with operators building their fortunes on stock manipulations in railroads. Few matched the audacity of Jay Gould, Jim Fisk, and Daniel Drew in their flamboyant war with Cornelius Vanderbilt in 1867 over the Erie Railroad. This brazen and prolonged struggle earned for the hapless Erie the sobriquet "The Scarlet Woman of Wall Street." But the titans were not alone in piling up plunder. Between 1865 and 1900 few roads escaped their own chapter of stock jobbing and financial manipulation. Most were left with bloated capital structures which even good earnings could not support; many slid into receivership and reorganization.

While Wall Street rang with the din of financial combat, the railroads fought their own competitive wars in which rate slashing and rebating were the chief weapons. These clashes, especially epidemic among the Trunk Lines and the Granger roads, unsettled rates and shipping everywhere. Though some shippers benefited from these disturbances in the short run, the constant disruption of business conditions antagonized everyone in the end. Neither manufacturers nor farmers could long abide wildly fluctuating rates and unsettled shipping schedules. To these disturbances were added the bitter and often violent rail strikes, the largest of which in 1877 and 1894 were crushed by troops.

The public response to this long parade of abuses was a swelling demand for regulation of the railroads. It began at the state level where, led by Illinois in 1871, laws were passed to curb discriminatory practices and in some cases to regulate rates. Several states, especially in the Midwest and South, established public railroad commissions for this purpose. These achieved some success but could not deal effectively with the railroads on an interstate basis. Moreover, the Supreme Court, which had originally ruled in favor of state regulatory efforts during the 1870's, reversed itself in the Wabash case of 1886 by holding that a state commission could not regulate shipment rates beyond its own borders.

At best state regulation achieved a disparate record, but railroads were in fact an interstate business for which only Congress could legislate satisfactorily. After lengthy hearings and much haggling Congress passed in 1887 the Interstate Commerce Act which, among other things, created a five-man Interstate Commerce Commission. Through this action the railroads became the first industry to be subjected to Federal regulation. Although the ICC floundered for years with inadequate powers against hostile Federal courts, the pattern for the future had been set. Later legislation, notably the Hepburn Act (1906) and Mann-Elkins Act (1910), strengthened the powers of the ICC, especially in the area of rate regulation.

Between 1900 and 1920 American railroads reached the zenith of their golden age. Having survived the era of turbid growth, fierce rate wars, and financial buccaneering, they emerged as an orderly, stable industry. Like other industries, they had brought order out of chaos through a process of consolidation and centralization. Unlike most other industries they had achieved that goal at the cost of incurring extensive public regulation. The colorful rail titans of the 19th century were dying off, to be replaced by managerial executives unknown to the public because they sat astride giant corporate bureaucracies.

In 1916 the American rail network reached over 254,000 miles, the highest figure it would ever attain. The following year saw America enter the war in Europe, and in 1918 the Wilson Administration took the unprecedented step of placing the railroad system under government control. For that brief spell the United States had what amounted to a nationalized rail system. When the war ended there was some sentiment to keep it that way, but the plan never gained enough support to receive serious consideration.

Shortly after the war ended the railroads were returned to their owners. However, Congress also passed the Transportation Act of 1920 which imposed the most stringent regulation thus far upon the railroads. The principles embodied in the act still endure as the basis for Federal railway legislation; its passage served as a harbinger of a new era for the railroads. The golden age of the locomotive was over. Ahead loomed the challenges of the automobile, the bus, the truck, and the airplane. No longer the dominant form of land transportation, the iron horse faced in the coming years a difficult struggle for survival. Unlike many other historical romances, the ending did not promise to be a happy one.

The Strategy of Southern Railroads

> This work appeared in the *American Historical Review* in 1968 and was one of three major articles spawned by my year at the Harvard Business School. Together they comprise my first fling at interpreting some aspect of railroad history. I believe these articles remain the standard interpretation of southern railroad history; at the time they represented a clear departure from past views on the subject. They also reveal my early interest in the patterns of railroad development, and my keen interest in the human element of decision-making at a time when econometrics was the fad of choice among many historians.

To contemporary observers and historians alike the amazing expansion of southern railroads after the Civil War seemed an economic miracle of the age. The wonder of it all lay not merely in rapid growth itself; northern and western railroads had extended themselves with no less alacrity. But expansion in the North derived from an already sizable and flourishing network that had grown considerably stronger during the war. The South, on the other hand, emerged from combat with its roads in ruins, the victims of systematic destruction and four years of unallayed wear. Where northern roads continued to grow the South had first to rebuild, and it faced the task shorn of most of the necessary resources for doing so. Capital was lacking, labor proved exceedingly scarce, and plant, tools, and equipment could be obtained only in the North or abroad. In addition, its shattered economy offered little hope of supporting the renovated lines for some time to come.[1]

Yet in less than thirty years the South more than tripled its railway mileage, and the worn, disconnected roads of 1865 were transformed into a cohesive network dominated by a handful of giant systems. The following figures trace the ratio of southern growth compared to the nation as a whole:[2]

Years	(A) South	(B) North	(C) Ratio of Growth
1860–70	.267	.915	.292
1870–80	.319	.882	.362
1880–90	.984	.750	1.312
1890–93	.080	.063	1.257

As the figures indicate, expansion proceeded at a rapid and highly uneven pace. It seems clear that both the tempo and nature of southern rail development changed significantly around 1880. Contemporary observers noted the shift, too, and ascribed it primarily to a growing trend toward consolidation.[3] Historians, on the other hand, have explained it in terms of a reviving southern economy and growing national prosperity, the emergence of a vigorous and ambitious new group of southern business leaders, an increasing interregional diffusion of capital, the growth of national markets, the heightened interest in railroad securities, and the effect of recurring business cycles during the late nineteenth century.

All of these factors contain important and perceptive elements of truth, but they tend to paint the broad canvas primarily from hindsight. Such a general picture of economic activity tells us little about the decision-making process that led to this end result. The importance of entrepreneurial decisions in shaping the economic environment has been well described by Alfred Marshall and Joseph Schumpeter, to say nothing of Adam Smith.[4] While much had been written about the general pattern of southern economic development, little effort has been made to relate it to decision-making activity.

The purpose of this article will be to trace the evolving strategy of southern railroad managers as they sought to cope with a rapidly changing economic environment. Strategy and entrepreneurial motivation are important because they illuminate the crucial question of resource (capital) allocation. They also offer insight into the equally important question of social versus private gains in an economy operating with fewer social restraints than exist today. The hope is that the analysis will suggest why the allocation of resources for one region proceeded as it did, and how the participants viewed social versus private gains.

For clarity it will be helpful to divide the period into two phases: the era of territorial expansion, 1865–1880; and the era of interterritorial expansion, 1880–1893. The division is somewhat arbitrary, and the dates will certainly not fit all roads with equal precision. It does, however, provide a useful conceptual framework for understanding the nature of expansion policy. This study will concentrate upon the more established roads whose origins antedate the war. Ten of these key roads comprise the nuclei of the major systems destined to dominate the South by 1893: the Richmond & Danville; East Tennessee, Virginia, & Georgia; Georgia; Central of Georgia; Louisville & Nashville; Nashville, Chattanooga, & St. Louis; Seaboard & Roanoke; Wilmington & Weldon; Norfolk & Western (Atlantic, Mississippi, & Ohio until 1881); and Savannah, Florida, & Western (Atlantic & Gulf until 1879).[5] As the oldest and ultimately most successful lines, these companies provide the continuity necessary for a study in strategy. They survived the entire period, confronted the major problems that arose, and formulated policies to deal with them.

The men who dominated southern railroads immediately after the war were for the most part the same group that had controlled them before 1860.[6] They belonged to the generation that had built the early railroads and represented powerful financial and commercial interests in the territory drained by the road, especially its key terminal city. Since their economic horizon rarely extended beyond that city or port, they assumed a naturally provincial attitude toward the road's function. They conceived it primarily as their most potent weapon in the growing commercial rivalry between leading southern ports and interior distributing centers. In formulating policy they sought to achieve three basic goals: long-term investment profit, localization of traffic at the principal terminus, and development of the economic resources of the region tributary to the road.[7]

From this localized perspective emerged the territorial concept that guided southern railroad policy making before and after the war. The road existed to service its key terminus and the region tributary to it. The welfare of city, territory, and company alike required that all concerned realize their mutually dependent relationship and the need to perpetuate it. Basic to this realization was the tenet of one road for one territory. The region drained by the road constituted its realm of control, much like a feudal barony, with boundaries determined by the line's terminals and connecting points. The description of western territorial strategy by Julius Grodinsky applies equally well to southern conditions:

To serve a territory with no railroad competition was the ambition of every railroad operator.... An exclusively controlled local territory, was a valuable asset, as long as it lasted. A monopoly of this kind was perhaps the most important strategic advantage of a railroad, provided, of course, the monopolized area either originated valuable traffic or served as a market for goods produced in other areas. Territory thus controlled was looked upon as "natural" territory. It belonged to the road that first reached the area. The construction of a line by a competitor was an "invasion." Such a construction, even by a business friend of the "possessing" road, was considered an unfriendly act. The former business friend became an enemy.[8]

In the antebellum period prevailing conditions nurtured territorial strategy. Competition within the skeletal southern network scarcely existed for through traffic and was virtually absent at the local level. The predominance of local traffic with its higher noncompetitive rate structure permitted many roads to achieve financial stability, retire part of their debt, and pay regular dividends. The strategy of stressing long-term goals by protecting the territory, constructing short feeder lines into yet untapped corners, maintaining the road by regularly plowing back earnings and paying dividends consistently had become both plausible and remunerative. The spurt of construction during the 1850's posed some threats to the territorial concept, but none serious enough to warrant rethinking of the strategy.[9]

Had the war not intervened, it might be supposed that continued construction would eventually have forced modification of the territorial strategy. The impact of the South's defeat, however, caused an immediate derangement in the economic environment. The cost of rehabilitation disrupted antebellum policies by burdening the roads with additional debt and thereby enlarging fixed costs. To service this extra financial load the roads would require more traffic at higher rates, but both proved difficult to obtain in the impoverished postwar South. The old reliance upon patient development of local traffic continued, but obviously could not provide immediate relief to pressing financial needs. For most managers the only feasible alternative lay in securing more through traffic to augment local income.

The desire for increased through traffic involved a host of problems. Unlike most local traffic, it brought distant and once neutral roads into fierce competition for an uncertain traffic at considerably lower and wildly fluctuating rates. Since through lines consisted of separate connecting roads, command of through traffic also demanded a high level of cooperation along the line. Competition for through tonnage could only be cutthroat and treacherous, and the returns extremely unstable. Most managers seemed reluctant to touch the problems involved, but economic circumstances forced a shift in strategy.[10] Traditional dependence upon local traffic would not do in the South's debilitated state. The fluctuation of crops in the overwhelmingly agricultural South further unsettled earning expectations, and later the advent of state railroad commissions helped depress both local and through rates. Under conditions that promoted uncertain traffic and steadily falling rates there seemed no feasible alternative but to adopt a policy stressing a heavy increase in tonnage carried.

The gradual shift in emphasis from local to through traffic constitutes the most significant factor in southern railway strategy. It would have a profound effect upon the development of large integrated systems, which evolved not from coherent planning but through a process of piecemeal expansion based upon momentary needs. It gave rise to the rapid expansion and consolidation movements characteristic of the 1870's and 1880's. The economic factors behind it affected policy decisions in virtually every company and often resulted in bitter fights for control. Perhaps most important, the financial difficulties created by its pursuit lay behind a change in profit motivation. In 1860 most southern railroad managers sought to realize profits through efficient operation of the property. By the late 1880's, however, the operation of most southern roads had ceased to be profitable.[11] The source of individual rewards lay instead in manipulation of the road's financial structure, usually to the detriment of the company.

In concrete terms the change in strategic thinking manifested itself most clearly in expansion policy. The need to assure stable through routes forced managers to reconsider the territorial concept. As an integral part of traditional policy they could not easily disavow it; nor did they wish to. In Schumpeter's terms they were prisoners of their pasts:

Past economic periods govern the activity of the individual. . . . All preceding periods have, furthermore, entangled him in a net of social and economic connections which he cannot easily shake off. They have bequeathed him definite means and methods. . . . All these hold him in iron fetters fast in his tracks.[12]

Unable to abandon the old strategy entirely, they tended to recast it into the notion of an enlarged territory suitable for controlling a through line but still capable of being sealed off from encroaching rivals. To achieve this end three alternative tactics seemed possible: cooperation, construction, and consolidation. The applicability of each for a given road depended upon its individual circumstances, but most managers attempted some combination of all three.

Cooperation assumed many forms. On the simplest level it involved agreements with connecting lines to promote through traffic at common rates. Sometimes the alliance sought to provide the road with entry into hitherto untapped territory, but more often it aimed at uniting several companies into a competitive through line.[13] Later in the period, protection of their mutual territories might prompt several roads to ally against invading lines and competing routes.[14] One of the most ambitious proposals, which never materialized, called for the formation of a pool composed of the Cincinnati Southern, Kentucky Central, East Tennessee, Virginia, & Georgia, Chesapeake & Ohio, South Carolina, and the Erlanger roads.[15] On a grander scale the managers attempted cooperation in two vital areas: fast freight service and maintenance of rates. The first occurred with the formation of the Green Line in 1868 and the second with the founding of the Southern Railway and Steamship Association in 1875.[16]

While this association proved to be the most successful major railway pool, it could not completely stifle rate cutting and other abuses; nor could it bring an end to competition. As commercial rivalry, aided to some degree by Reconstruction politics, spurred construction of new lines, managers quickly realized that cooperation alone was too tenuous a foundation for defense of the territory. Alliances once made could be easily unmade if better opportunities arose. The temptation to eschew long-term stability for short-term profits became especially irresistible to the hungrier roads. The opening of a new and "invading" line tended to alter existing relationships dramatically and to cause a shuffling of alliances.[17] And the stakes were high. Loss of a vital connector meant serious diversion of business and sometimes even a fatal blow to the company. The president of the Macon & Brunswick attributed the receivership of his road to just such an isolation:

The entire failure of our road is due to our having been blocked at Macon. The road never could have been built had it been supposed possible that lines north of that point could have been closed so effectually as has been done by the leases and amalgamations of these outlets northward.[18]

Fearful of isolation, managers naturally resorted to securing their vital connections on a more permanent basis. Hence began the growing reliance upon construction and consolidation as methods of achieving stability. Heretofore expansion had been perceived mainly as the construction of small feeder lines to develop local resources; now it came to be seen as the building or acquisition of larger roads to ensure through connections. The timetable of growth naturally varied, but no major road remained unaffected by the need. The potential dangers raised by the activities of rival lines spurred even the most reluctant manager to enlarge his domain. The Louisville & Nashville, having suffered no serious war damage and having been blessed with farsighted management, commenced expansion immediately after the war. It extended southward into the rich Alabama mineral lands, acquired connecting roads to Memphis, and built eastward toward a Tennessee connection.[19] By 1873 President H. D. Newcomb could report:

With the completion of the South & North Alabama Railroad the Company has now practically carried out the policy which was inaugurated some seven years ago under . . . the late Hon. James Guthrie, then President. . . . The importance of this enterprise cannot be overestimated; without it the Louisville & Nashville would be entirely dependent for its connections to the Southeast and Southwest upon other railroads, whose interests are not identified with ours, but are directly opposed to them. It would have been in the power of these companies to exclude us at any time from the business of the South, and make the property of this Company comparatively worthless.[20]

But the management of the Louisville & Nashville, though the road was a pacesetter in expansion, soon decided it had not gone far enough. Defense of the territory proved a difficult task, especially after the panic of 1873, and additional mileage meant additional realm to be protected. Growth of rival roads posed threats on every flank and prompted further expansion to meet them. Under the guidance of Dr. E. D. Standiford and Newcomb's brilliant son, H. Victor Newcomb, the company doubled its size from 921 miles controlled in 1873 to 1,840 miles in 1880. In the latter year young Newcomb summarized his goals and policies:

Unfinished Business

The year under review has probably been the most eventful and stirring in the history of your company. . . . your Board deemed it vital to the protection of your traffic, and the extension of your legitimate business, to secure, without delay, certain connecting lines, which it was feared might otherwise pass under control of interests inimical to yours . . . your system, as now perfected, is invulnerable to the attacks and assaults of any of its competitors. . . . it is the absolute conviction of your management that the vast command of territory now embraced by your lines of road, with the commanding and strategic position enjoyed by your company, renders the construction of new and competitive lines incapable of inflicting serious damage or loss of business upon your company.[21]

Most of the other roads followed a similar pattern on a smaller scale. The Danville, aided by the Pennsylvania Railroad, constructed a line into Atlanta and joined it to other, smaller acquisitions to form the "Piedmont Air Line."[22] The East Tennessee, itself the product of an 1869 consolidation, secured control of the Memphis & Charleston and gained outlets to the south via the Selma, Rome, & Dalton. To guarantee a through line it also formed an alliance with the Atlantic, Mississippi, & Ohio, which connected with the East Tennessee at Bristol and reached Norfolk.[23] The Central of Georgia, under the guidance of William M. Wadley, deplored the expansion trend, but lost no time joining it. By 1873 Wadley had leased the Southwestern Railroad, absorbed his connector to Atlanta, acquired a fleet of Savannah-based steamers, and bought into several smaller lines. No one could doubt that he had girded for battle:

New York is, and will continue to be, the great commercial centre of the country. This being recognized, and the fact that there are numerous land routes from the South and Southwest, terminating at New York, the question to be settled is whether an all rail or rail and ocean transportation is the cheapest. This contest is upon us, and, without the absolute control of ships, would be quite out of our power to make the issue, which, it is believed, must ultimately be decided in our favor.[24]

The strategy of territorial expansion, either by construction or consolidation, proved expensive. It often meant passed or reduced dividends and therefore required considerable justification to the stockholders. The most striking aspect of the expansion rationale was its essentially defensive nature. Most managers conceded freely that new acquisitions would not be a source of *direct* profit for some time.[25] They had acted from necessity rather than choice, and they sought mainly to protect instead of expand. Additions to the system drained valuable capital and usually brought more problems than benefits to the company, but they were needed to survive. Victor Newcomb insisted that

Your management has never contemplated . . . an aggressive policy in dealing with its connections or competitors, and what has been accomplished in the way of extension to your system, has been done solely with a view to the protection and extension of your natural and legitimate business, and in no single instance from a spirit of aggrandizement.[26]

Three years earlier the elder Newcomb justified the purchase of a small road by noting that "Forming part of a through line, it was, in conjunction with its connections, a constant disturber of rates to nearly every portion of the South and Southwest, and the injury it was capable of inflicting has been several times very apparent."[27] In defending his purchase of the Montgomery & Eufaula Railroad, Wadley argued that "That road is so situated that if in the hands of parties whose interests were in antagonism with this Company our interest could not fail to suffer seriously."[28] A later apologist for Wadley's policy recalled that "Indeed, it was at the time on the part of the Central a fight for existence, for it is a well-known fact that some of its best friends . . . very much feared bankruptcy."[29]

The strategy of territorial expansion had already drawn southern roads into fierce conflict by 1873, but panic and depression brought matters to a crisis. Only a steady growth of business could alleviate the financial burdens of restoration and expansion, the cost of which left even the strongest roads little margin for withstanding adversity. Policy makers had presumed that their efforts would create some stability among the roads, but the economic contraction hit them like a thunderclap. Unable to survive the blow, weaker roads succumbed rapidly to default and receivership.[30]

The failure of so many roads aggravated an already bad situation. Rates declined steadily as the bankrupt roads, freed from payment on their debt, undercut their solvent competitors ruthlessly to get whatever business offered. More important, foreclosure made the purchase of many key roads cheap and easy for rival companies. And since many of the defaulted lines had themselves pursued expansion by acquiring stock and bonds in connecting roads, purchase of the parent company often meant control over subsidiary lines as well.[31] The old defensive fears reasserted themselves in earnest after 1873. Managers of solvent roads, though struggling to keep their own companies afloat, could not resist the temptation to snatch up foreclosed roads in order to prevent rivals from doing so. By the late 1870's a new race toward consolidation had begun.[32]

In renewing their dependence upon expansion the managers sealed their own doom. Clinging faithfully to the territorial concept and reluctant to expand their economic horizons, they tried once more to isolate their domains. But their very efforts to preserve the territorial concept created the seeds of its destruction. Their attempts at defensive expansion under depression conditions deeply antagonized many stockholders. Conservative investors resented the sacrifice of dividends to the acquisition of insolvent roads and prophesied inevitable bankruptcy; impatient younger holders generally approved expansion, but opposed the grudging, piecemeal approach of the older managers.

Severe clashes over policy erupted on many boards. One by one the old managers fell victim to age, organized opposition, and obsolete policies as their roads passed into the control of a new generation. John P. King, who had helped build the Georgia Railroad and served as its president from 1841, was defeated for re-election after a bitter campaign in 1878.[33] Victor Newcomb mysteriously resigned the L & N presidency after less than a year in office. Wadley died in office in 1882 amidst powerful opposition to his policies. For a time his son-in-law, William G. Raoul, managed to pursue a modified version of the old strategy, but he too lost a heated election in 1887.[34] A. S. Buford of the Danville survived a transition in ownership in 1880, but fell out with his new employers over policy and resigned in 1886.[35] Others, like John Screven of the Atlantic & Gulf and William J. McGrath of the South Carolina, lost their roads through receivership.

The territorial strategy failed because it became increasingly inapplicable to the economic environment. A major cause of its demise, however, rested with the managers themselves and their inability to perceive the logical consequences of their policies. Expansion had proved ineffective as a defensive strategy. It could not succeed because it fed upon its own impetus. In trying to seal off the territories the managers only further exposed them by enlargement. The process of building new lines or of acquiring old ones brought previously neutral companies into direct confrontation, with each branding the other an "invader." Territories that once seemed distinct now developed overlapping zones of conflict, especially as rival companies pushed into hitherto untapped regions or sought entrance into some more distant commercial center. The result was not protection but increased warfare, not stability but competition at more places and on a grander scale.

One astute observer, Joseph Nimmo, sensed what was taking place, not only in the South but in the nation as a whole:

There is reason to believe that the managers of certain of the great railroad organizations of the country, in attempting to carry out their ambitious policy of railroad extension, failed to foresee the fact that they were creating competitive agencies more rapidly than they were gaining control over commerce.[36]

To be sure, the fast-departing managers were not unaware of their dilemma. Many recognized their problems only too well, but were helpless to find effective solutions. Buford of the Danville summarized their plight well in 1880:

This work amidst the extension, completion and reorganization of railroad lines now regarded as essentially necessary for their successful operation, has, by common consent, been found . . . one of the most difficult features of railway management. . . . Experience is daily demonstrating some of the requisites to the only safe policy in this regard, based upon an intelligent recognition of the just rights of each line of road, as well as those of the public, wherever conflicts of interest and competition naturally or circumstantially exist. The best methods of securing these important objects are yet, to a certain extent, experimental.[37]

The men who emerged as southern railroad leaders after 1880 differed markedly from their predecessors. They were of course younger, had virtually no previous personal identification with the company, and gained their business experience during the postwar period. Most of them were financiers with no practical railroad experience. Unhampered by local or regional loyalties, they possessed broader visions and more ambitious schemes. The old territorial concept held neither meaning nor relevance for them. They thought rather in terms of vast systems reaching into every corner of the South and vying for traffic at every important market. Coming to power just at the return of national prosperity, they had no fear of expansion. Indeed their major concern was that growth proceed rapidly enough for them to capture waiting markets. In their hands expansion became both an offensive and defensive weapon.[38]

The most significant aspect of this change in strategic thinking was the rapid growth of interterritorial competition. It constituted the logical alternative to the territorial concept: if a monopolistic territory could not be protected from invaders, then the best hope for increasing business lay in expanding the field of battle. The key to survival appeared to be a diversification of outlets for both through and local traffic. At the local level the old policy of developing local resources along the enlarged lines would provide the company with a reliable base for growth of traffic. Participation in the struggle for through traffic on a larger scale, meanwhile, seemed to offer better opportunities for stabilizing overall earnings. The new strategy appeared to promise greater flexibility. It would take time for new local traffic to develop sufficiently to turn a profit, and only a system large enough to cover losses in one territory with gains in another seemed able to buy that time.

The renewed expansion spawned by the receiverships of the 1870's furnished the impetus for the development of the major interterritorial systems. With startling speed the parent roads, most of them under new management, increased the mileage under their control. The L & N jumped from 966 miles in 1878 to 3,231 in 1883, the Danville from 448 to 2,503, the East Tennessee from 272 to 1,389, and the Central of Georgia from 861 to 1,754.[39] By 1881 contemporary observers, impressed by the swiftness of southern consolidation, could list seven companies as dominating southern traffic: the Danville; the Savannah, Florida, & Western, nucleus of a system being formed by Henry B. Plant; the East Tennessee; the Norfolk & Western; the Louisville & Nashville; the Central of Georgia; and the Chicago, St. Louis, & New Orleans, the southern subsidiary of the Illinois Central.[40]

The confrontation of major roads wrought by interterritorial expansion also fostered consolidation at a higher level. The clash of rivals over disputed ground often led to a fitting Darwinian climax, with one company absorbing the other. Thus Victor Newcomb, thwarted by the equally ambitious schemes of Edwin "King" Cole of the Nashville, Chattanooga, & St. Louis, proceeded to buy his adversary's company out from under him in 1880.[41] The following year the L & N joined the Central in removing a powerful competitor by leasing the Georgia Railroad.[42] In

1881, too, the Danville shut the Baltimore & Ohio out of the South by purchasing the Virginia Midland.[43] The culmination of this movement came in 1888 when the Richmond Terminal, a holding company, gained control of three major systems: the Danville, East Tennessee, and Central of Georgia.[44]

The desire to penetrate new territories provided the main impetus for the consolidation activities of the 1880's. So too did it spur new construction during the same period.[45] Growing systems generally built new lines for one or more of three reasons: to open new territories or reach new markets; to form new through connections with other systems; and to parallel an existing rival enjoying monopoly status. The Norfolk & Western, though richly endowed with heavy local traffic in coal and other ores, nevertheless embarked upon the construction of additional through routes. It built a new line to the Ohio River, pushed for new western connections with the East Tennessee, and completed the Shenandoah Valley Railroad as a rival route to the Danville's Virginia Midland.[46] The East Tennessee in 1882 finished a line from Rome, Georgia, to Macon that paralleled the Western & Atlantic Railroad and the Central's road between Macon and Atlanta.[47] In one of the most daring projects, the Danville completed the 566-mile Georgia Pacific from Atlanta to Greenville, Mississippi, by 1889.[48] Though the amount and type of construction naturally varied, no system remained aloof lest it lose ground to competitors. The necessity to expand revealed itself clearly in L & N President Eckstein Norton's somewhat contradictory remarks in 1887:

> The policy adopted by your management has been not to make any unnecessary extensions, but to encourage and build up local traffic. At the same time it has been found necessary to extend certain branches and to build new ones in the territory adjacent to your lines. . . .[49]

The strategy of interterritorial competition naturally produced friction and resentment. The Richmond Terminal report for 1887 noted tersely that "The Louisville and Nashville Railroad has invaded the territory of the East Tenn., Va. and Ga. during the past year at several important points. They claim the right, without notice, to build into any of its territory," and called for board action to meet the threat.[50] The Western & Atlantic, bitter over being paralleled by the East Tennessee, refused for a time to handle the latter company's freight.[51] The scope of interterritorial rivalries led to renewed efforts at cooperation. As in the previous period, alliances rose and flourished at least for a time. The East Tennessee formed a new pact with the Norfolk & Western, opened a cooperative fast freight line with the Danville, and closed a mutual nonaggression treaty with the L & N.[52] Perhaps the most ambitious effort involved the formation of the Associated Railways of Virginia and the Carolinas in 1885. Composed of the roads controlled by the Danville, the Atlantic Coast Line, and the Seaboard Air Line, the association reached agreement on joint management of all traffic, harmonizing of competition, no independent soliciting for traffic, common auditors to examine all accounts, mutual aid and protection when attacked by other lines, interchange of traffic wherever possible, establishment of an arbitration board to settle disputes, and specific arrangements for apportioning traffic.[53]

The basic tactics of cooperation, construction, and consolidation, utilized by the earlier managers, continued to serve their successors. The difference lay in the scale of operations and in the desired goals. The first resulted from the shift in strategic thinking from territorial monopoly to interterritorial supremacy. The second concerned, among other things, a change in attitude toward sources of profit. The financier-managers who created the large systems derived little personal return from operations. Their profits came instead from such varied sources as construction of the new lines, speculation in the securities associated with the company, transactions involved in the acquisition of other lines (in which they often held personal interests), and such external investments influenced by the railroad as real estate, mineral lands, express business, manufacturing, and industrial development.[54]

Because the financiers tended to think in short-term rather than long-term profits, they evinced little concern for the swollen capitalization produced by their policies. The financial effect of interterritorial strategy was to burden every system with considerably enlarged fixed costs that required additional earnings to service. During the 1880's, when general prosperity seemed to bless every enterprise, a constant expansion of business seemed almost inevitable. The centralization born of consolidation, moreover, promised reduced administrative costs and increased operational efficiency. Many companies had, in fact, rationalized the creation of large systems in terms of maximizing efficiency. Alfred Sully of the Richmond Terminal expressed feelings common to most of his peers when he declared:

The underlying principle which actuated the Board . . . in bringing into your ownership this extensive system has been the belief that the consolidation of the control of these roads must result in great economies, in less competition, and also enable the roads . . . to devote their attention to furnishing better facilities for the public. . . .[55]

By the end of the decade, however, serious flaws in the interterritorial strategy began to appear. The assumption of expanding business proved correct, but steadily declining rates prevented earnings from increasing in like proportion. Nor did the tactic of absorbing rival roads entirely reduce competition. The large systems expected to contend with each other, especially for through traffic, but they faced additional rivalry for local business. Besides its positive effect upon interterritorial expansion, the prosperity of the 1880's stimulated construction of smaller local lines as well. As a result the giants confronted an invasion of gnats, each capable of making severe inroads into local traffic. In 1889 the Central of Georgia bemoaned the opening of six new competing roads, and other companies echoed the complaint of the Mobile & Ohio that "Within the last few years competing lines have been built into the territory formerly solely tributary to the Mobile & Ohio."[56] The attempt to stifle or at least centralize competition had failed, and the policy of penetrating every available territory had created new weaknesses as well as new markets. The Central's president, E. P. Alexander, summarized the difficulties common to virtually all southern roads:

These four years have witnessed an unprecedented activity in railroad building in the territory served by this Company, its own prosperity being often the stimulus of other roads built to attract its business over shorter routes, or to other ports and lines. Under these circumstances this Company has been forced to occupy and develop the territory tributary to it, for itself and to control its own feeders. . . . As the . . . new roads built and acquired . . . are all of them branches and extensions into new territory, and necessarily enjoy much less business than our trunk lines and other established branches, it is naturally to be expected that the consolidated earnings of the system per mile would be diminished. . . .[57]

The pursuit of interterritorial strategy led nearly all southern roads into grave financial difficulties. Many of them toppled into receivership after 1893, but the old strategy did not die easily. The problems that had called it into existence still remained unsolved, and the decade of the 1890's witnessed further consolidation and construction.[58] An 1893 journal report predicting control of the South by only two systems proved exaggerated in degree but not in kind.[59] The change in strategic thinking that evolved around 1880 ensured that, for better or worse, southern railroads would proceed steadily down a course of further concentration and amalgamation.

A consideration of southern railway strategy, as outlined above, suggests some possible answers to a question of long standing. It was a notorious fact that southern railroads were poor investments during the postwar period. The dividend rate ranked well below the national average, and the number of paying roads remained small even during the prosperous years of the 1880's.[60] Why then did expansion continue to accelerate, and why did new capital continue to flow into southern roads?

Expansion continued because railway managers perceived it as a necessity for survival. Even in the 1880's it remained a largely defensive policy. Official optimism naturally predicted that it would ultimately prove profitable, but of course the end result could not be foreseen. The crucial point in the decision-making process was that it had to be done to protect the road's future, and that without it the company would die or atrophy. The change in strategic thinking after 1880 involved not so much a shift from defensive to offensive thinking as a greater willingness to incur the risks of expansion on a greater scale.

Capital continued to move into southern rail ventures because the financiers mobilizing it, as this article suggests, found sources of profit outside rail operations.[61] Lucrative returns from the manipulation of securities, consolidation transactions, and related investments all helped stimulate expansion even though earnings performances did not seem to justify the price being paid. The fruit of this activity was the rapid development of a rail network unwelcome to some of its creators, unplanned in any overall sense, but ultimately enduring.

To be sure, this constitutes only a partial answer to the question of continued investment in southern railroads. But understanding of entrepreneurial strategy and its consequent behavior patterns opens a crucial avenue of further research. The course of American industrial development in the late nineteenth century has become a familiar story; the process by which it occurred remains imperfectly understood and controversial. The work of Albert Fishlow has provided a comprehensive approach to the question of allocation of resources in terms of social return.[62] In taking the "outside" view, however, he made no attempt to deal with the "inside" perspective: the effect of entrepreneurial motivations. A full grasp of the historical process requires a synthesis of the two perspectives. Only when both receive consideration and are balanced properly will the process of economic development become clear.

Southern Railroad Leaders, 1865–1893: Identities and Ideologies

This article, published in the *Business History Review* in 1968, was in many ways a companion piece to the previous article, but with some differences that made it a favorite of mine. In it I tried not only to depict a pattern of change in southern railroads but also to capture that pattern through the men who fashioned it. Albro Martin, in his recent *Railroads Triumphant*, referred to my attempt to define two distinct types of entrepreneur as "provocative." It was considered even more so in 1968. Although the gist of these two articles was incorporated into *The Great Richmond Terminal*, both contain material that did not find its way into the book.

The development of the South's railroad system has become fairly well known in its broad patterns, but little has been written about the men who created it.[1] Few biographies of southern railroad men exist, and only one full-length study of southern railroads has been written since U. B. Phillips published his significant *A History of Transportation in the Eastern Cotton Belt to 1860* in 1908. In that one volume John F. Stover provided valuable sketches of the development of the major southern railroad systems after the Civil War.[2] Stover also focused attention upon the creators of those systems by advancing the thesis that southern railroads had succumbed to "northern men and money" by 1900.

In 1865, according to Stover, the ownership, financing, and operation of southern roads resided in the hands of southerners. But the acute need of capital for restoration and later for expansion, the growth of nationally integrated and interdependent traffic patterns, and an awakening speculative interest by northern financiers in southern roads all helped transfer control of 90 percent of southern lines to northern hands by the turn of the century.[3] To sustain his thesis, Stover analyzed the lists of directors for southern railroads given in Poor's *Manual of the Railroads of the United States* for the period 1865–1900. His findings are reproduced in Table 1. Largely on the basis of this analysis, Stover concluded that "The end of the century found northern men, money and management firmly placed in positions of dominance over the railroads of the South."[4]

Stover's use of Poor's directors' lists can be questioned on several grounds. In the first place, the address for a given director did not always remain consistent. To cite a few examples: in 1890 Patrick Calhoun's address is given as New York for the Richmond Terminal and Atlanta for the Central of Georgia (C. G.);[5] Thomas M. Logan was assigned to New York for the Richmond Terminal and Richmond for the Richmond & Danville (R. & D.) in 1882;[6] Walter S. Chisholm, a railroad attorney, was listed in New York for the Richmond Terminal and Savannah for the Savannah Florida & Western (S. F. & W.) in 1888;[7] and Charles M. McGhee resided in New York for the East Tennessee Virginia & Georgia (E. T. V. & G.) and Knoxville for the Memphis & Charleston (M. & C.) in 1889.[8] These discrepancies suggest the unreliability of the listed addresses, which often served charter requirements or some other purpose and did not always indicate the true residence of the person involved. Moreover, many individuals moved during the period, and the change of address picked up in Stover's analysis obscures the fact that the man involved remains the same. This is especially important for southerners moving north.

TABLE 1
Selected Indicators of Increasing Northern Control over Southern Railroads

	1870	1880	1890	1900
Southern Railroads	43	34	58	31
Southern Presidents	36	18	22	13
Northern Presidents	7	16	36	18
Northern Presidents	16%	47%	62%	58%
Southern Directors	345	210	302	118
Northern Directors	81	125	269	193
Northern Directors	19%	37%	47%	63%
Northern Controlled Mileage	21%	48%	88%	96%

Source: John F. Stover, *The Railroads of the South 1865–1900* (Chapel Hill, 1955), 282.

Secondly, the number of directors involved in Stover's calculations may be misleading. Several companies, especially in the later period, contained "dummy" directors who served to support those men actually in control or merely held seats until a suitable director could be chosen. In fact, the number of directors from North and South does not reveal where the real power lay. Certainly lines of influence and domination existed within individual boards, and it is entirely possible that one or two members of the board actually controlled the company through their influence over other board members.[9] And though the various boards did shape policy for their companies, they still represented only equity control. Stover's approach cannot get at the often powerful influence of bond and floating debt holders.

Apart from questions of methodology, however, a more fundamental objection to Stover's thesis can be raised. The terms "northern" and "southern" seem far too ambiguous to explain anything clearly. Should they be taken literally to mean that southern-born men had lost control of their railroads to northern-born men? If so, then the analysis breaks down because many of the "northerners" who came to dominate southern railroads after 1880 were, in fact, southerners who had gone north after the war. A list of such men important in the development of southern railroads would include John C. and Patrick Calhoun, Chisholm, John H. Inman, James C. Maben, John McAnerney, Charles M. McGhee, H. V. Newcomb, Eckstein Norton, Vernon K. Stevenson, James Swann, and Richard T. Wilson. In addition, several other southerners belonged to groups designated by Stover as representing "northern" interests: E. P. Alexander, R. R. Bridgers, Thomas M. Logan, and Samuel Spencer. On the other hand, many of the men long identified as representatives of local southern control—such as William M. Wadley, John M. Robinson, H. D. Newcomb, E. J. Sanford, and Milton H. Smith—were actually northerners who had come south.

The point is that Stover's "North-South" distinction does not explain very much about what happened. If taken to mean mobilization of capital from outside the region it still says very little about either the process or the personnel involved. If interpreted as loss of local control to "outsiders," it presents an inadequate explanation for that phenomenon and can be more confusing than clarifying. In 1883 and 1887, for example, the C. G. waged hotly contested elections that perhaps better depict this process of changing control than any other single event. Both contests developed quite distinctly around the issue of "local" versus "outside" domination. Yet the candidate for the "outsiders," General E. P. Alexander, was born and raised in Georgia while his "local" opponent, William G. Raoul, was a transplanted Louisianan who won the election of 1883 primarily because he obtained proxies for the 6,400 shares owned by none other than Hetty Green of New York![10]

The Stover thesis, then, seems inadequate to explain the struggle for control of southern railroads during the late nineteenth century. But this is not to say that it perceives the phenomena inaccurately. Important changes in control *were* taking place on a large scale, and marked, often bitter struggles for power *did* occur frequently. A significant change in the pattern of southern railroad development did become evident around 1880, and contemporary observers spilled a lot of ink trying to analyze and account for it. The leadership (as well as most other aspects) of southern railroads changed drastically between 1865 and 1893. The rest of this article will attempt to suggest an alternative interpretation for these changes in terms of the men most deeply involved in them.

The handful of systems that came to dominate southern transportation by 1893 emerged as the offspring of about ten parent roads. Though naturally possessing their own unique historical characteristics and circumstances, these parent roads had much in common. Each had established itself before the war as an important trade artery for some commercial center. Nearly all the roads lay along the strategic northeast-southwest or northwest-southeast routes that would eventually dominate the movement of through traffic. Table 2 lists these roads together with their length, terminals and year the main line opened.

As the nuclei of southern railroad development these roads played a role far out of proportion to their size relative to the South's total mileage; hence study of them sheds much light upon the process by which that development took place. Except for the A. & G. they comprised the strongest roads of the region and rehabilitated quickly from the ravages of war. Their stock tended to be widely distributed among a large number of holders, with the largest lots belonging either to the state or to prominent merchants and bankers of their main terminus.[11]

TABLE 2
Nuclei Roads in the Development of
Southern Railroad Systems

Road	Length (Miles)	Terminals	Year Opened
1. Richmond & Danville (R. & D.)	141	Richmond Danville	1856
2. East Tennessee, Virginia & Georgia (E. T. V. & G.)[a]	242	Chattanooga Bristol, Tennessee	1855–56
3. Georgia (Ga.)	171	Augusta Atlanta	1845
4. Central of Georgia (C. G.)[b]	295	Atlanta Savannah	1843
5. Louisville & Nashville (L. & N.)	185	Louisville Nashville	1859
6. Nashville, Chattanooga & St. Louis (N.C. & S.L.)[c]	321	Chattanooga Hickman, Ky.	1854
7. Seaboard & Roanoke (S. & R.)	80	Roanoke Portsmouth	1851
8. Wilmington & Weldon (W. & W.)	164	Wilmington Weldon	1840
9. Atlantic, Mississippi & Ohio (A. M. & O.)[d]	428	Norfolk Bristol	1852–57
10. Atlantic & Gulf (A. & G.)[e]	237	Savannah Bainbridge, Georgia	1858

[a] The East Tennessee comprised two roads, the East Tennessee & Virginia (Knoxville to Bristol) and the East Tennessee & Georgia (Knoxville to Chattanooga), which were consolidated in 1869.

[b] The Central extended originally to Macon and gained entry to Atlanta over the Macon & Western (opened 1846), which it absorbed in 1872.

[c] In 1865 the N. C. & S. L. consisted only of the Nashville & Chattanooga. The Nashville & Northwestern (Nashville to Hickman, Ky., on the Mississippi River) was acquired in 1870 and the two roads consolidated in 1872.

[d] The A. M. & O. in 1865 comprised three separate roads: the Norfolk & Petersburg, the Southside (Petersburg to Lynchburg) and the Virginia & Tennessee (Lynchburg to Bristol). The three roads consolidated in 1870.

[e] The A. & G. was originally intended as the first link of a through line to Mobile. By 1858, however, it had opened only as far as the small town of Screven. The extension to Bainbridge was completed in 1867.

Sources: Compiled from annual reports of the companies and Henry V. Poor, *Manual of the Railroads of the United States* (New York, 1867–1894).

The men who dominated these major southern roads during the first two postwar decades possessed forceful personalities and unusual administrative abilities. For convenience they are listed in Table 3 along with their age, tenure, and primary occupation.

A survey of biographical backgrounds suggests some significant similarities. Most of these leaders belonged to the same generation. They matured just about the time when the railroad began to demonstrate its

TABLE 3
Selected Data on Southern Railroad Leaders 1856–1880

Name	Road	Born	Tenure as Pres.	Primary Occupation
1. A. S. Buford	R. & D.	1826	1866–83	Railroad man, politician
2. Richard T. Wilson	E. T. V. & G.	1831	1871–79	Banker
3. John P. King	Ga.	1799	1841–78	Railroad man, manufacturer
4. William M. Wadley	C. G.	1813	1866–82	Railroad man
5. James Guthrie	L. & N.	1792	1860–68	Politician, railroad man
H. D. Newcomb	L. & N.	1809	1868–74	Merchant
E. D. Standiford	L. & N.	1831	1874–80	Physician, banker
6. Vernon K. Stevenson	N. C. & S. L.	1812	1848–65	Merchant, railroad man
Edwin W. Cole	N. C. & S. L.	1832	1869–79	Railroad man
7. John M. Robinson	S. & R.	1835	1867–93	Railroad man, engineer
8. Robert R. Bridgers	W. & W.	1819	1865–88	Railroad man, lawyer
9. William Mahone	A. M. & O.	1826	1865–76	Railroad man, engineer
10. John Screven	A. & G.	1831	1859, 1862–80	Railroad man

Sources: Based on information obtained from standard biographical dictionaries and obituaries. Since a complete listing would be impractical here, relevant sources for any specific individual will be furnished by the author upon request.

effectiveness as a means of transportation. Most of them played some role in antebellum railroad development as promoter, financier, investor, or engineer. The southern states, lagging somewhat behind the rest of the nation, did not embark upon their most extensive construction until the 1850's.[12] By that time, all the above except Robinson had gone into business, and the outbreak of war found every one of them well established in some career.

The importance of their "settled" condition must not be overlooked. Not all the men were native southerners and less than half still lived in his native state in 1860, but all had established strong local ties. Being essentially of the same generation, it seems reasonable to assume a fairly common fund of experiences, ideas, attitudes, and ambitions among them.[13] The prevailing attitude toward railroads in the South considered them to be localized enterprises whose primary purpose was three-fold: profitmaking; developing the commerce and other economic activity of its principal terminus; and developing the economic resources of the region tributary to the road. Although numerous grand schemes existed for the creation of sizeable through lines linking the sections together, most southerners took a more parochial view. The savage duel among southern ports for commercial superiority had already commenced and would increase steadily in intensity after the war. The advent of the railroad added certain geographically favored interior cities to the struggle. The merchant in Richmond, Louisville, or Atlanta tended to view his city's railroads as a major weapon against rival distributing centers; the farmer adjacent to the road regarded it as his opportunity to exploit his land to the fullest.[14]

In an atmosphere of ever increasing commercial rivalry, it should not be surprising to find our group developing strong community and regional ties. Ten of the thirteen men had some railroad experience prior to the war, and at least eleven of them had been associated in some capacity with the road they were to dominate after the war. Cole, Mahone, Robinson, and Wadley all had practical railroad experience; Bridgers, Guthrie, King, and Stevenson played significant roles in the promotion or construction of their roads; and Screven inherited the presidency of the A. & G. from his father, who had been the leading figure in it from its inception. Nearly all the group had external investments in local enterprises, so that their railroad work became a logical extension of their other financial interests.[15]

From this background emerged the heart of the concept loosely described as "local control." It meant keeping the company out of the hands of "outsiders," northern or southern, whose economic interests were not directly related to the road's territory. "Foreign" investors and bondholders would be tolerated, even cultivated, so long as they acquiesced in a policy of localizing as much traffic as possible at the chief terminus. But outside parties with interests in competing lines or cities were anathema. Time and again a railroad might rebuff the attempts of an enemy to absorb it; thus the Raleigh & Gaston in 1871 disdainfully rejected an offer by the R. & D. to buy 7,500 shares of its stock, fearing that "outside" influence might divert traffic from Raleigh to Richmond.[16] In each case, prominent local merchants and bankers dominated the boards of directors. Often they were virtually the same group that had run the road before the war, and many of them had been instrumental in building the line.[17] These men formed the power base upon which the president, seldom a major stockholder himself, retained his position. However strong-willed or domineering the president, he well understood his role as spokesman for directors and stockholders whose desires and interests extended beyond the railroad itself.

In the postwar era the presidents tried earnestly to formulate policies consistent with their role as representatives of this viewpoint. Indeed their general policies differed little from those practiced before the war. Basically their approach might be described as "developmental" in the sense defined by Arthur M. Johnson and Barry E. Supple.[18] Such a policy required that profits and development be conceived as long-term goals, that the company be run primarily to satisfy investors rather than speculators, and consequently that the stock be tightly held and protected from rapid turnover and fluctuation in value. This last goal was made substantially easier to achieve in those cases where the state held a sizeable portion of the outstanding equity.[19]

A key aspect of this policy involved what the presidents themselves called "development." Long-term success for the company depended heavily upon the cultivation of economic resources along the line whether agricultural, mineral or manufacturing. Especially was this true for the postwar South, whose shattered economy had suffered a severe depletion of population, capital and physical equipment. The presidents soon perceived the vicious cycle that confronted them: restoration of the transportation system was needed to rehabilitate the South's economy, but by the same token financial survival of the roads depended upon a revived economy capable of supporting them. The fact that local rates provided the most remunerative income added extra incentive to the task.

Managers of most of the roads worked actively to stimulate immigration into the regions along their right-of-way. They built branches and spur lines to provide access to market for infant industries and mining endeavors. Some created new traffic arrangements to foster the development of certain products. The W. & W., for example, worked arduously to cultivate the growth of truck farming, fruits and grapes in its territory.[20] "This Company, for several years past, has been boldly prosecuting a policy of development," proclaimed Buford of the R. & D. in 1872. "A necessity—the necessity of self-preservation, and of fulfilling faithfully its highest duties to its own interests as well as to the public—required it. . . . The result will be that which always follows well-meant and well-directed labor and enterprise, faithfully and manfully adhered to success! And if the measure of it be small at first, and its progress slow, its continuance is the more assured, and the benefits and blessings to those who have labored and waited for it, only the more permanent."[21] Other presidents echoed these sentiments with equal fervor if less rhetoric.

Developmental policy revealed itself in attitudes toward dividends and maintenance as well. Regular dividend payments seemed essential to any policy stressing long-term investment, and virtually all the presidents favored such a schedule. But the critical need for capital to repair and maintain the lines often clashed with dividend goals and forced unwelcome choices upon the decision-makers. Although six of the roads managed to pay regular dividends, all the presidents stressed the need to subordinate dividends to the necessity of plowing back earnings into maintenance and improvements. And most practiced what they preached. Wilson of the E. T. V. & G. insisted that "There can be no question . . . about the expediency of continuing the expenditure of money as rapidly as our finances will permit, and thus sustain its character as a first class road."[22] Bridgers noted more tersely that "This policy of rebuilding and improving the Road has been adopted, because a road in good repair, can be operated at less expense than one in bad repair."[23]

By the mid-1870's the presidents had come to resemble feudal lords presiding over their baronies. The policies they pursued coupled with their close personal identification with the company they served combined to render them conspicuous among the South's railroad men. They conceived of their road as having exclusive possession of the commerce in the territory tributary to it. Referring to this right as "the natural channels of trade," they resented any encroachment upon it and fought bitterly to seal off their territory from invasion.[24] To protect the interests of their companies, they did not hesitate to enter directly or indirectly into state and local politics.[25] In the confused political turmoil of Reconstruction each president stood out as a prominent representative of local interests. For them city, railroad and tributary countryside had become one inseparable economic unit constantly interacting for the prosperity of all concerned. With a keen sense of duty each strove to perform for his company and his state what Mahone called his "high mission in the development of Virginia."[26]

Unfortunately, a set of policies and perspectives derived from antebellum conditions proved woefully inadequate for the rapidly changing environment of the postwar South. Many of the assumptions behind traditional developmental policy no longer held true. The consequences of four years of war created new problems and frustrated attempts to apply tested solutions to older ones. While all the presidents perceived the changed circumstances clearly enough, they found it difficult to alter old habits of thought. Even those who did succeed in coping with the new environment found themselves engulfed by problems for which the old methods had no remedy.

The task of restoration posed the first such challenge. Traditional policy had called for financing the roads at a high equity to debt ratio, plowing back earnings for improvements and expansion and gradually extinguishing the debt. Such a policy required continuity and careful management, but the war had disrupted this pattern and left the roads in ruined condition. To renew operations, whole roads had to be renovated, rolling stock secured, and bridges, depots and other facilities restored.[27] Rehabilitation required a great deal of capital, and the prostrate South was in no position to supply it. Under the circumstances the presidents had no choice but to seek funds in the North or abroad. But an increase in the company's debt, placed in "outside" hands, harbored a potential threat to local control. Creditors would likely develop a heightened interest in the company and might be inclined to participate more actively in its affairs.

Despite this risk, most of the presidents hurried north in search of capital. Their efforts marked the beginning of a growing interest and involvement in the southern roads by "outsiders."[28] Wadley managed to sell $794,000 worth of bonds in New York during the summer of 1866. By 1873 Moses Taylor, who had served as trustee for the bond sale, owned the largest single block of C. G. stock, 2,999 shares, and had moved onto the company's board. Two other bankers, D. Willis James and Junius S. Morgan, also held sizeable blocks of the stock.[29] Eventually, most of the roads managed to find some northern market for their securities, though credit standings varied widely.

On the W. & W., Bridgers took what proved to be a momentous step. He appealed to Benjamin F. Newcomer and W. T. Walters, two prominent Baltimore merchants, to help refurbish the road. Both men had long been interested in luring more southern trade to Baltimore, and their involvement in southern railroads dated back to the 1850's. Presented with a fresh opportunity, the Baltimoreans took quick advantage of it. They bought control of the W. & W. when the state sold its stock in 1867 and maintained Bridgers as president. Then, with other northern capitalists, they proceeded in 1871 to organize the Southern Railway Security Company (S.R.S.C.).[30]

Probably the first important holding company, S.R.S.C. soon acquired large holdings in eight or nine southern roads, including the R. & D. and E. T. V. & G.[31] The stockholders in S.R.S.C. consisted of men interested in the Pennsylvania Railroad, New York bankers and firms holding either long-term southern railroad securities or short-term notes for rails and other equipment, Baltimore merchants, two Englishmen, and three Tennesseans deeply involved in the railroads of their state.[32] They soon joined the boards of subsidiary companies and seemed, on the surface, to present a formidable threat to local control. It was, after all, known that the Pennsylvania wanted its new southern connections primarily as a weapon for its war with the Baltimore & Ohio (B. & O.) and to block the latter's own southern expansion ambitions.[33] Some southern railroad leaders opposed this foreign intrusion. Mahone, for one, railed bitterly against both the Pennsylvania and the B. & O. and tried to play one off against the other.[34]

Yet the roads under S.R.S.C. influence offered curiously little resistance to the "outsiders," especially in comparison to the struggles of the 1880's. There was little opposition primarily because the change in control brought virtually no change in policy. The ambitions of the S.R.S.C. men proved quite compatible with those of the various presidents and their boards, and the presence of holding company representatives on the boards caused little friction or deflection of purpose. In fact some of them, like Wilson and McGhee of the E. T. V. & G. and Walters, Newcomer, and S. M. Shoemaker of the W. & W., had held seats on the boards for several years prior to the formation of S.R.S.C. Nothing better illustrated the continuity of policy than the fact that none of the major roads except the Charlotte, Columbia & Augusta changed presidents. Wilson had been on the E. T. V. & G. board since its consolidation in 1869. He assumed the presidency in 1870 on the death of Thomas H. Callaway and before the creation of S.R.S.C.[35] Buford, whose road remained longest under S.R.S.C. and Pennsylvania control, made his position unmistakably clear:[36]

In the Pennsylvania Railroad Company as your co-proprietor, you have a friend—not an enemy—identified by large interests with every movement in your history . . . a partner who has, and can have, no interest but that which is common to the smallest owner, the success, thrift and usefulness of your line of road, and the magnified prosperity of the communities and sections who use it.

The ordeal of rehabilitation, then, did not seriously disrupt traditional policies. It produced an increasing flow of stock northward and created a sizeable group of bondholders ready to assert their position should the presidents falter, but the threat remained largely potential until after 1873. "Outsiders" held considerable investments and influence in southern roads by that date, but their acquiescence to traditional policies rendered their presence inconspicuous. The fatal blow to continued domination by the presidents came rather from the changing economic environment and the nature of their response to those changes. The process by which their downfall occurred was intricate, complex and full of subtle shadings. It crystallized most specifically over the question of expansion.

Traditional developmental policy held the fundamental tenet of one road for one territory. The thinly populated, highly rural South could hardly support more than a single line carrying its products either to the road's terminus or to more distant markets via connecting lines. Arrangements with these connecting lines had to be made, and their junction in a sense marked the boundary between rival territories. The territorial concept presupposed the primacy of local traffic in providing income for the company with each road serving a secondary function as links in a larger system for through traffic. An orderly partitioning of this sort seemed vital for the survival of each road, and attempts to construct new lines in an occupied territory met with vehement resistance.[37]

The impact of war, however, wrought a severe dislocation to this dependence upon local traffic. Ultimately, each president wished to have his company sustained mainly by local traffic, but the exhausted postwar economy would take time to recover, and meanwhile the railroad had to live. Inevitably, they sought to stabilize their income by reaching out for more through traffic, and this in turn brought them into a situation characterized by heightened competition, declining rates, and increasing dependence upon connecting lines. Through traffic, carried at considerably lower rates than local, had therefore to be obtained in greater quantities and required stable relationships with connecting lines. But nothing proved more difficult to procure. Mutual suspicion and jealousy, the old local commercial rivalries, and the opportunistic desire to maximize traffic led to a constant spectacle of broken agreements and reshuffled alliances. Scarcely a president failed to lament the unreliability if not outright perfidy of his connecting roads.[38]

Seldom, too, did he fail to bemoan the growing spectre of competition.[39] Even in the late 1860's, the complaints over reckless competition and rate cutting had become a regular part of every road's annual report, but the chorus swelled in volume and intensity after the onset of depression in 1873. The fierce struggle for a dwindling traffic produced continual rate cutting, especially by those roads in receivership that had no bonded debt to service and could thus more easily afford a rate war. The goal of stable and reliable rates had always been a part of traditional policy, but it proved impossible to achieve in the postwar environment. The deteriorating economic atmosphere of the 1870's, coupled with growing uncertainties of income, traffic, and relationships with connecting lines, all demanded critical policy decisions by the presidents. It was these decisions, usually made reluctantly and under great duress, that impaled the presidents upon the dilemma of expansion.

Developmental policy naturally assumed a logical pattern of growth for the company, primarily in the form of constructing small branch lines as feeders to the parent road. But this aimed at developing local traffic and would require time. The immediate problem demanded expansion on a much larger scale to assure through connections. Three alternatives presented themselves to the presidents: the forming of alliances to insure through connections; the construction of one's own through line; and the acquisition of connecting lines by purchase or lease. All these methods were tried at one time or another. The first was of course cheapest but also the least reliable. The second required considerable capital and consumed precious time. The third could simplify connections quickly and at small immediate cost, but might saddle the company with unprofitable properties over the long run. None of the alternatives seemed particularly appealing, but the situation demanded action.

Forcefully, if reluctantly, the presidents responded to the crisis. Wadley absorbed his connector to Atlanta, paid dearly to lease the Southwestern Railroad, acquired a fleet of steamships to connect Savannah with major northern ports, and bought stock and bonds in other roads. Buford leased the North Carolina Railroad as a feeder, built a through line to Atlanta with generous help from the Pennsylvania, and pushed construction of connections to the northwest. King acquired connectors for the Georgia and invested heavily in the Port Royal Railroad, trying to develop that city as a rival seaport to Savannah. The L. & N. built or acquired connectors in all directions south of its main line, including a strategic penetration of the rich mineral lands in northern Alabama. The E. T. V. & G. acquired feeders, leased the M. & C., and formed a tenuous alliance with its principal connector, the A. M. & O. The other roads followed like patterns.[40]

Expansion came at great cost to every road. It proved extremely expensive for even the most solvent of lines and drained funds needed for maintenance and improvements on the main line. It added financial burdens to the company and, after 1873, resulted in the suspension of dividends for nearly every road. Strategically, it violated traditional policy by extending the company's authority beyond its territory. By overlapping rival lines and their terminal cities expansion threatened to weaken the hitherto cherished notion of one line feeding one commercial center. Rival interests might gain entry to the board and advocate policies diverting traffic to other cities on the expanded line, or rival lines might retaliate by expanding into one's own territory. In short, the creation of through lines threatened to strike a lethal blow at "local control" and the traditional policy of traffic localization. Moreover, expansion bred upon itself. It caused previously neutral companies to extend themselves into overlapping zones of conflict and tempted each road to resolve the clash simply by absorbing its rival. Once embarked on such a policy, it could not easily be checked.

The presidents realized these perils and sought to minimize them. They regarded expansion as essentially defensive and proceeded cautiously. Sensing the dangers to the notion of local control, they tried to seal off their enlarged territories anew, to create merely larger baronies or firmer alliances and agreements through such agencies as the Southern Railway and Steamship Association. Unable to disavow their traditional concepts, they attempted to reconcile the new environment and its conditions to the old tenets. Of all the presidents, King stood out as the strongest advocate of the old order. Throughout his tenure he opposed the building of extensive systems and argued for distinct smaller systems run by individual companies.[41] To lesser degrees most of the other presidents agreed, and in so doing enmeshed themselves in contradiction. Distrustful of expansion, they pursued it vigorously with an apologetic plea of necessity, and each successful step took them farther from their desired goals. The L. & N., reviewing its recent burst of expansion in 1880, concluded that:[42]

It is the absolute conviction of your management that the vast command of territory now embraced by your lines of road, with the commanding and strategic position enjoyed by your company, renders the construction of new and competitive lines incapable of inflicting serious damage or loss of business upon your company.

Increasingly, however, the thorny problem of expansion brought the presidents into conflict with their boards and stockholders. One road after another witnessed bitter disputes over policy and open rebellions against the president. Conservative directors and smaller holders resented the suspension of dividends and blamed it on the added financial burdens of expansion; a younger generation of businessmen carped impatiently at what they considered to be the parochial views of the elder statesmen. Under fire from all quarters, the presidents succumbed to the pressure. Only Robinson and Bridgers made terms with the new era and continued their reign undisturbed. The others either died in office while under fire or were ousted after an acrid fight for control. By the 1880's a new set of leaders, representatives of a new generation, had emerged. They are summarized in Table 4.

The new leaders, with the partial exception of Plant, constituted a distinct change from the old presidents and their developmental policy. Their previous experience prepared them for much different expectations and schemes than those of their predecessors.[43] Nearly all had been

TABLE 4
Selected Data on Southern Railroad Leaders 1880–1893[a]

Name	Road	Born	Tenure as Pres.	Principal Occupation
1. William P. Clyde	R. & D.	1839	none	Steamships, financier
John H. Inman	R. & D.	1844	1890–92	Financier, cotton broker
George S. Scott	R. & D.	1837	1884, 1888–89	Financier
2. Samuel Thomas	E. T. V. & G.	1840	1882–90	Financier, industrialist
Calvin S. Brice	E. T. V. & G.	1845	none	Financier, lawyer
3. Harry B. Hollins	C. G.	1854	none	Banker
4. C. C. Baldwin	L. & N.	1830	1881–84	Financier, merchant
Eckstein Norton	L. & N.	1831	1886–91	Banker
5. Clarence H. Clark	N. & W.	1833	none	Banker
6. Henry B. Plant	S. F. & W.	1819	1880–99	Financier, express

[a] The list of roads covered here is shorter than that in Table 3 for the following reasons. Robinson remained as president of the S. & R. throughout the period under study. Bridgers died in 1888 and was succeeded by B. F. Newcomer, who had been involved with the road since the end of the war. No additional president is given for the N. C. & S. L. because the L. & N. purchased control of that road and ousted Cole in 1879–80. The Ga. was leased jointly by the L. & N. and C. G. in 1881.

Sources: Same as Table 3.

uprooted by the war before they had developed careers; hence they emerged from combat somewhat at loose ends, unfettered by local ties, ripe for whatever opportunities happened along, and eager to make their fortunes in an environment extremely congenial to individual action. Their essential business training took place in the immediate postwar era with its emerging industrialism, rampant individualism, and extreme emphasis upon material values. Let loose in an environment stalked by commercial tigers, they learned the art of tooth and claw well.[44]

Not one of the new leaders possessed practical railroad experience. Most were financiers, and in fact their accession marked the beginning of a trend to separate the functions of financial and operational control. Some did not even become president but exercised their influence through control of the board. In these cases the president became merely the operational head. On those roads where the leader assumed the presidency, he tended to leave operations in the hands of a vice-president especially appointed because of his practical railroad experience. A specialization of functions wrought largely by expansion had begun to appear.

The policies created by the financiers bore little resemblance to the old developmental tenets. The most striking difference lay in their distinct lack of local or regional ties and loyalties. It was no accident that many of the new leaders, soon after their acquisition of control, made their company's stock more accessible by listing it on the New York Stock Exchange. Lacking the provincialism of the old presidents, they conceived of their roads not as distinct entities serving specific territories but as mere components of much larger systems spanning the entire section and free from dependence upon any one commercial center as an outlet. Usually, the railroad constituted but one of many diversified financial interests, many of them interdependent. Clyde, for example, moved to railroads as an extension of his interests in steamships; Plant did likewise from his involvement in the express business. Inman, Thomas, and Brice held extensive investments in southern coal, iron, and real estate. The bankers and brokers all did a considerable business in southern railroad securities. None of them made the railroad his exclusive business, and none localized his outside investments nearly as much as the old presidents and their supporters had done. The new leaders were, in the parlance of the era, "men of large affairs."

Nothing betrayed the difference in policy so much as the expansion programs of the new leaders. Instead of backing reluctantly into expansion, they embraced it willingly and on a hitherto unknown scale. Instead of fearing consolidation, they worked tirelessly to create gigantic systems capable of reaching beyond sectional limits for traffic and connections. Instead of sealing off a territory and defending it as their own, they aggressively penetrated every possible territory to compete with other lines organizing in like manner. The very scale of their consolidation efforts pushed competitors into similar policies and thus accelerated the process. Their impersonal approach and geographic indifference soon closed the era of individual territories and even the more recent development of individual competing through lines. In their place came a small group of sectional giants competing with each other in virtually every corner of the South. The financiers built and consolidated at an unprecedented pace. During the 1880's the South virtually doubled her railroad mileage: at the end of 1860 she possessed 9,190 miles; in 1870 11,587 miles; in 1880 15,469 miles; and in 1890 30,644 miles.[45]

The most conspicuous feature of this expansion to historians and contemporary observers alike was the creation of large systems. Unlike their forerunners, the financiers had few qualms about a low equity–debt ratio. They welded together their new giants through the free use of purchases, leases, and new construction. To finance the process, they resorted almost entirely to bond issues and thus greatly expanded company funded debts. The L. & N.'s funded debt, $16,484,230 in 1877, swelled to $59,572,778 by 1882, and the E. T. V. & G. from $4,110,100 in 1877 to $49,020,000 in 1883.[46] In some cases additional stock was issued as well but rarely to raise capital. Internal financing could not have begun to underwrite expansion on the scale taking place during the 1880's, and none of the financiers gave serious thought to it. The figures in Table 5 suggest the swiftness with which the systems arose.[47]

The justification given in annual reports for this rapid expansion was normally twofold: it protected the company's interests by extending its field of operations into new territories; and the earnings of the new roads, once a traffic developed upon them, would easily cover the cost of their acquisition or construction. On the surface, these explanations seemed compatible with traditional developmental policy, but in practice they were not. For one thing, time would prove the second assumption wrong. Then, too, the financiers seemed unwilling to wait for the final returns on their policies. Unlike their predecessors, the new leaders did not care to sacrifice dividends to underwrite expansion. They continued to pay dividends even though, in some cases, they were not earned. The

TABLE 5
Growth of Selected Southern Railroad Systems 1878–1893 (in miles)[a]

Systems	1878	1883	1893
1. R. & D.	448	2,503	3,429
2. E. T. V. & G.	272	1,389	2,633
3. C. G.	861	1,754	2,841
4. L. & N.	966	3,231	4,396
5. S. & R.	285	527	926
6. Atlantic Coast Line[b]	199	199	1,337
7. N. & W.	428	595	1,567
8. Plant System[c]	350	595	1,403

[a] Figures include all roads directly controlled by the parent system.
[b] The Atlantic Coast Line embraced the W. & W. and other roads.
[c] The Plant System was built around the S. F. & W., successor to the A. & G.
Sources: Calculated from the mileage figures for individual roads as given in the various Poor Manuals.

result of this policy tended to be the accumulation of a persistent floating debt and a diverting of funds needed for maintenance to meet financial crises.[48] By 1893, half the major systems had undergone a financial crisis and reorganization or change of management.

The reign of the financiers proved short and on the whole detrimental. They were poor builders, unwise administrators, and, on occasion, fraudulent manipulators. Their emphasis upon expansion turned out badly because additions to the systems were often ill-considered and consequently became a financial drain upon the parent road—though the transaction itself may have profited the financier handsomely. The most ambitious consolidation effort, the attempt to combine three major systems within a holding company called the Richmond & West Point Terminal Railway and Warehouse Company, crashed in ruins because of mismanagement and peculation.[49]

Their devotion to financial affairs, together with consideration of their biographical backgrounds, seems to offer the most adequate explanation for the performance of the financiers as railroad leaders. They differed most significantly from their predecessors in that they seemed more interested in short-term rather than long-term gains. They came not to build and patiently develop profits out of operations but to make their personal fortunes through construction of new lines and through speculation in and manipulation of securities in all the companies embraced within the consolidated system. Whether the systems they created prospered or failed over the long run seemed not to worry them greatly, for they profited chiefly from the transactions involved in the act of creation and could withdraw from management almost as easily as they had entered. Lacking the personal attachment of the old presidents to the company and the region, they had no scruples about sacrificing the interests of controlled or subsidiary lines to the needs of the parent company in which they were interested. A classic example involved the Richmond Terminal, which acquired control of the C. G. in a maneuver tainted with fraud and subsequently forced the latter to borrow $1,000,000 at 6 percent and lend it to the Terminal at 5 percent.[50]

If the old presidents resembled feudal barons presiding over clearly demarcated domains, the new leaders seemed like exiled princes ever in search of new lands to conquer. At their best they were conscientious financiers like Eckstein Norton, genuinely interested in erecting a sound transportation empire; at their worst they were rapacious freebooters bent on speculative fortunes. To the dismay of the historian they were often a complex mixture of both. Baldwin and Clyde, for example, both acquired unsavory reputations for speculating in their company's stock, yet Clyde made important and original contributions to the steamship industry. Inman, Brice, and Thomas all made fortunes centered around dubious transactions within their companies, but all played important roles in developing the coal, iron, and steel industries of the South.

In spite of their generally negative record, the financiers made genuine contributions to the development of the southern railroad system. Most important, they possessed a breadth of vision usually lacking in the older presidents. By transcending regional loyalties they freed southern lines from their basically local orientation and helped integrate them into a national network. However poorly or unwisely they built, they left the South a coherent and fairly complete rail system. Their ultimate failure lay in their inability to organize and administer efficiently what they had built. Though virtually all of them acknowledged the importance of that task, few displayed either the heart or the talent for it in practice. They took the loose materials and slapped them together in shoddy form, leaving it to more competent carpenters to fashion an enduring structure.

As early as the mid-1880's, when Baldwin was forced out of the L. & N., the financiers began departing the scene. The Panic of 1893 hastened their exit and paved the way for a third group of railroad leaders. The new leaders, all of them trained practical railroad men, would be the competent carpenters. They would reorganize and regroup the systems and give them the most efficient administration of their history. Included among their ranks were such men as Samuel Spencer, Samuel M. Felton, Jr., Henry Fink, Frederick W. Huidekoper, and Milton H. Smith. From their efforts would come the unified systems of the twentieth century, and their accession to power marked the end of what might be called the "adolescent" period of southern railroads.[51]

The Overland Route: First Impressions

> This piece originated as a paper given to the Lexington Group in Transportation in September 1987. It was reworked into another paper for the Mid-America American Studies Association in April 1989 and published in *Railroad History* that same year. Coming directly out of my research in the Union Pacific Railroad, it represented an attempt to capture the social significance and cultural impact of the first transcontinental road in something more than scholarly terms. Recently an editor (not of this press) complained that some of my writing was too "arty." I suppose that same charge could be made against certain passages of this piece, and to it I cheerfully plead guilty.

In an age where satellite communications can take us anywhere in the world within moments, we sometimes forget how short a time it has been since the interior of our own continent seemed as remote and foreboding as darkest Africa. To the generation that swelled with pride over the driving of the golden spike, the spanning of the continent meant something more than faster, easier travel. It offered access to a harsh but spectacular terrain that had long fascinated Americans. No part of the Wild West was more wild than the stretch traversed by the new transcontinental railroad. Apart from the Mormons, only a handful of whites lived there, and only soldiers, trappers, miners, explorers, adventurers, some hardy pioneers, and those who strayed from the Oregon Trail or wandered into the wilderness for purposes of their own had seen any of it.

When the project was taken up in the 1860s, the legend of the Great American Desert still flourished. The interior was forbidding terrain where the weather was fierce, water scarce, and the Indians hostile. Those who knew anything of that vast, desolate stretch across Nevada,

The Overland Route

Utah, and Wyoming were not encouraged at the prospect of its development. To the eyes that had seen it and the imaginations that had not, it seemed as remote and barren a landscape as the moon—which is exactly the right image for our purposes. The building of the first transcontinental railroad was to that generation what the moon project was to ours, the planting of a first tentative foot in unknown space.

A year before the rails joined at Promontory, Walt Whitman captured this sense of exhilaration in a verse from his "Passage to India":

> I see over my own continent the Pacific railroad
>   surmounting every barrier,
> I see continual trains of cars winding along the
>   Platte carrying freight and passengers,
> I hear the locomotives rushing and roaring, and the
>   shrill steam-whistle,
> I hear the echoes reverberate through the grandest
>   scenery in the world . . .

Here surely was one small step for man, one giant step for mankind. In building this ribbon of iron Americans had crossed a frontier of immense possibilities from which there could be no turning back. As always when reaching out toward a world larger than their own, Americans felt confident of making it smaller through familiarity. The pride and surge of excitement they felt at the driving of the golden spike spoke less to what had been achieved than to their anticipation of what was to come.

From the very first, then, the overland route meant much more than a glimpse at exotic scenery. It was a test, a challenge to the greatness Americans felt was their inevitable future. Even a destiny so obviously manifest still had to be acted out on the stage of history, and what grander or more fitting stage for this drama than conquest of this wondrous terra incognita. Far from being merely a route west, it was a path through the wilderness, a corridor of civilization along which the engines of progress would spread their irresistible influence. Some realized there would be losses as well as gains. A young engineer named Arthur Ferguson, toiling in one of the Union Pacific's survey parties during the summer of 1868, grasped this truth. "The time is coming, and fast too," he scribbled in his diary, "when in the sense it is now understood, THERE WILL BE NO WEST."[1]

As a prime instrument of that transformation, the overland route deserves more careful attention than the rhapsodic variations on the "Oh, wasn't it grand?" theme by the Lucius Beebe marching band and chorus. Of the route Beebe sang in his introduction to *The Overland Limited*:

> Its rails led without equivocation through the illimitable spaces of what had once been the land of buffalos and Indian scouts, of the processional covered wagons and the heart's desire of the American people. The pilots of its locomotives led straight to the horizon of the farthest ocean where, if the Manitou spoke sooth, was the edge of the world over whose rim the soul must one day plunge to everlasting forgetfulness.[2]

This sort of romanticism run rampant tells us as much about the real overland route as a Norman Rockwell painting does about family relationships. Like so much of human experience, the whole business seemed so much more appealing and uplifting in retrospect. One useful corrective to this glazing over process is to look at the impressions of those who were present at the creation. This paper offers a glimpse at some responses by people who helped build the road or traveled over its route during the first year or so of its existence.

Consider first what the construction of a transcontinental railroad meant in practical terms. After the Mexican war the United States found itself suddenly possessed of a continent without the means of transportation or communication to connect its opposite ends. Two thousand miles of apparent wasteland and rugged mountains separated the frontier town of Chicago from the burgeoning population of California. To reach the West Coast by sea from New York took thirty-five days to cover 5,250 miles if you sailed to Panama, risked crossing the malaria-infested isthmus, and boarded another ship. Or you could devote nearly five months to sail 13,300 miles around treacherous Cape Horn.[3]

The overland stage route from St. Louis to San Francisco cut the distance to a mere 2,800 miles and the time to thirty days for travelers who could endure the constant jouncing, the vagaries of weather, and the danger. All these routes found takers, especially after the discovery of gold in California and later in Colorado led to a flood of fortune seekers and camp followers heading west. The overland route owes its transition from a visionary scheme to a practical project to the growing demand for a cheaper, safer, more convenient way to penetrate this remote interior.

We sometimes forget how quickly the West changed in the national consciousness from remote moonscape to destiny's doorway. The Mormons knew painfully well how fast this transition occurred. They were the only large colony of whites inhabiting the area, having deliberately chosen the wilds of Utah as a haven from persecution. Once moved to the Salt Lake Valley in 1847, they hoped to dwell there forever without interference from the outside world. It seemed a reasonable hope, yet their isolation lasted barely a decade. One of their early visitors was Samuel B. Reed, an engineer sent west to find a route for the proposed transcontinental road.

When the Pacific Railway Act passed Congress in 1864, the question of what route the Union Pacific should follow had yet to be answered. The Platte River Valley offered an obvious and easy route from the Missouri to the Rockies. Over the years its path had been tramped by buffalo, Indians, fur traders, Mormons, and emigrants bound for Oregon or California. But there were problems even with this route, and huge question marks on the region through the mountains and beyond. In the spring of 1864 Sam Reed went out to explore the farthermost segment of the route from Green River to Salt Lake. Although he did not realize it, his journey offered a unique glimpse of the overland route as it was before the coming of the railroad.

In 1864 the train carried Reed only as far west as Grinnell, Iowa, where he caught a stagecoach for Omaha. Tired and cramped, he pulled into Omaha early on a Sunday morning in April and was surprised to find it bustling with people. Reed looked up one of Brigham Young's sons, who was there waiting to lead an emigrant train across the plains. The elder Young took a keen interest in the railroad project and had agreed to outfit Reed's party. His son provided helpful information, as did other Utah men.[4]

Reed found all the stages booked solid with fortune seekers bound for Montana, where gold had been discovered. "Hundreds pass through here every day," he noted in his dry way, "old men, young men, the lame and the blind with women and children all going westward seeking the promised land." He took a boat downriver to Atchison and managed to wrangle seats on a stage for himself and an assistant, Atchison too was crowded with gold seekers and also runaway slaves. The stage line had hiked its fare to $200 plus a dollar a pound for luggage above twenty-five pounds, which cost Reed another $150 for his instruments.[5]

The two engineers squeezed into a coach with seven other travelers. For thirteen days and nights the stage rattled monotonously onward except when storms or mud forced the driver to lay up. During one downpour the passengers found refuge on beds of hay in a stable; on another night they shared space on a rancher's floor. The hills of southern Nebraska struck Reed as dreary and desolate, broken only by an occasional cabin or stage station, where teams were changed and a meal of hard bread and bacon could be gulped down. At one stop everyone got sick from drinking alkali water. On the road the hours passed like days in the cramped, jouncing coach.[6]

A week after leaving Atchison the stage pulled into Latham Station, where the Denver passengers changed coaches. Reed and his assistant alone continued on through the mountains, crossing the divide at Bridger's Pass. There he got his first glimpse of the Rockies, the barrier through which he was expected to find an opening. At journey's end Salt Lake came as no less a revelation to the tired and dirty Reed than the massive ranges that shielded it from the outside world. Although he did not share the prejudice of many Americans against the Mormons, he was astounded to find that their Zion in the Wilderness was more than myth. "I have never been in a town of this size in the United States where everything is kept in such perfect order," he marveled. "No hogs or cattle allowed to run at large in the streets and every available nook of ground is made to bring forth fruit, vegetables, or flowers for man's use."[7]

Brigham Young greeted Reed warmly and provided him with three teams, tents, camp equipment, and fifteen men. Reed paused to give the men a week of training, then headed north to where the Weber River emerged from the mountains into Salt Lake Valley. By sheer coincidence he commenced his survey near the spot that five years later would become the western terminus of the Union Pacific Railroad. Entering the canyon, he was awed by the sight of a deep narrow gorge through which the river snaked between towering walls several thousand feet high. It was, he enthused, "the wildest place you can imagine." He had found Devil's Gate.[8]

For nearly four months the party hacked its way through thick brush and clambered along canyon walls. Occasionally they stumbled onto a valley tucked behind the ridges and were grateful for the relief from their exertions. At night they slept on the ground beneath buffalo robes. Food was plentiful while they lingered near the Mormon settlements scattered through the valleys. On Young's orders the faithful provided the surveyors with fresh mutton, butter, eggs, and milk. Reed's men caught trout and shot an occasional antelope to vary their diet of bacon, bread, beans, and fruit. "I can eat more at a meal than ever before in my life," Reed noted happily, "and don't care how often the meals occur."[9]

Field work had a bewitching effect on engineers, and Reed too felt its magic. The harder he worked, the better he felt. The challenge of finding a good line through the wilderness drove him joyously onward. He came to love the country and its spectacular beauty, the hard, clean brilliance of the air, the warm days and cold nights when ice as thick as window panes formed on the dishes even in summer. Life was elemental and palpable, stripped of all cant, transparent in its excitement as well as its dangers.

Reed had made in fact what would become in fiction the central theme of the American experience: the pilgrimage from civilization back to nature. He was far from being the only engineer to treasure that journey as a time when, for a few brief months, his life seemed to transcend the mundane level of ordinary affairs. Nor was he alone in failing to see the savage irony in his mission. He had come as agent of those forces eager to transform the wilderness by harnessing it to the blessings of civilization and progress.

Not all the engineers found their work so enchanting. In 1865 Arthur Ferguson ventured uneasily into the region between the Platte and Republican rivers, where some of the worst clashes with the Indians had occurred. "This is a terrible country," he wrote, "the stillness, wildness & desolation of which is awful. Not a hill to be seen, nothing but a succession of hill & valley." An army doctor tramping the overland route in July 1867 found along the north border of the Platte River "not a tree, bush, not even a stick of wood . . . nothing but one broad, level expanse of green land, dotted with little patches of prairie grass."[10]

Once into Wyoming, the good doctor found more congenial scenery. There he reveled in a prairie of "fragrant and beautifully tinted flowers. Diminutive purple morning glories, sweetly scented roses, yellow butter-cups, and crimson bell shaped flowers are blooming in luxurious profusion." In the bottomlands delicate lilies reared their white heads in numbers that carved winding streams of milk through the thick, wet prairie grass. "No plant is prettier than the cactus," he marveled, "which shoots forth its red and golden flowers in June and July." Beyond the heaving green sea to the west lay the snow-capped peaks of the Rockies shimmering in the sunlight. At night the doctor basked in the small pleasures of camp life, "the pipe of tobacco as you lie in the warmth of the camp-fire digesting your hearty meal, smoking and either engaged with your thoughts or listening to some legend that is always told among a party of officers."[11]

West of Cheyenne the country got decidedly less hospitable. That same summer the redoubtable Grenville M. Dodge, chief engineer of the Union Pacific and the man most responsible for seeing the road to completion, retraced the steps of Percy Browne, an engineer slain by Indians, from Fort Sanders across the continental divide. As he passed through wild, forbidding country north of the Medicine Bow range, Dodge found his mind dwelling on what a spectacle the scenery would make from the window of a passing train. In the Rattlesnake (now Saddleback) Hills he found a pass striking the head of Mary's Creek. He named the pass in Browne's honor and later gave the name Percy to a station at the head of Mary's Creek. Near the top of Browne's Pass the geologist in the party found immense deposits of coal at a place Dodge called Carbon. The company's first coal mine would be located there.[12]

A day after crossing the continental divide, Dodge ordered his party to fan out in search of water. Wandering southward with General John A. Rawlins, the close confidant of Ulysses S. Grant who was suffering from consumption and had come west for his health, Dodge struck a spring in the arid countryside gushing water from a bed of rock. Rawlins tasted the water and pronounced it "the most gracious thing" he had ever found. His endorsement prompted Dodge to name the place in Rawlins's honor. He also discovered that the spring had cut its way through the ridge beyond, making passage easy for a roadbed.[13]

Heading northward, Dodge was astonished to find that the mountains gave way to a series of basins, at the center of which lay a giant basin some 300 feet below the surrounding country. A vast plain running 200 miles east-west and 100 miles north-south stretched before him, with little vegetation and no living streams. It would, he realized, make an easy line if water could be found. He assumed the divide descended toward Green River; instead his party found itself plodding into the giant basin and through the alkali wastes of the Red Desert. On the third day their water ran out and scouts found only dry creek beds, the "shallow graves of deceased rivers." Burned and blinded by the sun, their tongues swollen with thirst, men and animals endured two days' march without water before stumbling onto an alkali lake. The water was not palatable, but they swarmed gratefully to it.[14]

Nearby they bumped into another survey party working east from Green River. They too had been without water for three days and were in terrible shape, some of them violently ill from stagnant or poisonous water they had found in the desert. Comparing notes brought Dodge to the realization that the continental divide had not one but two summits, at opposite ends of the giant basin. He led his party down an old trail in search of an outlet over the western rim of the basin to Bitter Creek, painfully aware now that it was "all-important to cross these plains on the shortest possible route that would carry our line from running water to running water."[15]

After some rugged going, Dodge's party struck Bitter Creek at Point of Rocks, the sandstone cliffs carved into bizarre shapes by the wind. Dodge guessed that an excellent line with low grades could be found across the divide by leaving the basin earlier and finding a gentler approach to Bitter Creek. He was right, but the engineer sent to find such a line did so only after months of great hardship and difficult work. From Bitter Creek, Dodge followed a splendid line run by James A. Evans in 1864 through the winding valley to Green River. There he met a survey party headed by Fred Hodges, who had been exploring the ground from Salt Lake to Green River via Bear River.

Hodges's report left Dodge uncertain as to the best route from Green River to Salt Lake. He decided to follow the line run earlier by Reed along Black's Fork to Fort Bridger, up Muddy Creek and across the divide to Bear River Valley and into Echo Canyon. Close inspection showed it was a good line that could be made better. From Echo his party wound its way into Weber Canyon and through the narrows to Salt Lake Valley. The trip convinced Dodge that the true line lay north of Salt Lake and probably along a refined version of Reed's original survey. Once again he was right.[16]

If this were not enough, Dodge also had a grand notion about a route all the way to Puget Sound via the Snake River. On his return trip he followed Hodges's line north to Soda Springs and beyond to Gray's Lake, where he reached the waters of the Snake. What he saw convinced him that a route along the Snake River Valley "would be by far the best line from the Atlantic to the Pacific, would avoid the high elevation of the Wahsatch [sic] and Sierra Nevadas with their heavy grades and troublesome snows." From atop a ridge he peered across a magnificent wilderness through which the Union Pacific would later build its Oregon Short Line.[17]

On this remarkable journey Dodge had done more than survey a major portion of the Union Pacific route west of the plains. Along the way he had mapped a part of the West, filling it with names and places that would become legendary—including Cheyenne itself, which he named after the dominant tribe of the region despite his hostility toward Indians. For all his own earnest swipes at self-promotion, Dodge has never received honor or recognition worthy of his immense achievement with the Union Pacific.

No one deserves more credit for the overland route than Dodge and his corps of engineers, who by 1868 had completed a line all the way to Humboldt Wells. Dodge was a fair but stern taskmaster; at Promontory Point he made the crews run a dozen lines until he got one that satisfied him. Nothing in the early history of the Union Pacific proved more impressive or enduring than the final route located through a forbidding, unmapped wilderness bristling with natural obstacles. Allowed grades of 116 feet by law, the engineers included none above ninety feet. History has demolished the charge that they made the line longer than necessary to garner more subsidy bonds from the government. When E. H. Harriman spent millions to improve the line, his engineers lopped only thirty miles off the original 1,032 miles to Ogden. The two major reductions came at points where the original survey had been altered over the engineer's protests.

Behind the engineers came the construction crews, who found the region west of Laramie as unpalatable as Dodge had warned. "It is not," wrote James Evans wryly, "a country where people are disposed to linger." Jack Casement, one of the brothers in charge of track-laying, did not mince words. "This is an awfull place," he grumbled about the desert, "alkali dust knee deep and certainly the meanest place I have ever been in."[18]

The crews did not wander into the wilderness alone, not even into the desert. On their trail came the porta-towns dubbed "Hell-on-Wheels," a motley collection of makeshift structures that housed an even more motley collection of camp followers who preyed on the construction gangs. They were the ghost towns of the overland route, unfolding overnight wherever the crews camped and disappearing in a wink once the men pushed farther west. The most miserable of these hellholes was Benton, set smack in the desert where the alkali dust was eight inches deep and inhaling it drew blood from the lungs.[19]

Benton, wrote a Cheyenne editor, "like the camps of the Bedouin

Arabs, is of tents, and almost a transitory nature as the elements of a soap bubble." Those hardy enough to visit the place came away with the feeling that they had glimpsed a suburb of hell. Novelist J. H. Beadle turned up there in August 1868. Tromping through the alkali in his black suit until he resembled a cockroach scuttling across a flour barrel, he found "not a green tree, shrub or patch of grass. The red hills were scorched as bare as if blasted by lightning." What did impress him was the "Big Tent," the drinking and gambling emporium that had served Julesberg, Cheyenne, and Laramie before making its desert debut.

A hundred feet long and forty feet wide, the tent had a floor for dancing and a raised platform for the band, which stood ready to play day and night. An elegant bar glittering with mirrors and paintings dispensed liquor in cut-glass goblets and pitchers. The rest of the space was devoted to tables for faro, monte, roulette, or whatever game of chance the reckless cared to try. Around the Big Tent sprang up a town of tents, shacks, and buildings of thinly painted pine that could be bought in Chicago for $300 and put up in a day by two boys with nothing more than screwdrivers.

Samuel Bowles, the genteel editor of the Springfield *Republican*, came to Benton and described it as "a village of a few variety stores and shops, by day disgusting, by night dangerous, almost everybody dirty, many filthy with the marks of lowest vice, averaging a murder a day, gambling and drinking, hurdy dancing and the vilest of sexual commerce." The alkali was "so fine and volatile that the slightest breeze loaded the air with it, irritating every sense and poisoning half of them." The inhabitants he referred to graciously as a "congregation of scum." It never occurred to Bowles that people were dirty because water cost a dime a bucket and once ran as high as ten dollars a barrel.

Located two miles west of Sinclair, Benton lingered no longer than any of the Hell-on-Wheels porta-towns. So wretched was its location that all the inhabitants followed the construction crews westward to Green River. Beadle revisited the site of Benton ten months later and found not a single house or tent, only the rubble of a few chimneys and the inevitable layer of alkali covering even the town's only surviving institution, the cemetery.

Camp followers were not the only visitors to the overland route in 1868. The construction gangs found themselves overrun by excursionists eager to see the West and inspect the progress on the great national highway. That summer W. C. Durant hosted a party of journalists headed by Charles Dana of the New York *Sun*, who dubbed themselves the "Rocky Mountain Press Club." A few weeks later Schuyler Colfax, soon to be vice president, toured the road, and behind him came a band of professors from Yale, who watched in awe as Jack Casement's men obligingly laid four miles of track one day. The visitors, complained Superintendent Webster Snyder, "have interfered with our work very much & have worn me out." Casement agreed they were "a great nuisance," but even in its infancy the overland route coveted good public relations.[20]

As the track snaked westward, excitement mounted over the prospect of the road's completion. "The day will soon come, we dare say," burbled the New York *Tribune*, "when it will be nothing unusual for a railroad to measure its length by thousands of miles, instead of by scores and fifties; but an unbroken line of rails so long as this is now almost unprecedented." Along the path new stations sprang up with names reflecting the harsh, exotic beauty of the country that would later delight travelers: Separation, Creston, Red Desert, Table Rock, Bitter Creek, Black Buttes, Point of Rock, Salt Wells, Rock Springs.[21]

After the driving of the golden spike, passengers flocked eagerly to the new overland route, not yet aware of the extent to which transcontinental travel was above all an endurance test. The Union Pacific ran one passenger and two freight trains a day in each direction. Westbound passengers made Promontory in fifty-four hours (an average of about nineteen miles an hour), while the eastbound trip required sixty hours. The usual train of two sleepers, two first-class cars, smoker, baggage, and mail cars could accommodate about 110 passengers who in August 1869 paid $63.33 apiece for the trip. Second-class or immigrant passengers paid only $26.81, but their spartan coaches were hitched to freight trains, which made the run in about four days going west and five or six days eastbound. An average freight train hauled twenty-two cars, and, after shedding four of five of them with way freight, climbed the mountains without help behind a forty-ton engine.[22]

Through service to Sacramento cost $111 and took about a hundred hours for passengers, not including the transfer delays at Promontory. A person boarding in New York arrived in San Francisco about a week later for a fare of $150. Along the way the train stopped a half hour or less for meals at eating houses. Although the trip was an ordeal even for first-class passengers, it was rapid transit compared to the horrors of what had gone before. By June 1870 fares from New York to San Francisco had dropped to $136 for first class and $110 for immigrants, whose coaches were now attached to passenger trains. This change alone cut almost in half the time immigrants had to endure the bone-rattling ride in the cabooses or converted boxcars used to accommodate them.[23]

Those who could afford it found some relief in the luxurious trappings of Pullman's Palace Cars. George M. Pullman came early to the Union Pacific with his newfangled sleepers, joining forces with Andrew Carnegie to offer a proposal in 1867. The result was creation in January 1868 of the Pullman Pacific Car Company in which the Union Pacific owned slightly more than half the shares. It may be true, as has been said, that Pullman's only real invention was railroad comfort, but on the long ride west that was no small blessing. His cars, with their plush, ornate interiors especially delighted British tourists, the exception being a parson who found it "an odd experience, that going to bed of some thirty ladies, gentlemen, and children, in, practically, one room."[24]

The demand for accommodations inspired Pullman to a bold experiment. In December 1869 he persuaded the two Pacific roads to cooperate in running a "Hotel Train" under his management. To his sleepers Pullman added new dining, drawing room, and saloon cars, thereby eliminating meal stops. By dropping the transfer as well, the weekly special advertised that it could make San Francisco from Omaha in only eight-one hours and, with good connections, New York to San Francisco in five and a half days. The train ran from October 1869 until June 1870, when the Central Pacific abruptly withdrew from the agreement. For a short time the Union Pacific ran it as far as Ogden, then discontinued the train altogether.[25]

Although the Hotel Train's life was brief, it offered a preview of what elegance on wheels could be. There were several reasons why the Central Pacific pulled out with such unseemly haste. The operations people on both roads complained that the heavier Pullman equipment, coupled with the faster speed of the special train, wore down the roadbed at a brutal pace. A more compelling reason had to do with a growing clash of interests between the Central Pacific and the Union Pacific, one that caught Pullman in the middle from the very beginning.

The Central Pacific took a dark view of through passenger service and was reluctant to cooperate in any such venture for one very basic reason: through service obliterated the separate identity of the Central Pacific, which could be clearly if inconveniently impressed on travelers by the transfer at Ogden. It had taken an arduous battle to bring the Hotel Train to life, and the battle did not end with its death. For three decades the same objection would confound attempts to offer premium through train service from Omaha to San Francisco.

Apart from the issue of corporate identity, the Central Pacific and Union Pacific also differed fundamentally on how to operate their passenger service. The Union Pacific decided early to entrust its sleepers to Pullman; the Central Pacific ran its own sleeper cars. This meant the hotel train was an extension of policy for the Union Pacific, a departure for the Central Pacific. Early in 1870 Pullman tried to lure the Central Pacific into joining the Pullman Pacific Car Company, which would in effect have made them all partners and let Pullman manage the service over the entire line. A meeting was scheduled to finalize terms, but the deal got entangled in a dispute between the two roads.[26]

In fact the Big Four of the Central Pacific disagreed among themselves over what to do. Charles Crocker knew the company's own sleepers were already running to capacity and could not handle the load if the Hotel Train sleepers were eliminated. He favored consolidation, arguing that "we will make the most money by running Sleepers through from Omaha to S. F. & I believe Pullman will manage the line better than we do." Mark Hopkins disagreed vehemently. "The less of mixed management," he growled, ". . . the better it would be for us."[27]

Hopkins opposed what he called "this Pullman humbug" because it siphoned profits that he thought belonged to the road, and he bitterly resented the Hotel Train. "The effect of . . . permitting *them to do it*," he railed, "has been to give them the opportunity to disparage our own regular sleepers, as 'second rate,' 'rattle traps,' & 'entirely unsafe' &c &c—and they have blowed hard & made the most of their opportunity." Hotel trains also discouraged the growth of eating stations, which were needed for regular passenger trains and which, Hopkins thought, were useful in building up towns and industrial interests along the line.[28]

Huntington sided with Hopkins and the consolidation never occurred. Whatever the benefits for the Central Pacific, the lack of premium through service did nothing for the traveling public. For all the exotic and romantic flavor of the overland route, the actual journey was taxing enough to test the hardiest traveler. Skeptics still doubted whether the road could operate in winter. A few days after the golden spike one old mountain country hand assured readers of the New York *Tribune* that "the present route can never be relied on for a Winter route." Early experiences with blizzards nearly proved him right. It was a long time before easterners comprehended the severity of a plains blizzard.[29]

The Overland Route

Other dangers menaced the early traveler. The first fatal accident occurred on July 15 that first summer, when heavy rains undermined the track and derailed a train, killing the fireman and a passenger. Indians killed a section hand in May 1870 and kept passengers jittery for months over an attack or derailment. Fires and storms sweeping across the prairie raised hackles on travelers' necks, as did crossing the spidery Dale Creek Bridge. For most, however, fatigue and discomfort were the worst of it. There were long delays making connections in Chicago and interminable waits to cross the Missouri in what one passenger called a "rickety old ferry boat."[30]

Omaha itself was a mudhole or a dust bowl, its depot a swirl of confusion from which trains departed with no more warning than the abrupt shriek of a whistle and a cry of "All Aboard!" from the conductor, leaving those caught by surprise to jump aboard moving cars. The coaches were stifling in summer, freezing in winter. Open windows inhaled a cloud of smoke and hot cinders from the engine. With few exceptions the food at eating houses ranged from bad to awful, with the usual fare being steak, fried potatoes, fried eggs, and tea for every meal.

The pleasures came mainly from the passing spectacles of nature: waving oceans of prairie grass sprinkled with flowers, the bounding tumbleweeds of autumn; herds of antelope racing the cars; the playful antics of prairie dogs in their villages; occasional packs of wolves or coyotes or elk, or a lone bear, and sometimes even a few buffalo; farther west the snow-capped mountains and soaring profiles of rock looming above Echo and Weber canyons; the forlorn isolation of Thousand-Mile Tree, Castle Rock, Hanging Rock, Devil's Slide, and the slashing course of the Weber River along its jagged bed; the sudden entry into the forbidden land of the Mormons; and beyond that the barren desert, steep, rugged mountains, and the descent into the lush valleys of California.

For tourists this glimpse of worlds unknown to them was the thrill of a lifetime as it can seldom if ever be to our generation. The overland route still lives, but in a very different way. Except for some of its most durable scenic monuments, the West as it was has long since left us. Indeed, like so much of nature, it began changing the moment we laid eyes and hands on it. Equally important, we are as changed as the West. To a large extent we have lost that sense of wonder and innocence that was part of life a century ago. In our time we see places a hundred times over before we actually come to them. There is scarcely anything left to us like the original overland route except the mysteries of outer space.

First impressions are by their very nature a beginning, and they have a way of lingering long after the world has become a very different thing to us. For that reason it is only fitting to close this look backward with the reminiscence of Alva B. Cady, who grew up on a farm near Grand Island and became an agent for the Union Pacific:

In travelling on the great Overland Limited now [1922], you will see thousands of these old maple trees on the old Cady place, and also on the Dye and Beaman farms near the growing city of Lockwood, Nebraska, where, as a boy, I watched the old Union Pacific No. 1 and No. 2, with their great two-wheeled engines, pass through one corner of our farm daily. I used to stand and watch them, wondering what was behind the western horizon, and envy the trainmen who wore nice blue uniforms and did not have to milk cows, feed hogs, hoe corn in the hot sun, and run for the cyclone cellar when the "jimmycane" came up suddenly and unroofed the straw roofed barn.[31]

Here in a very real sense was the overland route that mattered most. It didn't run across prairie or mountains at all. Instead it ran through the imaginations of countless boys like Alva Cady, and there it will endure unchanged and unchanging for as long as dreams last.

1. **Pride of place:** railroad crew poses proudly in front of their Kansas Pacific locomotive, Abilene, Kansas, 1887.

2. **Where the officers worked:** the Omaha office of William R. McKeen, Jr., superintendent of motive power and machinery for the Union Pacific Railroad and inventor of the McKeen Motor Car in 1905.

3. Where the shopmen worked: the machine shop of the Union Pacific Railroad in Omaha, probably 1900s.

4. Building the Overland Route: a work crew pauses in its labors above the construction train in the barren Bitter Creek Valley, Wyoming.

Building the Overland Route: construction over the Weber River at Devil's Gate, called by engineer Samuel Reed, "the wildest place you can imagine."

The Overland Route: a later view of the line reaching into Weber Canyon.

7. **On the inside looking out:** a buffet-lounge car interior, 1907.

8. **Plenty of free parking:** on main street in Salt Lake City, Utah, 1865.

Man of mystery: Jay Gould ponders his next move.

10. **Late bloomer:** E. H. Harriman captured in a rare moment of repose.

11. **Not all heroes were baseball players:** a profile of E. H. Harriman in the June 1936 issue of *Railroad Stories*.

12. Reconstructing the Overland Route: progress on a giant fill in the Papio Valley, Nebraska, part of Harriman's modernizing of the Union Pacific line.

13. Creating something from nothing: the new Union Pacific depot looms over the scattered buildings of a budding new town in the desert called Las Vegas, 1906.

14. Grooming the Iron Horse: machinists at work on a locomotive in the Omaha shops of the Union Pacific Railroad, 1908.

5. The shape of things to come: one of William R. McKeen's new motor cars, 1905 or 1906.

6. King of the beasts: a Union Pacific 4000-class "Big Boy" locomotive, first built in 1941 for freight service and the largest steam locomotive ever built.

17. Dressing up for the future: a Mountain-class Union Pacific steam locomotive, streamlined for passenger service, 1937.

18. The real thing: a diesel locomotive pulls the Union Pacific passenger train "City of San Francisco" past Riview, Wyoming.

19. The new breed: a diesel unit hauls a train of PFE refrigerator cars eastward at Inkom, Idaho, near Pocatello.

20. The new railroad doesn't always run on tracks: one of the early trucks used in combined rail-truck service on the Union Pacific Railroad.

21. The dawn of a new era in technology: an early Centralized Traffic Control board at East Los Angeles on the Union Pacific Railroad.

In Search of Jay Gould

> This article originated as a paper given to the Organization of American Historians in 1976. It marked the beginning of what turned into something between an odyssey and an obsession with Gould. I had originally intended to do a novel based on Gould's life. When I took the idea to a Boston publishing house, the editor persuaded me to do a short biography as part of the research for the novel. While fulfilling that task, I kept discovering source materials that I had been assured did not exist, and my small biography turned into a large one and a major piece of revisionist history. This destiny had not yet been revealed to me at the time I reworked the paper into this article, which appeared in the *Business History Review* in 1978. Although considered an important piece of work at the time, it was overshadowed by the biography eight years later.

In their use of biography, historians have often assumed too much from too little. Individual lives by themselves do not "explain" what an age is all about; nor are they "explained" by broad social forces, abstract laws, or even the play of serendipity. In the succinct if somewhat oversimple observation of John A. Garraty, "The individual makes history; so does chance; so do social forces."[1] To depict a person as a product of his or her era reduces the complex multiplicity of both the individual and the age to an appealing but distorted simplicity.

While American history abounds with examples of this dilemma, no individual illustrates it more perfectly than Jay Gould, whose historical image hovers somewhere between legend and cliché. Historians have had no more success in understanding Gould than the businessmen who dealt with him. Then, as now, he seems so much a man of his time that it is difficult to separate the one from the other. Our image of his era, whether we call it the Gilded Age, the Age of Excess, the Great Barbeque, the Age of Enterprise, or the Search for Order, derives largely from the activities of Gould and other businessmen. No other group challenges them for center stage during the post–Civil War years. Their careers have been interpreted in varying ways: Allowing for distinctions and finer shadings, they have been cast by different historians as Robber Barons, Industrial Statesmen, and as key agents of far-reaching institutional changes in American society.[2]

However historians interpret their behavior, they agree that Gould and his peers exemplify the elemental forces of their age. They were the prime movers, the architects of industrial America. This characterization has in turn done much to color our impressions of them as individuals, to suggest not only what they did, but who and what they were and even their worth as human beings. Once enlisted as raw data for historical generalizations, they were stripped in large part of their distinctive personalities and reduced to colorful, one-dimensional stereotypes.

This process has exacted an especially harsh toll from Jay Gould, who occupies an unenviable niche as the supreme villain of his era. With few exceptions, contemporary and modern critics have heaped opprobrium upon his name with a vigor that is astonishing in its duration and depth of feeling. Even those who admired Gould's talents did so with a mixture of awe and revulsion, as if they were fascinated by the movements of some exotic but deadly predator. A consensus of catcalls emerges from even a cursory sample of opinions past and present. Daniel Drew, ruined by Gould after an unsuccessful attempt to double-cross him, said simply that "His touch is death."[3] James R. Keene, another disaffected ex-ally, denounced Gould as "the worst man on earth since the beginning of the Christian era. He is treacherous, false, cowardly and a despicable worm incapable of a generous nature."[4]

This vituperation was echoed by other embittered rivals, business associates, stockholders, assorted moralizers, and editors. Newspapermen especially had a field day. Joseph Pulitzer called Gould "one of the most sinister figures that have ever flitted bat-like across the vision of the American people." A New York *Herald* editorial argued that "he should be called the Skunk of Wall Street, not one of its ubiquitous Wolves and Wizards." In England a financial journal declared that "like the Ishmaelite of old, his hand is raised against every man, and every man's hand is against him.... But to attempt to sketch the character of Mr. Jay Gould in its true colors would be futile, since no language is equal to the task."[5]

Silver-tongued orator Robert G. Ingersoll, finding himself counsel in one of the countless lawsuits brought against Gould, sputtered, "I do not believe that since man was in the habit of living on this planet anyone has ever lived possessed of the impudence of Jay Gould."[6] The fastidious Henry Adams described Gould as "small and slight in person, dark, sallow, reticent, and stealthy, with a trace of Jewish origin" and said of him, "there was a reminiscence of the spider in his nature. He spun huge webs, in corners and in the dark, which were seldom strong enough to resist a serious strain at the critical moment."[7]

Except for Julius Grodinsky's monumental study and Lucius F. Ellsworth's recent article on Gould's career in tanning, the views of more recent writers have varied little in tone and even less in substance.[8] Textbooks, general histories, and monographs usually dismiss Gould as one of the more spectacular freebooters of the crass Gilded Age. According to John A. Garraty, "Gould's career encompasses almost every known variety of chicanery, from stock watering and industrial blackmail to bribery, market manipulation, and union busting."[9] One leading textbook labelled Gould "the most notorious land pirate of all the railroad barons."[10] Matthew Josephson, who called Gould "the capitalist par excellence," admired his talents and lack of self-deception as much as he loathed the destructive ends to which they were put: "Where certain of his rivals, intoxicated with power, learned to crave glory too, Jay Gould seemed to place himself above such human vanities. Nor did any social interest, or any sentimental consideration, as to the size or beauty of an enterprise, deflect him for a moment from his marvelously logical line of movement. No human instinct of justice or patriotism or pity caused him to deceive himself, or to waver in any perceptible degree from the steadfast pursuit of strategic power and liquid assets."[11] Cochran and Miller too marveled at Gould's abilities, while deploring their effects. Of Gould's market manipulations they wrote, "he knew his instrument like a virtuoso, knew every permutation and combination of its possibilities, knew how to exploit them till he hovered again and again on the very brink of failure but never once fell over."[12] As a businessman he learned the knack of "using the stock market as his lever to force combinations." Between his booming promotions and bear raids he "milked the assets of his companies until they became in fact the carcasses he had claimed they were when he started his bearish machinations. Gould improvised many variations on his favorite theme of profits through destruction."[13]

Only one critic, Gustavus Myers, bothered to inquire why Gould had been singled out as the *bête noire* of his age. After all, Myers argued, "it was only in degree, and not at all in kind, that he differed from the general run of wealth builders. The Vanderbilts committed acts of as great enormity as his, but they gradually managed to weave around themselves an exterior of protective respectability." Yet no one outstripped Myers in his excoriation of Gould: "Gould was impeached as one of the most audacious and successful buccaneers of modern times. Without doubt he was so; a freebooter who, if he could not appropriate millions, would filch thousands; a pitiless human carnivore, glutting on the blood of his numberless victims; a gambler destitute of the usual gambler's code of fairness in abiding by the rules; an incarnate fiend of a Machiavelli in his calculations, his schemes and ambushes, his plots and counterplots."[14]

Alongside the composite portrait that emerges from these descriptions, Dorian Gray seems but a choir boy in comparison. Gould looms as a dark, sinister figure of almost supernatural powers in judging men, markets, and manipulative possibilities. A cold, calculating loner, his eye ever on the main chance, he crushed rivals, betrayed friends, fleeced unwary investors, corrupted judges and legislatures, tyrannized workingmen, and flouted every standard of decency and morality.

If this were a complete and true picture of Gould, he must indeed have been something more or less than human, the grandest villain in all American history. But there is more to the story. Scholars have neglected virtually everything about Gould except his business career. Little has been written about his personality, attitudes, social behavior, or his psychological and emotional characteristics. Historians, and even biographers, too often fail to deal with the whole person. They have rigorously investigated the effects of business upon life, but rarely explored the effects of life upon business. An artist is more than his technique; so is a businessman. It is important to know about Gould the businessman, but that knowledge alone cannot inform us about the whole man. Close attention must also be given to the broader context of his life and personality.

Gould's Defenders

Even Gould's severest critics concede that his private life was as unblemished as his business career was tarnished. Gould had no vices and indulged in no excesses except overwork.[15] He ate little, did not smoke or drink, and kept no stables of horses or mistresses.[16] He loved his wife and children and was devoted to them with a regularity that put even Victorian convention to shame. Fashionable society meant nothing to Gould; he shunned formal entertainments ("unescapables" he called them) whenever possible. Unlike most of his peers he made no effort to translate his wealth into social standing. While the fashionable played golf or rode to hounds, danced their cotillions, or exchanged snippets of malice at elegant soirees, Gould was content to curl up in his library with a good book. His few social intimates, like the Russell Sages, themselves tended to be outside the social whirlpool.

It was not that Gould lacked pleasures but that his pleasures were simple.[17] He was no puritan in Babylon. While his association with the Falstaffian Jim Fisk may have occasionally caused him discomfort, he never publicly censured Fisk's roisterings. When Fisk died, Gould sobbed openly and later eased his widow's bereavement with financial assistance, an act of charity he was to perform for others as well. For himself, he loved to read; his library overflowed with thick volumes on an incredible range of subjects. He had a passion for flowers, owned the largest and finest private greenhouse in America, and took special delight in his orchid collection. Horticulture became a passion with him that extended beyond the greenhouse to the grounds of Lyndhurst, his estate at Irvington-on-Hudson. Besides books and horticulture Gould allowed himself the luxury of a floating palace. If his 243-foot yacht *Atalanta* seemed a wanton extravagance, it was put to modest service.[18] Unlike others of his class, Gould used his yacht not for extramarital dalliances and rarely for racing but rather for family excursions, for commuting between New York City and Lyndhurst, and for long cruises to revive his fragile health.

In his personal habits and tastes, then, Gould was as sober and conventional as he was daring and unpredictable in business. Of course details about his private life, while they provide a fuller picture of the man, do not alter the facts of his business career. But even in that realm the case is not as clear-cut as Gould's critics have put it. Later sections will take up this discrepancy in more detail, but its dimensions can be outlined here.

If Gould had critics by the legion, he also had faithful allies and disinterested defenders who did not regard him as a perfect engine of perfidy. Collis P. Huntington, who fought many a savage battle with Gould, said of him, "I know there are many people who do not like him. . . . I will say that I always found that he would do just as he agreed to do."[19] The son of Ezra Cornell, who succeeded his father on the board of the Gould-controlled Western Union, stated that "He was the most misunderstood businessman in the country. . . . I regard Mr. Gould as one of the most remarkable men America has produced. . . . He was the soul of honor in his personal integrity."[20] Similarly E. Ellery Anderson, who had been appointed by Grover Cleveland to the commission investigating the affairs of the Union Pacific Railroad, admitted that "I have always found, even to the most trivial detail, that Mr. Gould lived up to the whole nature of his obligations. Of course, he was always reticent and careful about what he promised, but that promise was invariably fulfilled."[21]

Since none of these men were cronies or lackeys of Gould, one may allow their testimony as much weight as that of his antagonists. Those who worked closely with Gould—Russell Sage, Sidney Dillon, Judge John F. Dillon, Samuel Sloan, Giovanni P. Morosini, Washington Connor, Norvin Green, and several of his employees—attest to this same view. Taken together, their statements share at least two common themes: that Gould was grossly misunderstood by most men and that, in Connor's words, "The people who spoke unkindly of Jay Gould were those who in many instances had never seen the man and . . . never had any business dealings with him."[22]

Gould's Secretiveness

Nor is Gould's reputation as an unrestrained wrecker of values and properties so clear-cut. Two factors obscure his precise role in individual market operations. First, his secretiveness was so complete that in any given activity we do not know exactly what he did, much less why he did it and what if anything he gained from it. Even his closest associates confessed ignorance of his true designs.[23] A thick cloud of rumor and confusion obscured every Gould transaction, the effect of which was to produce a host of speculations about his real intentions. Since all the facts rarely came out, even long afterward, much of Gould's market career remains shrouded in mystery. As one journalist wrote in 1872, "Gould is not the sort of man to leave his tracks clearly marked in the dirt."[24]

Secondly, every Gould market operation attracted both friendly and hostile camp followers. Gould may have been a lone wolf but his reputation lured many speculators into divining his purpose and trying to profit from following his lead or opposing it. Brokers and journals alike ascribed to Gould an almost mystical power over the market. One journal called him "undeniably the most potent person in the speculative ranks."[25] In December 1881, a Philadelphia paper attributed a sharp break in the market to Gould's maneuvers: "It was a striking instance of the immense power which one man can exercise. Jay Gould has done more in a single week, without the aid of a solitary bear event or disaster, than all the Vanderbilts, Mills, Cammacks, Keenes, Sages, and Osbornes were able to accomplish with the assistance of an assassination, a change of administration, a tight money market, a railroad war, a short crop, a drought, and a flood, so long as the little dark man was not in sympathy with them."[26] While these accounts exaggerated Gould's influence, they did not diminish the interest of traders in his pronouncements and activities. The flurry of speculation that followed helped conceal Gould's own actions and make it impossible to measure his actual effect upon the market.[27]

Gould's record with the properties he controlled also defies easy generalization. Some companies did suffer grievous financial wounds during his tenure. Yet three of his most important holdings, Western Union, Manhattan Elevated, and the Missouri Pacific, evolved into solid, stable properties in which he retained deep interest until his death and which comprised the bulk of the large fortune he bequeathed to his children.

In short, a close inspection of Gould's life reveals far more shadow and shading than historians have put into their sketches of him. Perhaps the most remarkable thing about the man is how little we actually know about him. Few persons of such public prominence achieved so complete a personal privacy or guarded it so jealously as Gould. In his private life no less than in his business affairs, he frustrated the curiosity of reporters, associates, enemies, and general public alike. This aura of mystery may be the single most important clue to the enigma of Jay Gould. His contemporaries knew no more about him than we do, and one wonders whether they despised the mystery about the man more than the man himself.

Whatever the case, Gould remains a figure of shadows for whom contemporaries and historians alike have filled in the substance largely from their own imaginations. From this license has arisen the stereotype of Gould as Robber Baron and financial vampire *par excellence.*

While there is some truth in the Gould legend, it is not the whole truth because the mystery surrounding him goes well beyond conflicting interpretations of the man and his career. It concerns the basic facts of what he did and did not do, what powers he did and did not possess, what the effects of his actions were, and why he did what he did. Anyone in search of the real Jay Gould must therefore start by separating fact from legend. Since the data themselves are so elusive, the most basic questions turn out to be the hardest to answer: Who was Jay Gould? What did he do? Why did he do it? Why was he so universally disliked and condemned?

The Literature

A good place to begin is the existing literature. It is predictably meager. The historiography on Gould resembles a hall of mirrors in which contemporary and modern accounts reflect one another without adding depth to the image. No scholarly biography exists, and only Grodinsky has ventured to study Gould's business career in detail. Except for a few scattered letters, Gould left no wealth of personal papers similar to those that enriched recent biographies of Andrew Carnegie and James J. Hill.[28] The most reliable source of Gould's own words consists of testimony he gave before various Congressional and legislative committees, but on these occasions Gould was inclined to conceal more than he revealed. Most of his testimony betrays serious omissions and discrepancies when compared against other evidence, and in any case one finds little that is personal there.[29]

In addition to this testimony, later writers drew their information on Gould from four basic sources: newspapers, family memoirs, the Adams brothers' *Chapters of Erie*, and the "hack" biographies that appeared soon after Gould's death in 1892. Beginning with the Erie imbroglio of 1868, the New York press fastened upon Gould as a prime source of copy. For a quarter century, the papers poured forth accounts of Gould's activities, interviews with and quotations from Gould, and editorials about Gould. As a source, the newspapers are easily the most comprehensive but also one of the most suspect.

The reasons for handling these press accounts gingerly extend beyond the usual caveats about journalistic accuracy. Gould owned one major New York daily, the *World*, for a time and was rumored to control or at least influence several others in both New York and other cities.[30] Moreover, no financial reporters had access to the full details of Gould's byzantine maneuvers, or possessed the acumen to discern their significance.[31] Since Gould's own associates and brokers seldom knew his ultimate purpose, one could hardly expect even the most diligent journalist to uncover the whole story. Compelled to operate in the dark, the papers traded heavily in rumor, innuendo, and speculation generously spiced with sensation. While this approach sold papers, it misled as much as it informed.

All this suited Gould's own purposes nicely. Part of his genius lay in his ability to use both public statement and public reticence as an effective tactic. Speaking of Gould's trading career prior to 1884, Grodinsky concluded that "during these years he gave few public interviews, and much of what the newspapers and financial press said about him was mere surmise."[32] Later, when Gould's market position had shifted, he resorted to issuing statements as a device for bulling his properties. He grew adept at the art of telling people what they wanted to hear. For that reason, and because he was not a man to let unguarded statements pass his lips, his press quotations must be taken with a grain of salt. The bias of most editors and reporters against Gould, coupled with their ignorance of his true activities, tarnish the value of their observations about him. Anyone who mines the press for information about Gould must be prepared to wade through a mountain of dross in search of nuggets.

Three accounts of Gould's life appeared the same year as his death.[33] Predictably all were "quickie" narratives that drew extensively upon newspaper material (often quoted verbatim and at length), Gould's Congressional testimony, reminiscences, and public documents. All three rehashed the familiar episodes of Gould's life and wrapped them in homilies without scratching the surface of his business career or offering fresh insights into the man.[34] The Adams brothers attempted a serious study in *Chapters of Erie* but their analysis bogged down in righteous indignation. They succeeded mainly in popularizing Gould's image as villain.

Family memoirs add little because only one reaches closer to Gould than his children. Marquis Boni DeCastellane, a cheeky, extravagant Italian noble who sought to cure his family's hereditary poverty by marrying Gould's daughter Anna, left some vivid impressions of the family; unfortunately he arrived on the scene in 1894, two years after Gould's death.[35] A second daughter, Helen Gould Shepard, achieved renown as a philanthropist, charity worker, fundamentalist, and do-gooder of such sweetness and light as to provoke Mark Twain into muttering that "we all belong to the nasty stinking human race, & of course it is not nice for God's beloved vermin to scoff at each other; but how can I help it when the Abendblatt pukes another mess of Helen-Gould adulation unto me."[36]

Two recollections of Helen Gould exist, one by a daughter-in-law and one by a cousin.[37] The daughter-in-law never knew Gould and mentions him only as the curio that provided the family fortune. The cousin, Alice Northrop Snow, wrote a personal memoir of Gould. A blend of nostalgia and apologia, it occupies over half of her book on Helen Gould. While her account contains a wealth of personal detail about Gould and his family, it must be handled with caution. Alice Snow wrote as an old woman recalling scenes she witnessed as a young girl. She knew nothing of business or finance, and saw in the Gould household only what her limited experience enabled her to see, which was seldom more than the surface of things. There are glaring omissions and misinterpretations, yet the book remains a valuable source. She loved her uncle deeply, and her book alone bathes his portrait in affection and sympathy.[38] But the inner Gould puzzled her young mind no less than it did more distant observers. Her recollections offer some shrewd insights into Gould's character but still concede that he was an enigma beyond her powers to penetrate.

Outside the family, a few memoirs by financiers and other figures of the era touch briefly upon Gould, but their total contribution is slender and unsatisfying. Of the financiers Henry Clews offers the fullest account but he provides more anecdote than insight, as does Edward Bok, the magazine editor, who once served as Gould's stenographer. Other individuals, like Alexander D. Noyes and Clarence W. Barron, either dismiss Gould with a wholesale condemnation or mention him only in connection with some specific episode.[39]

Upon this modest base later writers have erected the modern image of Jay Gould. Three popular biographies of Gould do little more than rehash the older materials in more vivid and less charitable terms. Robert I. Warshaw, writing in 1928, insisted that "this story of Jay Gould preaches no moral, urges no reforms, demands no changes. But in the very telling of the story of his operations, the evidence seems to convict him."[40] Of what charges he does not make clear. Writing in the 1960s, Richard O'Connor and Edwin P. Hoyt had the benefit of Grodinsky's study, which appeared in 1957. Both quote Grodinsky on occasion but leave the impression that they understand neither the intricate convolutions of Gould's career nor Grodinsky's explanation of them. Both works gloss over their superficial grasp of business and financial matters with a colorful style and sure instinct for piquant anecdotes.[41]

Grodinsky's Book

Besides these works, and some briefer accounts of Gould in more general works, there remains only Grodinsky's monumental study.[42] In his preface Grodinsky states explicitly that "this volume is an examination of the policies of a businessman in the field of speculative or equity capital in the free enterprise era between the Civil War and the Theodore Roosevelt Administration. It is not a biography."[43] Having disclaimed any intent of depicting Gould's life or interpreting his character, Grodinsky then spent 610 pages in a searching analysis of Gould's business career. The result is surely one of the most remarkable books ever written by an American scholar. While Grodinsky's work is massively documented, the most striking fact about his citations is the paucity of references drawn from Gould himself. This point can best be made by citing a few figures. The book contains 1188 footnotes in which there appear about 1235 different references.[44] The sources for these references break down as follows; direct citations of Gould (correspondence and legislative testimony) total only 1.4 percent of all citations:

Type of Sources	Number of Citations	Percent of Total
Newspapers	601	48.8
Journals, periodicals, magazines	231	18.7
Correspondence by individuals other than Gould	147	11.9
Correspondence to or from Gould	10	0.8
Legal decisions and documents	20	1.6
Government documents, legislative testimony	87	7.0
Legislative testimony by Gould himself	8	0.6
Annual reports of railroads	19	1.5
Railroad company documents: minutes, pamphlets, etc.	16	1.3
Published primary source materials	14	1.1
Secondary sources	18	1.5
Explanatory or textual reference notes	64	5.2
Total	1235	100.0%

Unfinished Business

This is not to disparage Grodinsky's research methods or to minimize his achievement. On the contrary, he fashioned a *tour de force* from the meagerest of resources. Nevertheless, even Grodinsky fails to penetrate many of the mysteries attached to Gould's career. Working from such limited resources, he had to rely heavily upon his own calculated guesswork to fit the available and often disparate pieces of the puzzle together in some coherent manner. Whatever its other merits, Grodinsky's book must be regarded as a masterpiece of detective work.

Through this approach Grodinsky discovered quite another Jay Gould than that found by other writers. His study is not, as some critics have asserted, an apologia for Gould; indeed Grodinsky seemed less interested in Gould than in the economic milieu in which Gould played so prominent a role. While denying none of Gould's faults or misdeeds, Grodinsky displayed no interest in flogging the financier for his villainies. His concern was rather to portray the economic environment in which Gould operated and to show how Gould grasped that environment more thoroughly than most other men and utilized it in ways that were breathtaking in their boldness of innovation and breadth of vision. In effect, he performed a scholarly autopsy upon Gould's career and declined to keep a scorecard of moral judgments.

Although it is impossible to summarize Grodinsky's analysis, necessity compels at least a brief survey of his conclusions. The principal chapters of Gould's business career include the Erie Railroad, the so-called Gold Conspiracy of 1869, the Union Pacific Railroad, Wabash Railroad, Missouri Pacific system, Western Union, and Manhattan Elevated. Dozens of other projects and properties also claimed his attention for varying lengths of time, either separately or as pawns of some greater scheme. Leaving nothing to chance, Gould acquired an encyclopedic knowledge of properties, local conditions, and future prospects on every project. His command of detail, his dedication to business, his concentration, and his ability to keep so many irons in the fire at the same time can only be described as awesome.[45]

But what of his record with these enterprises? Under Grodinsky's close scrutiny, it proves a mixed one, limned in subtle shadings rather than blacks and whites. Gould profited from some ventures and lost in others, wrecked some properties and developed others into strong concerns. Above all, Grodinsky shatters the image of Gould as a mere predator intent upon ruining properties and destroying values for his own profit. In its place, he depicts a complex career that falls into two broad, overlapping phases, the first of which was primarily speculative and predatory and the second largely conservative and constructive. In effect the first phase of Gould's career changed his business position dramatically. Finding himself in a new situation, he was compelled to redefine his business role and adopt new tactics to fit that role. The result was quite a different Gould than either the financial community or the public had known from their earlier experience with him.

Prior to 1880 Gould amassed his fortune—and his unsavory reputation—from trading operations and the manipulation of properties from the inside. Even then he often fared poorly on the market except when his trading resulted from an active role in the company whose stock he boomed or broke. In Grodinsky's words, "He could not, however, long remain in action purely as a trader. In that role he was not at his best. He found it essential to operate in the securities of a given company, and by participating in its management to master the details of its business. With such knowledge he could trade against the general run of traders."[46] This period culminated in the crisis of 1878–1879 during which Gould's miscalculation of the market led to heavy losses and near ruin. So complete was his rout that one Wall Street operator was quoted as saying: "Nothing that Gould undertakes will ever amount to anything."[47]

Yet within two years Gould rose phoenix-like from the ashes of disaster to become one of the country's most powerful business figures. Grodinsky exaggerated little in asserting that "the transformation of Gould from a trader into a business leader of national proportion was one of the most startling events in American business history. His accomplishments in the three years of 1879, 1880, and 1881 were unprecedented in the business and financial life of the country, and in a sense have never been repeated since."[48] His achievement was all the more remarkable in that he had few allies and only the resources he could personally muster. Most of his financial resources came from market profits, from borrowing against securities (it was his heavy debt position that got him into trouble in 1884), and from skillful use of pyramiding techniques. He had no inherited wealth or social capital upon which to trade; nor did he have the support of any important commercial or investment banks. He did possess a genius for securing control of large corporations with a minimum outlay of capital.[49]

Between 1879 and 1881 Gould first unsettled and then restructured the pattern of railroad relationships on both sides of the

Mississippi. Through a coup in Union Pacific stock in February of 1879 he paid off his trading losses and filled his coffers for expansion. In rapid succession he acquired the Wabash and Kansas Pacific railroads, reacquired the Union Pacific (to which he sold the Kansas Pacific for a large profit), gained control of several railroads in the Southwest, utilized the power of his railroads to seize control of Western Union, and won a spirited battle to dominate Manhattan Elevated. Grodinsky calculated that on December 31, 1881, Gould dominated 15,854 miles of railroad or 15 percent of the national total, in addition to telegraph lines, terminals, bridges, elevateds, water transportation, and other properties.[50]

From this triumph arose a vision of empire unmatched by any of his peers for sheer breadth and audacity. Buoyed by his success, Gould conceived of a transcontinental system that haunted him the rest of his days. To fulfill it he bought railroads in every section of the country, built new lines and extended old ones at a furious pace, disturbed existing relationships everywhere, precipitated rate wars, signed agreements, broke them and remade them, and devised new techniques to advance his purpose. He took upon his frail shoulders a staggering burden and everywhere encountered tough, powerful adversaries. In the East it was William H. Vanderbilt, in the Midwest Charles E. Perkins, and in the West Collis P. Huntington. By 1890 his dream of continental empire had collapsed, leaving intact only the systems in the Southwest and Great Plains. Gould failed not for want of vision or energy but because he had attempted too much with too little against too many imposing opponents. The wonder is that he got as far as he did.[51]

During these years Gould acted primarily as a railroad man, not as a speculator, and he was far more a builder than a wrecker. To have done otherwise would have been to destroy the properties that formed the basis of his own fortune. In fact his absorption in railroad strategy and affairs of empire caused him to neglect his exposed market position. In borrowing heavily against the securities in his enterprises to finance expansion, Gould allowed his debts to accumulate to a dangerous level. This oversight, coupled with another serious misreading of the market, left Gould unprepared for the Panic of 1884, in which the plummeting of stock prices threatened the collateral behind his loans and jeopardized his financial position. A powerful group of bear operators, sensing Gould's exposed position, hammered relentlessly at the stocks of his companies. Their determination to break Gould once and for all plunged him into the gravest crisis of his career.

Slowly the light dawned upon Gould. The possession of an empire changed his role from the hunter to the hunted. His need was no longer to attack vulnerable properties but to defend them, not to break the market but to sustain it at all costs. Nothing better illustrates his altered role in business affairs. After a taxing struggle Gould extricated himself from disaster in typically bold fashion: he confronted his tormentors and threatened to ruin all concerned by announcing publicly his inability to meet his obligations. Since the resulting crash of security prices would destroy even the bears, they came to terms, took a handsome profit, and the crisis passed. Over the next two years Gould sold off many of his extraneous holdings, used the cash to fortify his position, and declared himself out of the speculative market forever. Although few Wall Streeters took him seriously, he appears to have kept his vow.[52] From this episode Grodinsky concluded that: "His experience had also changed his financial outlook. . . . He had by this time learned a lesson which others had learned in the same way—apparently the only way in which lessons of this kind are taught, by repeated instruction in the school of experience. Scott of the Pennsylvania in the middle seventies, Stanford in the early eighties, and Huntington in the middle nineties were others who after long experience decided to remain no longer in debt."[53]

The fierce struggle of 1884 also broke Gould's health and left him a changed man. He had been frail and sickly since childhood, a condition he overcame by driving himself to the limits of endurance.[54] After the ordeal of 1884 he gradually lost three of his most precious gifts: his demonic energy, his intense concentration, and his icy imperturbability in the face of conflict. Unable to work his usual long hours or attend to so many projects at once, Gould required longer and more frequent vacation trips.[55] During meetings his inscrutable demeanor sometimes collapsed into outbursts of agitation and hysteria, an astonishing spectacle to men unaccustomed to witnessing Gould betray even a flicker of emotion.

As his physical condition declined, facial neuralgia plagued him constantly. His delicate stomach, which had always denied him a rich diet, reduced him to fare that a prisoner would have scorned. Fits of insomnia drove him to a small island of sidewalk outside his Fifth Avenue mansion where, under the drowsy eye of his bodyguard, he paced away the long night hours like some caged and tormented animal. When at last his physician told him he had tuberculosis, Gould studied every book about the disease he could find, seeking perhaps some opening to exploit much as he had probed the vulnerabilities of his business rivals. In the end it proved the one enemy against which he was helpless.

During the last eight years of his life Gould's operations moved on still another plane. Having lost the eastern and midwestern wings of his rail empire, he reorganized his southwestern system, launched an expansion program in Kansas and Colorado, and defeated all rivals to Western Union in a campaign Grodinsky called "the greatest success of Gould's career."[56] In his railroad wars Gould alternated between policies of competition and cooperation, first slashing rates and then working hard to stabilize them. His shifts in tactics betrayed a genuine uncertainty as to what changing conditions required. On one hand, he had perfected his own line of attack, disturbing rates and destroying traffic arrangements through rate wars and expansion drives, conciliations and counterattacks. On the other hand, he seems to have realized that the new circumstances demanded stability instead of disruption, and he yearned to don the unfamiliar robe of statesman in the emerging railroad order.[57]

Both circumstances and his business rivals denied Gould this aspiration. As Grodinsky observed, "he was now to learn that his financial ingenuity and ruthlessness in interpreting agreements in accordance with their strict letter instead of their spirit, had cost him the support of many railroad officers. Many refused to attend meetings or join in plans if they were arranged or proposed by Gould."[58] The mantle of conciliation fell instead upon J. P. Morgan, who was not disposed to seek Gould's counsel or heed his advice. Nettled at being ignored by Morgan, Gould still vacillated between tactics of aggression and cooperation. He experimented with both tacks, seeking stability as his ultimate goal but unconvinced of the surest road to it. His distaste for Morgan's intrusion did not prevent him from working with the banker if it promised results, but when schemes of harmony fell through he retreated to the old device of rate wars and pressure applied on every front. Gould went to his grave without finding the solution.

Gould's Legacy

What had Gould accomplished in a lifetime of struggle? Aside from his influence upon individual properties he left an imposing legacy for American transportation. It was not in the field of service; the Gould roads were notorious for their wretched physical condition and inefficient, unsafe operation. To some extent Gould glossed over these operational inadequacies through his skill as a promoter, but neither his customers nor his employees were fooled.[59] Nor was he an administrative or technological innovator.

His achievement lay rather in the broader realm of strategy. Gould profoundly influenced the development of railroad systems during the 1870s and 1880s. His invasion of the territory west of the Mississippi River destroyed the equilibrium of rates and agreements there. It compelled rival roads to respond to his threats by lowering rates, building new lines, and forming new arrangements. In this way he accelerated the economic growth of the whole region between the Mississippi and the Rocky Mountains. Between 1879 and 1892, according to Grodinsky, Gould-controlled companies constructed 4,231 miles of new road and prompted the construction of many thousands more by rival companies.[60] New towns sprang up everywhere along with new industries and their economic ancillaries. To that extent he helped generate an economic boom that benefited millions of Americans who hungrily desired such a boom whatever their feelings about Gould.

Most important, Gould did much to lower the cost of rail transportation. His rate jiggling may well have damaged the properties themselves and wrought short-term havoc with shippers, but the long-run gains outweighed these effects. On that point Grodinsky is both insistent and convincing. The final words of his study are worth quoting in full:

> As a leader in the railroad industry he built many new roads; he broke down local territorial monopolies, destroyed traffic pools, and wrecked railroad rate structures. As a leader in the arena of speculative capital, he transformed millions of dollars of paper profits into productive wealth in the form of new railroads. Gould made fortunes for many of his followers, and produced losses for others. What his followers in the security market gained, many did not permanently retain. The public did gain permanently, so far as anything permanent can be assumed to exist in economic life. Through the use of funds obtained from speculative followers and which could not have been obtained from investors, he built many new railroads. At the same time, in the process of disturbing existing business values, he reduced permanently the price of railroad service. To Gould, as much as to any other single business leader, goes the credit for that far-reaching reduction in rates that characterized the growth of the American economy in the generation after the Civil War.[61]

Gould's Talents

Leaving Gould's personality and private life aside, Grodinsky convincingly swept away much of the myth surrounding Gould's business career. For this reason it is easier to assess Gould's talents as a businessman than to estimate him as an individual. There is some irony, usually overlooked, in the fact that if any stereotype fits Gould's career it is that most cherished of American myths, the rags-to-riches fable. Gould started with nothing, drove himself unmercifully hard, accumulated some capital as a youth through clever dealings, and entered the Wall street jungle in 1859 at the age of 23.[62] Beyond his own ambition, perseverance, and talents, he had no other asset except a respectable father-in-law from an old Murray Hill family.[63] Working mostly on his own and in direct opposition to the financial "establishment," he pyramided these modest resources into an astounding success story. If he did not display the probity and purity of conscience so prominent in Horatio Alger heroes, neither did the vast majority of businessmen. The sad truth is that there were few Luke Larkins or Dick Hunters on Wall Street or in industry.[64]

What qualities brought Gould to the top? Several have already been mentioned. He was clever and inventive, with the ability to think and act on a scale unimagined by most men. Where others saw difficulty or confusion, Gould saw possibility. Once decided upon a scheme, he moved with a vigor and subtlety that generals might envy. Charles E. Perkins, finding himself hamstrung by the conservative directors of the Burlington, once complained that "Gould moves so rapidly it is impossible to keep up with him with Boards of Directors."[65] His lightning strokes prodded the most cautious and unimaginative businessmen into action. Most adversaries did not challenge Gould so much as respond to his challenges. His tireless quest for the initiative left others little pause for rest or contemplation.

Knowing well his own strengths, Gould was also a keen judge of other men's character and motivations. He hired able men to work for him, treated them well, and usually retained their loyalty.[66] In his dealings with other businessmen he displayed an uncanny instinct for adapting his tactics to their temperament. He sensed who would fight and who would not and under what circumstances. To William H. Vanderbilt's craving for compromise he fed a steady diet of pressure and maneuver; to the stolid intransigence of Collis Huntington he discarded threats for conciliation and sweet reason. Above all he never bluffed or blustered.

His dark, deep-set eyes, which impressed so many of his contemporaries as bottomless pools of mystery, might betray icy contempt or anger but never fear or uncertainty.[67]

Gould's reputation as a technical genius in finance seems deserved. Few American businessmen have shown more originality or diversity in their methods. He excelled at the art of controlling large enterprises with minimum holdings of varying types. To gain command or keep it he utilized not only equity control and funded debt but also floating debt, flaws in contracts, receiverships, and especially legal technicalities. Gould was a master of what Grodinsky called the "art of judicial interference.... By the fall of 1881 Gould was probably the most successful litigant in American history. His court suits had been almost phenomenally successful."[68] Gould used the courts to attack and to defend, to confound and to obfuscate, to delay and to deflect. Many suits operated as a smoke screen to conceal his intentions and movements.[69]

Above all Gould was a supreme realist in his policies. If he was a master at deceiving others, he was careful never to deceive himself. He did what the situation required and he did not hesitate to face up to that requirement, however difficult or unpleasant it might be. His mistakes, and they were many, were mostly errors of judgment, miscalculations rather than misperceptions. He had a superb sense of timing and a gift for doing what was least expected of him. And he did his homework. Gould's ability to find an adversary's weak spot stemmed largely from his thorough command of the facts of the situation. Rarely did he launch a campaign without a full reconnaissance.

Thoroughness coupled with imagination produced in Gould a knack for doing the unexpected. He mystified his contemporaries because they could not catch his drift or his depth. Like a chess master Gould usually grasped the whole position well enough to stay a move or two ahead. He found combinations that escaped duller minds. Recognizing that a straight line was the shortest distance between two points but not always the best or safest route to travel, he rarely took it. Gould's ability to find unorthodox responses to apparently straightforward situations perplexed observers in several ways: it masked his true intentions and sometimes concealed the fact of his involvement for a time; it bred confusion and uncertainty from which he might extract some advantage; and it led critics and rivals alike to misinterpret his victories as blunders.[70] To this streak of originality Gould added a reservoir of patience.[71]

Gould's Unpopularity

This impressive array of talents confirms Gould as a true business genius but leaves many questions unanswered. One of the most important and certainly the most intriguing of these is why he was so universally disliked. Why was Gould singled out as the chief pariah of his age? On this question neither Grodinsky nor any of the other writers offer much insight.[72] There is no simple answer; the explanation lies in a tangle of factors.

A part of the answer has already been suggested. Businessmen hated and feared Gould because he outsmarted and sometimes destroyed them, and because they could not comprehend the man or his actions. He brought constant change, uncertainty, and risk to men who preferred constancy, certainty, and assurance. Fear and mystery bred suspicion, one effect of which was to credit Gould with powers he did not possess. His legendary influence upon the stock market made him a natural target for the wrath of disappointed speculators who had never even met Gould. As Warshaw noted, "every ten-share trader who lost six points on some stock Gould never heard of blamed Gould for it."[73] Similarly, many of the larger fish who got hooked in their dealings with Gould preferred to blame their misfortune upon his evil magic instead of their own shortcomings.

The myth of Gould's malign omnipotence sprang not so much from Wall Street as from the newspapers, which found in him an ideal whipping boy for a public that relished such floggings.[74] In New York Gould's detractors were legion, but none spiked their criticism with more malice than James Gordon Bennett. On one occasion Bennett contrived to drag Gould's name into a divorce suit and thereby provoked him into a slashing, intemperate retort, the only such rebuttal Gould ever attempted.[75] While anti-Gould sentiment ranged from sincere outrage to righteous sermonizing to scurrilous sensationalism, it surfaced everywhere and lost little of its intensity over the years.

Several factors help explain this hostility if not the extremes to which it went. Gould's exploits aroused great interest among a public eager to feed upon the derring-do of the business titans. That so much of Gould's legerdemain was cloaked in mystery only heightened its appeal and encouraged journalists to flesh their vague accounts into any design they chose. Reporters disliked Gould because he spoke little and said even less. When he did speak it was either to advance some purpose of his own or, on rare occasion, to trick reporters into thinking he had answered their questions when he had in fact evaded them.[76]

On this point the contrast between Gould and Jim Fisk is revealing. The irrepressible Fisk cavorted genially with reporters and furnished juicy copy with his personal exploits. His accessibility, his Falstaffian personality, and his willingness to spin colorful yarns on any subject, insured him good relations with the press regardless of how much disapproval his behavior incurred or how much blarney his tales contained. With a man like Fisk there might be misunderstanding but not mystery; with Gould there was no understanding at all.[77] Gould's personal habits offered little meat for news-starved newsmen. His devotion to family and quiet leisures, however commendable, resisted efforts to humanize his public image through an inventory of his personal or moral eccentricities. Unlike Fisk he had no redeeming social vices upon which the public might fawn and forgive. His private rectitude seemed so proper as to be inhuman, and reporters, like Dante long ago, learned that virtue made dull copy.

On the whole, then, Gould enjoyed perhaps the worst press of any American of his era. While he accepted this fact as the price of his privacy, it clearly bothered him as the years wore on.[78] Even his acts of charity, which were numerous but usually unpublicized, were twisted into expiations of a guilty conscience to the point where Gould simply gave them up rather than defend them. As one broker sympathized, "Mr. Gould has many properties but a brass band is not one of them."[79] To these attacks Gould found no effective response beyond a retreat into stoicism. "I never notice what is said about me," he told a reporter. "I am credited with things I have never done and abused for them. It would be idle to attempt to contradict newspaper talk and street rumors."[80] To another reporter he complained, "If I denied all the lies circulated about me I should have no time to attend to business."[81] In an interview he admitted that "I do not object to criticism, provided it is only fair. Sometimes, however, I get, as I think, unfair knocks. I asked a certain editor at one time why he abused me so. 'Mr. Gould,' said he, 'there are only three of four men in the country worth abusing, and in my opinion you are one of them'."[82]

From this abuse emerged the popular image of Gould as a cold, delicate figure with a subtle and devious mind, an insinuating manner, and an instinct for the jugular. As caricatured in print and cartoons, Gould betrayed little feeling for anything or anyone. He performed his heinous deeds with the detached air of a surgeon dispensing his ruthless precision upon friends, foes, and innocent bystanders alike. He purred like a cat and struck like a cobra. It is a cold, clinical figure that stalks the dailies; the image harbors much that seems inhuman and little, beyond illness, that softens or suggests weakness. He seems nothing less than the ultimate financial technician.

Reasons for Unpopularity

It is idle to speculate on the degree to which the press manufactured or merely reflected Gould's reputation as "the most hated man in America."[83] The point is that the reputation did exist and something more is needed to account for it. The answer cannot be found in his ideas and beliefs about business or other matters, for in this area if nowhere else Gould was orthodox to the point of banality. His statements cleave firmly to the standard tenets of laissez-faire, free enterprise, rugged individualism, and economic patriotism. At the same time there is little indication that he permitted these verities to interfere with the business at hand. It was not as a heretic that Gould stood convicted at the bar of public opinion.

What, then? Two other possibilities are suggested here. The first is that Gould incurred dislike because he did not fit the "manly mold," the image of masculinity held by most American men; the second is that Gould was an unsparing realist in age that preferred to cushion the harshness of social and economic change with bloated sentimentalism. Both characteristics ran against the grain of his culture and made him a loner in the true sense of the word.

It seems plausible that Gould was hated because he was so different from other men that they could not identify with or understand him. He marched to the beat of a drummer whose rhythms baffled and disturbed others for reasons they seldom grasped or expressed. Gould recognized the presence of this difference and seemed in fact to relish it. Whatever the personal cost, he carved out his own path early in life and stuck to it.

Nearly every aspect of Gould's life, from his physical appearance to his tastes and habits, departed from the manly mold. A slight, fragile man with delicate hands, small feet, and large dark eyes, he spoke in a low gentle voice that seldom rose above *piano*, and seemed incapable of sounding a raucous note even under stress. Just as Gould's eyes fascinated some observers, so his voice intrigued others with its soft purring charm, its almost musical power of insinuation and persuasion. These attributes struck some contemporary observers as effeminate, a word that was occasionally applied to Gould.[84] Certainly nothing in his appearance or manner inspired visions of masculinity by whatever criteria or stereotypes one chooses; he was not hardy or robust, loud or forceful, gruff or domineering, strong or clumsy. He slapped no backs and crunched no bones in a handshake. There was nothing of the peacock in him; he was in manner and dress probably the most inconspicuous titan of his era.

His tastes and pleasures reinforced this impression. Gould competed in no game more rugged than croquet, and his passion for books and flowers was hardly a basis upon which to build a reputation for *machismo*. He was not, and never cared to be, a *bon vivant* or "one of the boys." Gould realized the difficulties his tastes posed for him. On one occasion he admitted frankly that:

> I have the disadvantage of not being sociable. Wall Street men are fond of company and sport. A man makes one hundred thousand dollars there and immediately buys a yacht, begins to drive fast horses, and becomes a sport generally. My tastes lie in a different direction. When business hours are over, I go home and spend the remainder of the day with my wife, my children, and my books. Every man has normal inclinations of his own. Mine are domestic. They are not calculated to make me particularly popular in Wall Street, and I cannot help that.[85]

By any definition of "manly mold" Gould deviated from the conventions of his era. None of this would have mattered much had he not risen to a position of wealth and power by besting more "masculine" but less talented rivals. There is evidence to suggest that some men resented losing to Gould because he did not fight "fair" or "like a man," not as a Titan but as a Siren, elusive and beguiling. Combat with him was not two rams locking horns but the deadly maneuver of spider and fly. It was not that Gould lacked a taste for combat. He relished a good struggle but on his own terms and in his own way.[86] Did it infuriate the "sports" in Wall Street to be outsmarted, even ruined, by this puny creature whom physically they could crush underfoot but against whose machinations they were often as helpless as babes? Gould's contemporaries repeatedly accused him of physical cowardice. "Everybody knows that Jay Gould is a coward," commented an observer in 1884.[87] Others made the same point less baldly and linked physical cowardice with Gould's "sneaky" business methods. The image of Gould as a furtive figure operating always in the shadows reinforced the impression of a man anxious to avoid not only the light of publicity but also direct physical confrontation with his rivals.

Even so, those confrontations could not be evaded. Throughout his career Gould faced a steady stream of physical threats. Some were more bluster than belligerence, such as the day after Black Friday when Henry N. Smith, Gould's brokerage partner, shook his finger in Gould's face and roared, "I will live to see the day, sir, when you have to earn a living by going around this street with a hand organ and a monkey."

"Maybe you will, Henry, maybe you will," Gould cooed softly. "And when I want a monkey, Henry, I'll send for you."[88]

More serious threats could not be fielded so easily. In 1873 Joseph J. Martin, a lawyer engaged in a frustrating suit against Gould and Fisk, approached Gould during lunch at Delmonico's and hit him in the nose. His attack won him the applause of newspapers critical of Gould.[89] But the most notorious assault upon Gould involved two California plungers come East, James Keene and Major A. A. Selover. In 1877 both speculators entered a pool with Gould to drive down Western Union. As Keene and Selover sold heavily, they discovered some unknown buyer snapping up their stock. In the word of Henry Clews, "it was gravely suspected that Mr. Gould was the wicked partner who was playing this absorbing game behind the scenes."[90]

The enraged Selover, a husky six-footer, responded western-style. He intercepted Gould on New Street one day, smacked him in the face, and pitched him down a flight of stairs. The newspapers applauded Selover's assault and quoted his remark that Gould was "notoriously treacherous."[91] Gould's response to this humiliation was no less revealing than the incident itself. He issued no threats and pressed no charges against Selover. Instead he waited patiently to execute a market operation which, by Clews' estimate, cost Selover $15,000. Later, when Keene attempted a corner in wheat, Gould smashed it in a bear raid that cost his antagonist several million dollars.[92] It did not fit the Code of the West, but it worked effectively.

That was Gould's forte: he led with his strength and exploited his enemy's weaknesses. His style provoked cries of cowardice and treachery even among traders who relished a fast coup when it worked in their favor. The implication was that Gould did not play by the rules. Yet the crux of the matter was not that Gould played unfairly but that he played better than most in an arena where the rules were at best malleable. Nor did the charge of treachery stand close scrutiny. Gould's alleged "sellout" of Keene and Selover was a commonplace maneuver on Wall Street, one which only a naive or reckless operator would overlook. Contrary to legend, Gould possessed no clear-cut record of disloyalty and double-dealing. As one perceptive journalist noted, Gould's reputed treachery was not so simple an issue: "It was his business to utilize for personal ends the follies and passions of his fellow-men, and he probably accepted philosophically whatever penalties his vocation imposed.... And yet, though Mr. Gould was widely accused of failing to keep the faith, there were many among his harshest critics who were ready to admit that he seldom, if ever, turned upon an associate without having had previous reason to believe that the associate was turning upon him."[93]

The extent to which Gould's "unmanly" demeanor colored contemporary impressions of him cannot of course be measured. It is clear that he was an alien creature to many of his generation, and like most things alien he both fascinated and repelled. If some measure of his difference from others lay in his "unmanliness," so too did it lie in the cold realism by which he conducted his affairs and his life. By realism I do not mean that Gould viewed everything in a "true" light, whatever that is, but rather that he usually grasped the facts of a situation, accepted them for what they were whether he liked them or not, and acted on that basis. He was perhaps more unfettered by cant, less cowed or deceived by illusions than anyone of his age. He did not cling to shibboleths or axioms. He might invoke them in testifying before a committee or boosting a project, but he was far too flexible to let them impede or deflect his course.

Therein lies one of the cruelest ironies about Gould. Critics despised him for his dishonesty, treachery, and double-dealing. Yet the impression lingers that many of them loathed Gould because he was too honest for minds used to dealing with reality under wraps. Gould was a man of unflinching purpose. He knew what he wanted, went after it, and did not mouth pieties to justify his course or disguise himself in airs of respectability. By eschewing polite society, he cut himself off from the surest and safest road to cleansing a tarnished reputation. He recognized the game of business for what it was and played with few illusions and fewer pretenses. If the markers of success were wealth and power, he meant to win them; in that sense his purpose was as frank and open as his methods were devious and closed.[94] Even his modest but numerous philanthropies took place behind the scenes. As the Atlanta *Constitution* commented, "the trouble with Mr. Gould was that he did not make arrangements with the newspapers to herald his deeds of benevolence, and the result was that no one outside of his small circle of intimates and familiars knew the extent of them."[95]

Gould's personal beliefs displayed no less aversion to cant. His deep love of family instilled in him a fierce devotion to their interests above all else. Throughout his life religion occupied but never absorbed him. Never a strong sectarian, Gould made no pretense of piety nor any effort to cover his business dealings with a glaze of Christian virtue.[96] His lack of hypocrisy in religious matters was the one characteristic that even hostile editors applauded.[97] He valued the friends he had and never wavered in his loyalty to them. Most of all he knew himself and the world about him. Behind the cold logic and rigid detachment one senses a current of skepticism, even cynicism. Theodore Dreiser caught this attitude in portraying Frank Cowperwood, a character who, although supposedly based upon financier Charles T. Yerkes, bears some striking similarities to Gould as well: "Judges were fools, as were most other people in this dusty, shifty world. Pah! His inscrutable eyes took them all in and gave no sign. His only safety lay, he thought, in the magnificent subtlety of his own brain, and nowhere else. You could not convince Cowperwood of any great or inherent virtue in this mortal scheme of things. He knew too much; he knew himself."[98]

Conclusion

Gould's magnificent subtlety has lain buried beneath the rubble of Gilded Age and Robber Baron clichés for too long. Whatever judgment one makes of Gould, his values, or his behavior, he remains a richly complex and distinctive individual. If we are patient enough to probe that complexity and detach it from misleading or misapplied generalizations, we may learn much more about the man and his era.

Under the heat of recent scholarship the old images and interpretations of the Gilded Age are fast melting away. In their place have come more complex analyses, which have shredded the old synthesis without providing a substitute of equal compactness and convenience.[99] Here as elsewhere advancing knowledge has shattered existing syntheses in favor of a galloping multiplicity. The situation resembles that described by Peter G. Filene in his autopsy of the Progressive movement:

At this point in historical research, the evidence points away from convenient synthesis and toward multiplicity. . . . The present state of historical understanding seems to deny the likelihood of a synthesis as convenient and neat as "the progressive movement." In their commitment to making sense of the past, however, historians will continue to search for conceptual order. . . . But if that is to occur, the "progressive" frame of reference, carrying with it so many confusing and erroneous connotations, must be put aside. It is time to tear off the familiar label and, thus liberated from its prejudice, see the history between 1890 and 1920 for what it is—ambiguous, inconsistent, moved by agents and forces more complex than a progressive movement.[100]

So too with the Gilded Age and with the biography of Jay Gould and other figures of that turbulent era. As our grasp of its complexities deepens, we may finally stop stirring the clay of the Gould legend and commence the search for more reliable artifacts. At that point our search for Gould will have begun in earnest. In the quest for so enigmatic a figure it may be that Dreiser has revealed the most promising path. Perhaps what Gould requires is not a conventional biographer but a novelist willing to trade on his license in imagination and invention—willing, in short, to take the same sort of gambles and incur the same risks to fulfill the larger vision that Gould himself so frequently undertook.

The Man Who Saved the Railroads

My most recent biography (not yet published) has been of E. H. Harriman, for whom I developed a fascination while doing the history of the Union Pacific Railroad. This piece was written for a popular magazine, the *American Heritage of Technology & Invention*. At the time I turned it in, however, *American Heritage* was preparing to launch a new magazine called *Audacity*. The editors thought my article a good piece for the new magazine's first issue and, with my consent, traded it to *Audacity* for a future draft pick. The version printed there in 1992 was cut and shaped differently than the original, which appears here for the first time.

For much of the nineteenth century railroads dominated the American industrial and commercial landscape. From modest beginnings in the 1830s they wrought an economic revolution by giving the young American republic what it needed most: a reliable form of transportation to carry its restless, ambitious people into the remote interior of a huge continent and haul back the prodigious output of their labors. No other technology did more to fuel the industrial transformation that reshaped the whole of American life in the nineteenth century.

The triumph of the railroad was as swift as it was stunning. By 1900 a network of 206,631 miles of track laced together a nation that only half a century earlier boasted proudly of having 9,021 miles of rail. To the generations born in that era, the locomotive loomed as the dominant symbol of power, progress, and prosperity—the hallmarks of what they deemed the most advanced civilization on earth. Yet by the 1890s the mighty rail industry tottered on the brink of collapse, the victim of forces spawned by its rapid rise to the forefront of the American economy.

Frenetic expansion during the 1880s triggered a series of rate wars that sapped the financial strength of even strong roads. A host of abuses and controversies provoked an outcry of public wrath that led to regulation of the carriers first by state agencies and then by the federal government under the Interstate Commerce Act of 1887—making railroads the first industry to be scrutinized by the federal watchdog. Unfortunately, this mounting public antagonism against the railroads peaked on the eve of the worst depression the country had yet endured. Between 1893 and 1897 nearly a fourth of the nation's rail mileage sank into receivership. The casualties included such major roads as the Union Pacific, the Northern Pacific, the Atchison, Topeka & Santa Fe, the Erie, and the Philadelphia & Reading.

For two decades rail managers had groped unsuccessfully for some form of self-regulation to defuse the criticism heaped on them. Haunted by the twin fears of financial ruin and external control, they realized that the depression had struck a death blow not only to reckless wars of expansion but also to an era of overcapitalized companies, wasteful competition, and inefficient operations. In the piquant phrase of Albro Martin, "The final hour had struck for the Victorian railroad corporation."[1]

The breathtaking growth of the rail system had relied on conditions unique to the era: declining prices that made labor and materials cheap, low interest rates, an insatiable appetite among communities throughout the nation (especially west of the Mississippi River) for a railroad of their own, and an imperious ambition among railroad leaders to forge giant systems and capture distant markets. As more railroads reached more cities and towns, competitive wars erupted that drove rates steadily downward despite vigorous efforts to maintain them.

The great need of the region west of the Mississippi River had been for a far-flung rail system, however flimsy or ill-equipped, to penetrate unsettled areas of the country and expedite their development. The roads did not have to be first class because the traffic for them in many cases had yet to be created and could not be until some way existed to get the crops or goods to market. Their task was not simply to haul freight but to help create the towns and farms and factories that would generate the freight.

In this atmosphere rail leaders devoted more time to constructing lines and forging them into systems than to managing them efficiently. The depression exposed the weaknesses of this strategy with cruel precision: bloated capital structures, too many roads chasing too little business in hard times, physical plants that were outmoded in the case of older roads and flimsily built in the case of newer ones, managements that were hidebound in their ways, and organizations that lacked the efficiency and flexibility to adjust to changed conditions.

Clearly the rail industry had reached a turning point in its history, but where was it heading and who would lead it into the new era? The generation of leaders who had dominated the expansion era were dying off or retiring. Of those giants only James J. Hill and Collis P. Huntington remained, and Huntington was 76 years old in 1898, the year the depression finally lifted. Knowing eyes looked to Hill to lead carriers out of the wilderness, and indeed he played a pivotal role. The true catalyst for modernizing the railroads, however, was a figure little known outside Wall Street until he flashed onto the railroad scene like a bolt of lightning.

No one could have foreseen that E. H. Harriman would be the Moses who dragged the rail industry into the modern era and laid the foundation for its survival. In 1898 he was known in financial circles as a shrewd, conservative banker whose firm had prospered through good times and bad. He sat on the board of the powerful Illinois Central Railroad and had served briefly as its vice president. Insiders on Wall Street gave him credit for helping that road weather the depression storms in fine shape, but no one thought Harriman knew much about managing railroads.

Fifty years old in 1898, Harriman seemed destined to follow the well-worn tracks of his fellow bankers into comfortable old age. Yet in three years he all but eclipsed Hill as the best-known railroad man in America and maintained that position until his death in 1909. He was more than a late bloomer; he was a force of nature—unpredictable in his arrival and elemental in his impact.

There was nothing heroic in his appearance. Small and slight of frame, with deep-set eyes hidden behind thick spectacles, his thinning hair offset by a thick droopy moustache that was, quipped banker Frank Vanderlip, "as unkempt as if it had been worn by a Skye terrier,"[2] dressed in plain clothes and an overcoat that seemed to swallow him, Harriman looked more like a clerk than the latest Napoleon of the railways. But his chin had a pugnacious thrust to it, his eyes gleamed with energy behind their mask of glass, and his walk had the bow-legged jauntiness of a jockey.

Despite his frail appearance, Harriman was wiry and athletic, a bantam rooster with a fierce competitive streak in everything he did. Off duty he was a gregarious and sociable person devoted to his family and the eternal verities of God, mother, and country by which he had always steered his life. On the job, however, he was a curt, unsmiling dynamo who resented wasting a minute or a dollar and once boasted that he got through his morning bath, shave, and breakfast in only twenty-five minutes.

Nothing in Harriman's early life even hinted at what was to come. He was born February 25, 1848, in an Episcopal rectory at Hempstead, Long Island, the son of a minister who was the financial black sheep of an otherwise old and respectable family. His father was a good, well-meaning but impractical man, his mother a strong, well-bred, haughty woman who held the family together and left a deep imprint on all her children. Harriman quit school at fourteen to launch his career on Wall Street as an office boy; by 1870 he had done well enough to open his own office as a broker with the help of a loan from his uncle.

During the next three decades, through expansion booms and depression blights, Harriman earned a reputation as a savvy banker who watched the market's every wiggle, seldom speculated on his own, and was utterly reliable with his clients' funds. He married the daughter of a prominent upstate banker, entered the best social circles, bought a large estate in Orange County which he named "Arden," and settled easily into the life of a well-heeled financier who had overcome the long shadow of ineptness cast by his father. Although his eldest son died young, Harriman had three daughters and two younger sons as well as an intelligent, devoted wife within a family circle that remained unusually close.

During the 1880s Harriman had dabbled in some smaller upstate New York railroads, but his role had been largely financial. His longtime friendship with banker and prominent socialite Stuyvesant Fish landed him on the board of the Illinois Central when Fish needed allies to modernize the company's management and policies. When Fish became president in 1887, Harriman moved up to the vice presidency and began to expand his knowledge of the road beyond its finances. So rapidly did his education proceed that he soon clashed with his friend and mentor Fish. The tension between them, though well concealed from public eyes, forced Harriman to leave the vice presidency in 1890 and return to his post as chairman of the finance committee.

This experience had a profound effect on Harriman. From his brief stint as vice president—including a summer overseeing the Illinois Central while Fish was in Europe—he not only mastered the principles of railroad management but also leaped to a vision of the industry's future and what was needed to realize it. Through the funereal gloom of the 1890s he brooded on these larger vistas while struggling to keep the expanded Illinois Central system solvent as other roads around it collapsed. Deep within him, unknown to anyone else, there hatched a fierce ambition to become a major player in the industry at a time when he had nothing to prove to anyone except himself.

The opportunity came in 1897, when he wangled a seat on the executive committee of the reorganized Union Pacific. That road, part of the first transcontinental line, was just entering a new phase of its history, free for the first time of its old federal charter that had made it a political football in Congress. Harriman was the most obscure financier on its executive committee, yet by May 1898 he had so impressed the others with his ability that they elected him chairman. That moment marked his emergence onto the national stage, and he was quick to seize it.

Less than a month after becoming chairman, Harriman boarded a train to tour the entire Union Pacific system in what proved to be the most fateful trip of his career. In 23 days he covered 6,236 miles, inspecting not only the railroad but the country through which it ran, wearing out his officers and locals alike with an endless stream of questions. It was his first look at the West, and it provided him with a vision that was to transform his own life and the railroad map of America.

What Harriman found was a typical nineteenth-century western road with light rails, little or no ballast, heavy grades over mountain ranges, and inadequate equipment. The receivers had done a good job of maintaining the road, but they were as old fashioned in their thinking as the Union Pacific was in its equipment and operating procedures. Like other roads, the Union Pacific had retrenched during the depression. As the oldest transcontinental line it was the most hidebound in its outlook, with officers and men who had hunkered down for so long that a defeatist attitude came naturally to them.

All of this Harriman took in, but he saw something more—something that seemed to have escaped those around him. After four dismal years of depression the West was rising from the dead. Crops were burgeoning, mines were awakening, and cities and villages were humming with signs of fresh activity and optimism. On the distant horizon Harriman thought he saw the faint outline of an onrushing wave of prosperity hurrying toward the West. He concluded that the railroad must be made ready to receive this flood of business that was about to crash down on it. Near the end of his tour, he telegraphed New York for authority to spend $25 million at once on new equipment and improvements.

The directors gasped in astonishment. To lavish such an amount on a road barely out of bankruptcy, cried one of them, would quickly put it back there. But Harriman argued that new business was coming, and with labor and materials still at depression prices the time to act was now, before a reviving economy drove them upward. In the end he got his way, not once but repeatedly. Over the next decade Harriman spent a staggering $160 million modernizing the Union Pacific at a time when the total expenditures by the federal government averaged only $561 million a year.[3] In the process Harriman also created the most efficient railroad for its size in the West and probably the nation.

The key to his vision lay in grasping earlier than most that railroads had entered a new era in which profits had to be made by hauling greater loads at lower rates as cheaply as possible. Hill had shown the way by extending his Great Northern road to the Pacific coast on the very eve of the depression and then demonstrating how a well-built and well-run line could make money even on low rates in hard times. But Hill had started with a road located and constructed to his own specifications. Harriman faced the herculean task of rebuilding older, meandering lines with shaky financial pasts; he had to overcome history as well as geography.

Later critics dismissed Harriman as merely having had the good luck to appear on stage just in time to catch the new wave of prosperity. But plenty of other players were there, too, and none of them assumed the leading role he seized for himself. Harriman had not only the vision to see what was coming but the nerve to stake his future—and that of his company—on it. His unabashed optimism and confidence in his own judgment were as crucial to his success as his keen insight into what was happening.

The reconstructed Union Pacific bore little resemblance to its former self. Its new line was 54 miles shorter, had 4,470 feet less grade, had eliminated enough curvature to make 26 complete circles, and was laid with heavy rail, new ties, and plenty of ballast to provide stability and drainage. A straighter line with lower grades and a first-rate roadbed allowed engines to haul longer trains with heavier loads at greater speeds on less fuel. Mountains were tunneled and cuts filled with tons of material to straighten the line. The hardest work lay west of Cheyenne, where Harriman's top engineer, John B. Berry, had to cope with a line across the heart-stopping Dale Creek bridge and the highest point on the line, Sherman summit, while working around traffic over the most overtaxed division on the railroad.

After several false starts, Berry solved the problem by locating a new line 250 feet below the original one, relocating thirty miles of track, and boring an 1,800-foot tunnel through solid granite. He amassed a work force that ultimately totaled 131,332 men armed with eight giant steam shovels and fifteen locomotives pulling strings of giant Rodger dump cars. Electric lights were strung so that the work could proceed around the clock. The Dale Creek bridge was eliminated by a fill 900 feet long and 120 feet high that swallowed 475,000 cubic yards of gravel. This new line boasted a standard grade of 43.3 feet across the Black Hills (except for one short stretch) compared with former grades ranging from 68 to 98 feet.[4]

Harriman did nothing by halves. On one troublesome stretch in southwest Wyoming, he allowed Berry to transform twenty-one crooked miles into eleven straight ones by boring a 5,900-foot tunnel that consumed two and a half years of exasperating and costly work. East of Cheyenne, Berry got rid of the infamous "ox-bow" that had snarled traffic for three decades by creating the Lane cutoff with some spectacular fills.

Along with these projects work also progressed rapidly on a second track, an unheard of luxury on western lines. Heavier engines and larger rolling stock were acquired, which in turn meant rebuilding bridges and widening the roadbed. Large sums were invested in automatic block signals, still a rarity on American roads, making Harriman a leader in the field. By 1909 the Harriman system had already installed more than 5,000 miles of block signals; twelve years later only 39,000 miles of the nation's railroads had them.

Nothing on the line escaped Harriman's eye. Everything from water tubs to coal chutes to depots and section houses was upgraded. Shops were modernized with new machinery and electric lights. The telegraph line was overhauled and expanded, and telephone wires soon followed. Older, lighter engines and rolling stock were replaced by newer, heavier

The Man Who Saved the Railroads

models, allowing each train to haul much larger loads. Most of the new cars had steel frames instead of wood. Between 1899 and 1909 the fleet of locomotives increased only 11 percent and that of rolling stock 20 percent, yet tonnage carried tripled over a system that had grown in mileage by 36 percent.[5]

In May 1906 Harriman tested his new railroad by making a record dash from San Francisco to New York in 71 hours and 27 minutes. Even he was amazed at how well the new line rode. Early one morning, east of Cheyenne, he sent for the superintendent, who arrived at Harriman's stateroom to find him shaving.[6]

"Why are we running so slowly?" Harriman growled between strokes.

"Slowly?" stammered the officer. "Why, we are running sixty-five miles an hour."

Harriman paused, then raised his shade and peered outside. "Are we on time?" he asked.

"Yes sir, to the minute."

Another pause. "This track rides a little smoother than I expected it would," he said, returning to the mirror.

The Union Pacific became a marvel to travellers and shippers alike, demonstrating that a western road could match the superior performance and standards of the best eastern roads. Harriman was the harbinger if not the prophet of a fact that would not become obvious for decades: in the new century the future of railroading belonged to the western lines that were the most efficient and had the longest hauls.

Those who scoffed at Harriman's insistence that a flood of business was coming soon ate their sneers. The revived economy swamped the nation's rail system with traffic, forcing most companies into belated modernization programs while struggling to cope with unprecedented demand. Thanks to Harriman's foresight, the Union Pacific fared better than most. With its newer and larger equipment, an average train in 1909 carried 552 tons of freight, nearly double its load in 1898. The operating ratio (ratio of operating expenses to gross earnings) dropped from 63.6 percent in 1898 to 47.2 percent in 1909 even though costs rose steadily and rates were held in check.

The once marginal transcontinental road became a cash cow that has never ceased to pay dividends. Anyone wise enough to have bought Union Pacific shares in 1900 would have pocketed 60 percent in dividends by 1909 and seen the stock itself soar from $44^{3}/_{8}$ to 219. Between

1900 and 1908 Harriman sold $208 million worth of new bonds, yet fixed charges increased only $3 million a year while net income jumped 125 percent and the surplus 188 percent. All outstanding bonds were funded at a low 4 percent rate.[7]

If Harriman had done nothing more than rejuvenate the Union Pacific, he would have left an indelible mark on railroad history. But at no time did the Union Pacific occupy his full attention. Rather it served as a launching pad for Harriman's rise to a dominant position in American railroad affairs. In rehabilitating the road he acquired two powerful allies, Jacob H. Schiff of Kuhn, Loeb and James Stillman of the National City Bank, who had access to all the capital Harriman needed to carry out his grand plans.

Fortified by their unwavering support, and by his own shrewd sense of finance and strategy, Harriman stunned the railroad industry with a series of lightning moves. He regained control of the Union Pacific's Oregon lines, which had drifted loose during the receivership, and reestablished the company's presence in the Northwest. He led syndicates that took charge of the Chicago & Alton and the Kansas City, Pittsburg & Gulf, two troubled roads with a legacy of cutting rates and unsettling schedules. In the East he moved onto the board of the Baltimore & Ohio and later the Erie, using his influence in both cases to get the companies to spend heavily for improvements and modernization.

Through these and other moves, Harriman tried to create what came to be known as a "community of interest" in which a handful of major players would impose order on the rail industry and maintain it with help from the bankers. Harriman entered eagerly into arrangements leading to this end, but he was never content merely to be one among many. He craved power unabashedly and loved nothing more than a challenge. Viewing himself as an apostle of progress—and better equipped than anyone else to lead the way to it—he insisted on doing things his way. Harriman, said rival George Gould ruefully, "aims to dominate, and if he don't like us he'll throw us out."[8]

More a warrior than a diplomat, Harriman moved to impose his own brand of order. When the venerable Collis Huntington died in 1900, Harriman bought control of his Southern Pacific, then the largest transportation system in the world. Although the company was saddled with a huge debt, Harriman promptly applied his formula of spending huge sums to upgrade the road and its physical plant. In eight years he poured $247 million into making the Southern Pacific equal to the Union Pacific.

The most spectacular of his projects eliminated the old bottleneck that took the combined Union Pacific–Southern Pacific line over the mountains north of the Great Salt Lake to their historic meeting place at Promontory. In one of the great engineering feats of the age, Harriman's men built a new line straight across the lake. Known as the Lucin cutoff, the project was hailed by one expert as "perhaps the most noteworthy engineering achievement ever attempted in bridge-and-fill work."[9]

At the same time Harriman tried to gain control of the Chicago, Burlington & Quincy, the most efficient and well managed of the four Iowa lines between Chicago and the Missouri River. An alarmed Hill, backed by his banking ally J. P. Morgan, thwarted Harriman by using the Northern Pacific, which they dominated, as a vehicle to acquire the Burlington. Undaunted, Harriman launched a bold campaign to scoop the Northern Pacific, and with it the Burlington, from its unsuspecting owners. The result was a titanic struggle that triggered a panic on Wall Street in May 1901. Forced to compromise, Harriman reluctantly joined Hill in creating a giant holding company called Northern Securities, which kept the disputed roads securely under Hill's thumb.

Still Harriman pushed on. He fought a pitched battle with mining baron William A. Clark over construction of a line from Salt Lake City to Los Angeles, then secretly agreed to share the road with him. Ultimately it ended up in the Union Pacific system as one of the most profitable roads in America. With Schiff's help he bought a large interest in the powerful Atchison, Topeka & Santa Fe and neutralized its competitive struggle with the Southern Pacific. By 1904 he had emerged as the giant of the industry and therefore the primary target of its critics.

The scope of Harriman's power was formidable, but he did not merely collect railroads. Everything he touched was whipped into shape through large outlays for improvements. Harriman also worked hard to improve management and to integrate key functions with connecting lines. Once in command of both the Union Pacific and Southern Pacific systems, he devised a radical new organization that shocked and outraged traditional rail managers.

To integrate the managements, Harriman first assumed the presidency of both systems. He then centralized the three most critical functions of a railroad—operations, maintenance, and traffic—in the hands of officers located in Chicago, hundreds of miles away from either system. These two officers, who reported directly to Harriman, took charge of routing and soliciting all traffic, overseeing all major construction projects, systemizing maintenance work, and distributing rolling stock from what amounted to a pool of all Harriman roads to insure maximum efficiency. The authority of the general auditor was extended over all Harriman lines along with that of the purchasing officer, who bought goods in huge quantities for all the systems at substantial savings.[10]

While railroaders clucked dubiously over these heresies, Harriman launched a host of other new programs. His pioneering safety campaign revolutionized the way railroads dealt with this sensitive topic and opened it up to public scrutiny for the first time. The Union Pacific also launched education programs for its workers, enabling them to receive instruction in any area they chose as a spur toward promotion. Everywhere, from the top down, came a constant prodding for quality work and efficient service.

After 1904, when his old friend Theodore Roosevelt attacked Northern Securities, critics turned Harriman into a public enemy by charging that he had become too powerful and arrogant. But no one ever questioned the value of what he had accomplished, and by the time of his death in 1909 his public image had been restored despite a long and bitter fight with Roosevelt.

Harriman himself never doubted the value of what he had done. He had led the rail industry into a new era, shown open minds the path to a future that stressed a modernized physical property hauling large volumes at low rates as efficiently as possible. He had demonstrated that money spent wisely on modernization, even in huge amounts, reaped dividends in the end. Despite repeated blows from new competitors on the highways and in the air, the railroads remain a vital component of the nation's transport system. After Harriman's death, legal action by the federal government separated the Union Pacific and Southern Pacific, but Harriman's influence remained strong in both roads. The Union Pacific has never ceased to pay dividends and remains one of the strongest systems in the United States.

Once, during an interview, Harriman surprised the reporter by pulling out a sheet of typewritten data on the improved Union Pacific. "As he read from it," recalled the reporter, "I realized it was the *apologia pro vita sua.*"

"But the public assails and attacks you," ventured the reporter when Harriman had finished, "and impugns your motives and accuses you of all sorts of things. Doesn't the thanklessness of the job ever embitter you?"

In response Harriman slapped the sheet of statistics and said defiantly, "*That* remains."[11]

And so it has, for nearly a century.

Competition and Regulation: The Railroad Model

> This study originated as a paper given at the Business History Conference in 1988. Hewing to my belief that the purpose of papers should be to explore ideas, I used the opportunity to develop a model for one of the most complex and perplexing issues in railroad history. A revised version was later published in the *Business History Review* minus the opening and closing references to science fiction, which were deemed too unscholarly. The original version is reprinted here, beefed up with the documentation added for the printed article that was not necessary for the paper.

Let me begin with science fiction, surely an appropriate lens for viewing the American brand of competition. There is a story by Ray Bradbury in which an alien, the last of its kind, tries to survive on Earth by using its power to become whatever someone wishes it to be. But its attempt to please is mistrusted, and the creature is destroyed. There is too an old "Star Trek" episode about an alien, also the last of its race, who uses the same ability not to please but to kill in order to obtain from victims the salt it needs to survive. Somewhere between these extremes lies an instructive analogy for the role of competition in American life.

The point is not that it's a jungle out there whether you hail from this planet or another one, or that only the fittest survive. It is rather that competition has survived in this culture by assuming as many forms and shapes as two centuries of theorists and practitioners could devise. Probably no concept except democracy has been more extolled or less understood by Americans than competition. For all that has been said about the subject, it remains a stranger in a strange land, a mutant whose meaning is still, like beauty, in the eyes of the beholder.

The railroad offers valuable insights into the nature of competition and its alter ego, regulation, because it was the formative industry that shaped the American conception of both. We know the story of the rail experience by heart, so often has it been told, yet there are still gaps, even mysteries, that render our overall grasp unsatisfactory. Why is it, for example, that so few interpretative histories have been written about so well-trod a subject? Why is there no definitive general history of American railroads?[1]

The answer may be that our understanding of the rail experience is less complete than we realize, and that one major area of weakness concerns the railroads' relationship to the roles played by competition and regulation in the economy. To explore this possibility, I want to sketch a historical model of this relationship and to discuss the state of confusion and contradiction that has long existed among those who have grappled with the problem.[2]

The model arranges railroad history into three periods: (1) the transition from competition to regulation, 1860–1920; (2) cartelization and the new competition, 1920–58; and (3) restructuring and deregulation, 1958–present. In many respects it confirms the old saw that history is just one damn thing after another. Like so much else, transportation systems did not arise by planned, rational means but through a process of accretion. As E. Porter Alexander aptly observed in 1887, "The prominent features of modern railway practice ... have come about from necessity, not choice.... Like Topsy they are not creations but developments."[3]

The railroad emerged at a time when no serious competition existed among modes of transportation. By the Civil War or soon afterward it dominated the field, a position it held unchallenged for half a century. During this upward march the railroad played three distinct roles: it introduced transportation where none had existed before; it supplemented existing forms; and it replaced other inadequate or less efficient modes. Only in this last function did the railroad compete with other transportation methods. The true paradigm for competition as we know it arose not from these early intermodal clashes but from intramural strife among the carriers.[4]

During this first period certain baffling characteristics of the railroad emerged. Although defined early as a common carrier, the railroad was very much sui generis and its development, as Charles Francis Adams stresses, "little else than a constant succession of surprises." Much confusion and wasted energy resulted from the failure of Americans to grasp the unique aspects of railroads that made them poor models for public policy dealing with competition, regulation, and most other issues. One perceptive critic of regulation, himself a former Interstate Commerce Commission (ICC) member, complained in 1936 that "At no time from the inception of the railroad industry has public thinking on the subject been clear."[5]

Foremost among these characteristics was the fact that the railroad discriminated. Many industries discriminate in some way, but the railroad had more types affecting more people more directly in more ways. Three distinct forms of discrimination arose early: geographic, classification, and individual. The first was inherent in the very nature of railroads, as it is in any form of transportation. The second was a logical response to difficult pricing problems, whereas the third resulted largely from pressures brought to bear by shippers and the railroads' own fierce scramble for traffic.

These discriminations provoked most of the public wrath against carriers that led to regulation. This wrath in turn derived largely from confusion over another characteristic of railroads: no one knew how to calculate costs in a manner that made them a meaningful basis for rates. Without any cost basis, rate structures had necessarily to evolve from experience, trial and error, and a witches' brew of internal needs and external pressures. They were called tariffs for good reason; if there was a model for how rates were made, it was the tariff system, where logic took a back seat to expediency, pressure, and self-interest. The result was a common carrier lacking rational means to calculate either its costs or its pricing structure, which made public defense of its rates lame and unconvincing.[6]

Still another characteristic compounded the problem of discrimination. Two different rate structures emerged: one based on local or noncompetitive traffic, the other on through or competitive traffic. The railroad exercised monopoly power over the first type but was at the mercy of competitive forces in the second type. From this duality arose vast confusion over the question of whether the railroad problem—and therefore the target of regulation—was one of monopoly or excess competition. This was further aggravated by a tendency to lump two very different conditions under the rubric of "monopoly": the domination of whole traffic routes by merging systems, and the domination that any line exercised over local shippers who lacked other outlets.

The rate structures that evolved were based on local rates with through rates figuring in effect as marginal income. Rail managers had no choice; given their lack of a cost basis, they had to peg prices to their most constant source of business if rates were to have any stability at all. Seen in this context, the decision to base rates on the value rather than on the cost of service was both logical and necessary. Unfortunately, it produced a classification system so complex that its inherent and artificial discriminations became yet another inviting target for critics.[7]

History then played some cruel tricks on rail managers. First, patterns of discrimination turned rate structures into a crazy quilt; then competition for traffic drove rates steadily downward. Triggered by rapid construction that brought more roads into common markets, and fueled by the hard times after 1873, this early brand of competition was so reckless and profligate that it aroused widespread public indignation.[8]

Perceptive rail managers realized that once rates were knocked down, shippers would clamor to keep them down. They were more right than they knew. The broadside attack on carriers denounced monopoly, excessive competition, and all forms of discrimination with equal vehemence. As the clash grew more politicized, a fateful reversal took place. The rhetoric of protest managed to gain acceptance for the argument that *all* rates should be based on competitive rates, which kept falling, rather than on local rates, which were denounced as "unnatural."[9]

Rail managers paid dearly for failing to establish the premise that local rates were the proper basis of the price structure, but once the issue moved into the political arena it is likely that their argument would have been ignored anyway. As a result the exception became the rule: local rates came to be viewed as artificial and competitive rates as "real." A. B. Stickney, a maverick rail president who strongly favored rate regulation, conceded nevertheless that the immediate effect of the Interstate Commerce Act was the lowering of some noncompetitive rates to competitive levels. He also noted tersely that "competition cannot reduce cost."[10]

The return of good times brought not peace but the equally bitter expansion battles of the 1880s, which broadened the theater of war and the scale of losses. As rates plunged inexorably downward despite repeated attempts by the carriers to stop the bloodletting through pools and other agreements, the public outcry forced government to intervene—first at the state level during the 1870s and then at the federal level in 1887. All sides were anxious to restore stability but disagreed widely on the source of disturbance. Federal regulation thus made a curious debut as a remedy for either excessive competition or monopoly, depending on whom you consult.[11]

Stickney believed the Interstate Commerce Act would fail to prevent unjust discrimination because it tried to preserve competition, which was in his view the source of discrimination. Alexander warned that laws against unjust discrimination amounted to "legislation against the competition which produces it." Scholars have divided over the issue for a century. Some, like Richard Waters, argue that the act's purpose was "to curb unfair practices born of excess competition," whereas others, like James Nelson, label it an attempt to curb "excesses of rail monopoly power." George Hilton called it an effort to stabilize rail cartels. Still others have declared it a mixture of both.[12]

"From simple and coherent beginnings," observed Nelson, "transport regulation has grown very complex and detailed." He was wrong; the beginnings look anything but simple or coherent. It is hard to escape the conclusion that the ICC began life with several missions that were incompatible with each other or with the realities of railroad economics. It tried both to prevent monopoly by enforcing competition and to outlaw discrimination. As Stickney and others pointed out, however, a policy designed to preserve competition also perpetuated discriminations. By 1898 the ICC shared this belief; Adams got to the heart of it as early as 1870. The basis of the whole transportation problem, he declared, was that *competition and the cheapest possible transportation are wholly incompatible.*"[13]

In characteristic fashion Americans wanted both. They harbored a long and deep hatred of monopoly, whether in royal, private, or public hands. As Thomas K. McCraw has noted, any policy favoring monopoly "bore a crushing burden of negative national prejudice." The result was a policy gridlock with roots deep in the national culture. The law banned discrimination but hedged its definition of the various forms and how they related to competition. It barred pools but left other forms of collective ratemaking in legal limbo. If the object was to stabilize or cartelize the industry, banning the most popular vehicle for carrier collusion seemed an odd way to go about it.[14]

Whatever the disease, the remedy proved ineffective. The competitive wars grew steadily worse until the depression after 1893 swallowed many of the roads in receivership. Once the depression had run its course, a new generation of rail giants led by E. H. Harriman caught the rising crest of prosperity by overhauling the railroads into efficient modernized systems on a scale never before witnessed. Clearly a new era in railroad history had dawned. Determined not to repeat past mistakes, these leaders tried to rationalize competition in a variety of ways ranging from private understandings to mergers on a grand scale to interlocking directorates. This "community of interest," as it was popularly known, sprang from a vision of a few giant systems ruled by men who trusted each other and played the competitive game by shared rules.[15]

Ironically, the systems forged by Harriman and others in the 1900s came remarkably close to the railroad map that emerged in the 1970s, but the policy puzzle made the road between a long and tortuous one. Americans could not let go of the belief that competition was essential in the rail industry; as a result public policy down to 1918 consistently encouraged it. The new systems were denounced as a bald attempt at monopoly, and both the ICC and the courts attacked key mergers, most notably the Northern Securities Company and the Union Pacific–Southern Pacific combine. The Supreme Court applied the Sherman Act to the railroads in ways that made clear its determination to keep them competitive.[16]

Not everyone shared this view. "The benefits supposed to result from railroad competition," said former ICC chairman Martin Knapp, "I believe to be greatly exaggerated." A former pool official and ICC commissioner observed that "The phrase 'free competition' sounds well as a universal regulator, but it regulates by the knife. Unless the weapon in turn itself is held in check it is too dangerous an agency to be endured." The ICC itself argued that competition was wasteful, and noted in 1898 that while nearly every nation regulated rates, only the United States tried to enforce competition. In the next breath, however, it warned against the threat posed by the vast rail combinations forming to suppress competition.[17]

It is hard to read the reports of the ICC commissioners during these years and not sympathize with their frustration. A decade's experience had given them some good insights into the nature of the problems confronting them, but they could not get either carriers, shippers, or Congress to share their vision. Nor could they shake entirely free of the inherently contradictory belief that both combination and competition were dangerous. By the time their views had an impact on policy, the realities of the railroad problem had shifted ground.

While the Supreme Court upheld the banner of competition, the ICC gradually gained new powers from Congress until by 1910 it exerted full control over rates and therefore over much of rail competition. Between 1903 and 1916 power drained steadily from the carriers to the regulatory agencies. Then the unexpected occurred: American entry into the First World War led to the government's taking over the railroads. Regulation gave way to a form of domination that gave the roads better treatment than they had ever received. Once responsible for the roads' performance, the government could not help but view their problems in a more sympathetic light.[18]

The war's end forced Americans to confront directly the issue of what should be done with the carriers. By then the mood of the country had changed radically. Most of the prewar reform fervor had exhausted itself in the Crusade for Democracy, and the wartime experience had revealed certain undeniable advantages in a rail policy stressing cooperation under government supervision. From this chrysalis emerged a sharp reversal of regulatory policy embodied in the Transportation Act of 1920.

Instead of enforcing competition, the act sought to create a protected cartel under tight regulation. It permitted pooling of traffic and earnings. Mergers that had been attacked only a few years earlier were now actively encouraged so long as they conformed to a master plan that combined strong roads with weak ones. The object was to create a limited number of systems of equal strength that might compete in healthy ways. As Ari and Olive Hoogenboom observed, "Consolidation became the panacea competition had been in the decades surrounding the turn of the century." Machinery was devised to guarantee roads a minimum return, and the ICC received power to fix minimum rates, decide questions of extensions and abandonments, and oversee the issuing of new securities.[19]

A new era dawned in which the transition from unbridled competition to regulated monopoly seemed on the threshold of completion. Many rail leaders, dazed by the rapid forced march through ever stricter regulation, government control, and an unfamiliar postwar world, welcomed the new structure of things, if only because they craved stability no less than the public did. With the ICC possessing virtually absolute control over rates, competition among railroads shifted from rates to service.

Too late rail managers discovered that this brand of head butting could be very expensive and wasteful in its own fashion.

Unfortunately, the 1920 act came a generation too late. Its primary effect was less to blaze new trails than to institutionalize certain ironies. Seeking the best of all possible worlds, it decreed in effect that there should be competition without losers. The mechanism for preserving competition was to be the same one rail leaders had used earlier to eliminate it: a consolidation plan. Nothing better illustrates the confused thinking on the subject than the contradictory aims of this consolidation policy.[20]

"A major purpose of the transportation act," declared the ICC in a 1929 decision, was to preserve "substantially the whole transportation system." This was to be done by a "union of weak with strong lines" to ensure the survival of all. In other words, strong roads would be rewarded for their efficiency by being saddled with weak roads according to a master plan concocted not by them but by the ICC. And the final product was intended to be at bottom not monopoly but an updated brand of competition. "A greater amount of actual and effective competition in service," intoned the commission in a 1926 decision, "may be assured by a limited number of well-articulated systems than by a greater number of systems less complete."[21]

It seems not to have occurred to the architects of this policy that strong roads were strong and weak ones weak for reasons that went beyond their horoscope or hard luck. If rail managers had learned one lesson from the bitter expansion wars of the 1880s, it was the folly of eliminating unprofitable competitors by absorbing them. The best roads had worked hard to rid themselves of mileage that failed to pay its way; now Congress proposed to force more on them in large, unpalatable doses.

Small wonder that strong systems shunned the plan and shed no tears when the scheme collapsed in failure after a decade of futile efforts to enact it. Unfortunately, the 1920 act contained another poison pill in the form of the provision giving the ICC sweeping authority to approve extensions and abandonments. It also allowed the commission to compel carriers to construct new mileage in certain circumstances. On occasion the ICC permitted new construction of competitive track on the grounds that "competition, within reason, rather than monopoly, is in the public interest."[22]

On these questions as on so many others, the commission was a house divided. One commissioner, noting the emphasis placed by his colleagues on the role of competition in one key decision mandating construction of a new line, said bluntly that "The theory of competition as applied to railroads and a more or less dogmatic reliance upon it has been in my judgment the greatest single error in our national policy toward railroads." He was joined by a fellow commissioner who reminded his brethren that " 'Monopoly' is not necessarily synonymous with inadequacy. 'Competitive' facilities are not 'necessary' merely because they are 'competitive.' "[23]

No one could have predicted that in the long run the railroads would suffer more from being forced to maintain service—that is, not abandon mileage—than from being told when and where they could (or must) lay down new track. But history played another cruel trick on the carriers. The act of 1920 bound them in a straitjacket of regulation at precisely the time they fell victim to a technological revolution.

For seventy years railroads had dominated the transportation industry because no new forms had risen to challenge them. After 1920, however, several new modes appeared on the scene, and older ones like pipelines and water transport were reinvigorated. The automobile, truck, bus, and airplane all utilized the internal combustion engine and new lightweight alloys to gain significant competitive advantages over railroads. Within a few years there emerged a vicious contest for business among modes of transport competing less with each other than with other modes.

The railroads and their regulators had put their house in order only to find that the action had moved outside. Suddenly the ground rules of regulation required a complete overhaul. Nothing in them even remotely anticipated the nature or dimensions of intermodal competition. How could they? Unlike law and custom, technological change is neither linear nor predictable. After enduring largely unchanged for a century, the structure of competition in the transport industry was revolutionized within a decade, and more change loomed on the horizon. Once the Depression intensified the scramble for traffic, the nation found itself gripped by yet another transportation crisis.

Two broad policy alternatives existed. Congress could loosen the regulatory straitjacket binding railroads, or it could try to fit the other modes with jackets of their own. Some carriers were itching to compete, not only by cutting rates but also by diversifying into other forms of transportation themselves. Contrary to their image as business fossils, many if not most major systems redefined themselves as transportation companies during these years, adding truck and bus service where the law allowed. Some, like the Union Pacific, contemplated buying airlines to make themselves into complete transportation firms. The obstacle always was whether regulation would permit it.[24]

Given the potency of competition as a cultural value, it may seem strange that this course was not chosen. But the times were all wrong for it. The Depression cast business in an ugly light, and to many people the proposed transportation companies raised the old specter of monopoly. Moreover, the New Deal administration, grappling with huge problems of unemployment and deflation, showed no interest in forms of competition that threatened to drive rates even lower, incur higher deficits, and ruin more firms. Coordination and control were the bywords of the new era. Some way had to be found for all modes to coexist under federal supervision with each one carrying the traffic best suited to it as efficiently and economically as possible.[25]

After the usual exhaustive public debate fortified by a fresh generation of statistical input, policy followed a predictable course: the transport jumble was rationalized on familiar terms by bringing the new modes under regulatory strictures similar to those already in force for the railroads. A series of acts beginning with the Motor Carrier Act of 1935 and culminating with the Reed-Bulwinkle Act in 1948 applied to the new modes the old formula of regulatory cartels that suppressed competition and stabilized rates.[26]

The Transportation Act of 1940 became the cornerstone of this effort. It inserted a preamble into the Interstate Commerce Act defining the national transportation policy as the "fair and impartial regulation of all modes of transportation ... to recognize and preserve the inherent advantages of each." The ICC was to pursue policies that created a transport system adequate to the needs of commerce, defense, the postal system, and "sound economic conditions" among the carriers. To fill this tall order, it had to protect each mode from competition in the form of rate cuts by other modes. The object became not only coordination but perpetuation of services.[27]

This was simply the traditional American approach of taming the unfamiliar by fitting it with familiar harness. The problem was that almost nothing in the rail model fit the other types of transport; in many cases regulation was not only ineffective but simply irrelevant. All railroads were regulated, but all private automobiles, most trucks, and 90 percent of inland water carriers were exempt. The railroads might be cartelized, but large sectors of other modes were not and could therefore exploit their competitive advantages. Instead of protecting the railroads, the heavy hand of regulation left them even more vulnerable to the new competition.[28]

The competitive environment had changed radically and in ways that hurt railroads the most. This became painfully clear when the Second World War with its blizzard of traffic ended, and rail traffic suffered a precipitous fall that confronted the nation in the late 1950s with the next round of the transportation problem. This deterioration of the railroads' competitive position was all the more shocking for having occurred during a period of relative prosperity. Trucks swept away much of the high-value freight traffic, and airplanes were fast scooping the long-haul passenger business. Even long-haul freight, the staple of rail earnings, was being nibbled away on several fronts.[29]

Slowly, grudgingly, the machinery of institutional change cranked up to meet a crisis that threatened to throw giant systems into ruin. The Weeks Committee among others discovered in 1955 what some industry people had been shouting since 1920: the railroads had long since ceased to be a monopoly threat and need not be clamped so rigidly in regulatory irons. Scholars and analysts edged gingerly onto the bandwagon, proclaiming that regulation in the transport industry was neither efficient nor economical. Where the generation of the 1930s had sought coordination and control, the new era emphasized cost efficiency—an objective better reached by a freer market than through tight regulation.[30]

The result was a gradual reversal of past policy beginning with the Transportation Act of 1958 and continuing with the formation of Amtrak in 1971, the 3R Act of 1973, the 4R Act of 1976, and the Staggers Act of 1980. Together these acts deregulated the railroads in a way that gave them a freedom of action they had not possessed since the nineteenth century. Apart from regaining control over most of their rates, they were able to shed at last the common carrier burdens that had required them to continue unprofitable operations. "Freed of its medieval shackles of common carrier service obligations," predicted one scholar, "the railroad industry should continue to play an important and profitable role in the U.S. economy for many years to come."[31]

By 1980 the railroads seemed to have come full circle in their *totentanz* with competition and regulation, and the trip had cost them dearly. Only a handful of once-proud systems remained; the rest had been swept into bankruptcy or into a new wave of mergers that buried their original identity forever. The reorganized industry was leaner and meaner, with most roads being creatures of holding companies formed to spin off nonrail assets that in many cases had become more valuable than the railroad itself. Some of these companies have even gone out of the railroad business, and many large roads have vanished, littering the countryside with old roadbeds that are fast assuming the status of burial mounds among cultists.[32]

What does the experience of the railroads tell us about the American way of competition and regulation? Obviously it suggests that the usual time lag between policy and reality has grown steadily worse over the years. Regulatory policy, like old generals, seems doomed always to fight the last war, partly because in our system it takes so long to recognize new problems and then to build a consensus for change. At bottom regulation involves a quest for some viable equation reconciling economic efficiency, social justice, and political acceptability. The more complex regulatory mechanisms become, the more difficult it is to adjust them or get rid of them when necessary, let alone tie them to these objectives.

Since the pace of change wrought by new technology continues to gain speed, the gap between policy and reality widens daily despite all efforts to close it. In the modern world policy cannot possibly keep pace with change of all kinds. The renewed emphasis on deregulation in recent years may reflect a growing realization that the market mechanism, whatever its other shortcomings, provides faster and more accurate signals about changing realities.

Another obvious conclusion is that the railroads were unique in too many ways to be a useful model for regulating competition. More important, the slowness of Americans to grasp these aspects as unique helped to distort their larger understanding of what competition entailed in business. The railroad experience confounded one dubious set of preconceptions about competition, and in the process did much to create an even more dubious set of preconceptions. It led policy down wrong paths on which considerable time and energy were wasted for the return trip. This was probably unavoidable, given human fallibility, but it ought to caution us against any hasty application of regulatory machinery as a cure for problems.

In a broader sense the railroad experience reinforces a behavioral pattern common to our culture. The market mechanism seems to be popular so long as it produces good news. When it produces bad news, however, a clamor for restraint and regulation arises. Put another way, the true American obsession is with winning, not competing. We relish, even glorify, competition in the abstract until we come out losers from it—and historically we have often been poor losers.

This attitude extends well beyond athletics and business to wider forums of policy. There was a healthy dose of it in the bitter debate over Vietnam and in the current rage for Japan bashing, to suggest but two examples. Our inability to accept that in competition we cannot always win, and indeed may have reached a point in world affairs where we will lose more often than we win because we cannot dominate as we once did, has had tragic consequences in the past and will likely have them in the future.

The flaw lies in a failure to understand competition as a process rather than an outcome—and least of all an outcome foreordained in our favor. "Competition," said Adams, "has been a great educator for railroad men. It has not only taught them how much they could do, but also how very cheaply they could do it." But the tuition has been high, and the need now is to find less costly ways of learning new lessons.[33]

Which brings us back to science fiction. In the Bradbury tale the alien was slain by those who could not accept the blessings it bestowed for what they were. They could not embrace its marvelous diversity as a fact of nature; to them it was something unnatural and therefore dangerous. In the "Star Trek" episode, the more lethal creature perished because in a changed, hostile environment it could survive only at the expense of others, by making them see it as something they wished it to be. Once seen for what it actually was, the alien was doomed.

Judging by the American railroad experience, the name of either creature might well have been "competition."

The Turning Point in American Railroad History

In recent years a number of invitations to give papers has allowed me to explore a variety of broad themes and ideas relating to railroad history. This paper was to be part of a colloquium on transportation and industrialization held in Madrid in January 1990 as a preconference to the International Conference on Economic History. Unhappily, circumstances prevented my going to Madrid at the eleventh hour. The paper went without me and was presented by one of my American colleagues. Later it was printed as part of the conference proceedings. Among other things it emphasizes the significance of the Northern Securities case, which has been woefully slighted by historians.

The primary role of railroads in the development of the 19th-century American economy has been well documented, as has the merger movement in American business that exploded onto a shocked public during the years 1898–1904. Less is known about the interaction between them or about the critical turning point American railroads reached in their history during these years. This paper will outline the efforts of rail leaders to rationalize their own tendency toward consolidation through an approach known popularly as "community of interest," and suggest the reasons for its ultimate failure.

In half a century American railroads moved from their initial stage of development to an explosive expansion that forged a rail network totaling 169,780 miles of main line track by 1893. Four years of depression brought this era of unprecedented growth to a decisive halt as companies owning nearly a quarter of this mileage plunged into bankruptcy. From the financial debris of these failures emerged reorganized systems that were leaner and more attuned to the changed business environment of the post-depression era.

The period of prosperity after 1897 offered carriers a golden opportunity to thrive if they could avoid the pitfalls that had brought them to ruin prior to 1893. Foremost among these evils were the savage rate wars that bled companies dry and provoked costly expansion programs. "A war of rates," warned one disgusted rail official, "is about as catching a disease as ever was seen." His words became the epitaph for a generation of rail leaders who discovered that it was no more possible to fight a limited war than it was to have a limited epidemic.[1]

During the 1880s a vicious cycle had erupted: rate wars bred expansion, which in turn bred more severe wars until the cost of war put an end to expansion. Rail leaders were proud men with an exaggerated sense of independence. They did not desire war but could find no way to peace. Every attempt to resolve disputes through diplomacy bogged down in mutual suspicion and recrimination.

"Misery is so fond of company," sighed Charles E. Perkins of the Burlington, "that we are pretty sure to be driven together like quails in a snow storm." But how? For two decades the pool had been their refuge despite its many and glaring weaknesses. Pools were easily violated, could not be enforced, and multiplied like rabbits. Their mechanisms were elaborate and often ingenious, but none of it worked. Despite long, tortuous hours of negotiation, agreements broke down faster than they could be patched up.[2]

The failure of the rail industry to regulate itself forced government to intervene—first at the state level during the 1870s and then at the federal level in 1887. The pool, having lacked any standing in law, became an outlaw after passage of the Interstate Commerce Act. A fear of anarchy haunted the industry and prompted two more dogged efforts at self-regulation before the depression swept the weaker lines away and the stronger ones to cover.[3]

Once the depression ran its course, a new generation of rail leaders led by E. H. Harriman caught the rising crest of prosperity by modernizing the railroads into efficient systems on a scale never before witnessed. The bitter wars of the 1880s and bankruptcies of the 1890s left a deep imprint on this new generation of managers, who resolved to prevent such a thing from happening again.

The most painful legacy of these two decades was the steady decline of rates. Since little prospect existed for reversing this pattern, the formula for success became one of hauling a high volume of traffic at low rates. To do this profitably, roads had to operate at maximum efficiency, something they had rarely done when expansion drained most of their resources. This required a drastic rebuilding of physical plant. The new century marked an end to the age of construction and the beginning of an era of reconstruction.

While the rebuilding of American railroads lacked the drama and romance of the pioneer era of construction, it occurred on a colossal scale. The object was to increase the payload per train since the size of a train could be doubled for much less than twice the cost of a smaller train. But increased payload required more powerful engines and larger cars, heavier rails, more ballast, reduced grades and curvature, stronger bridges, modern signals, more durable ties, and other improvements.

The staggering cost of this transformation was made possible by the flood of traffic that poured onto the rail system after 1898 and a capital market that absorbed one enormous issue of securities after another without complaint. The reorganizations of the 1890s had not only streamlined the capital structures of many roads but also strengthened the role of bankers in their managements. Their presence added a moderating force to rail diplomacy, for the bankers understood even better than railroad managers that prosperity depended on another crucial element besides modernization: peace among the major systems. This could be achieved only by curbing the competitive wars that had brought the roads to ruin earlier.

In 1907 an Interstate Commerce Commission investigation sought to prove in ponderous detail what intelligent rail managers already accepted as gospel: that Harriman and men like him were bent on eliminating competition from western railroads. Their minds equated competition with low rates, costly wars, overexpansion, and perpetual strife, all of which was wasteful and inefficient. This generation of railroad men had been to the slaughterhouse in their youth and did not care to go again. It had been their Munich, the pivotal experience that shaped their views of what future policy should be and must never again become.

The logical alternative to their nightmare was consolidation on a grand scale coupled with what became known as a "community of interest" among the leaders of the giant systems that were emerging. Put the rail network in the hands of a select few who would impose order and maintain it with help from the bankers. Harmony among the systems would assure efficient service for shippers, solid returns for investors, and security for workers. The result would be, said Jacob H. Schiff of Kuhn, Loeb, a "community of interest between railroads, shippers, and labor."[4]

Community of interest involved the rail leaders buying stock in each other's roads and serving as directors in them to learn firsthand what was going on. This exchange of hostages provided a convenient forum for mediating conflicts before they erupted into crises. The bankers sat on the boards as well and used their influence to smooth over differences. Critics denounced this cozy arrangement as one more conspiracy to stifle competition and jack up rates; proponents insisted the object was rather to avoid the reckless overbuilding and rate wars that had disrupted the industry earlier.

The beauty of this approach was that it seemed to stay within the bounds of law. Formal consolidations could be attacked under state law or the Sherman Antitrust Act, which so far had not been applied to railroad mergers. But no law forbade men of large interests from cooperating with each other on an informal basis. "They see," stressed the *Wall Street Journal*, "that the principle of community of ownership is beyond legal interference and that it affords a sure road to the desired end."[5]

But not entirely sure. Community of interest demanded cooperation among ambitious, strong-willed men accustomed to having their own way. Could they do better than the previous generation of rail leaders who had bickered and schemed like petty nobles for every scrap of advantage they could gain? The danger, mused the *Journal* perceptively, was that "human nature will be found very much the same in the controllers of great railway systems as it is in other people. Kings when bound together by the strongest political and family ties have not been able to agree."[6]

Therein lay the fatal flaw of community of interest. Kings might be fewer in number than the nobles beneath them, but they were no better at reconciling their differences or subordinating their ambitions to the greater good. They too had their weaknesses and their distractions, their vanities and vices. And kings no less than nobles were fond of posing as apostles of peace while awaiting the moment to steal a march. For all their good intentions, they had yet to learn the fundamental truth that peace was more than a matter of power; it was a matter of attitude.

The grand hopes placed in community of interest ran their short and unhappy life cycle in barely five years. Most observers traced the movement's origins to January 1900, when the Pennsylvania Railroad bought large blocks of stock in the rival Baltimore & Ohio, the Chesapeake & Ohio, the Norfolk & Western, and some other roads. At the same time the New York Central acquired control of two key lines and bought some Chesapeake & Ohio stock as well. Privately the managers of the two giants agreed to keep the peace and maintain rates in the coal regions, with the Pennsylvania overseeing the tidewater soft coal interests and the New York Central taking care of the anthracite region.[7]

In fact, the roots of community of interest traced back to attempts at securing peace in the Northwest during 1898, and to a syndicate formed a year later to buy the Chicago & Alton Railroad. E. H. Harriman played a prominent role in both cases, rejecting shared rule in the Northwest while promoting it in the Midwest, where there were many more interests and relationships were far more complex.

In a confidential letter Harriman explained the reasons for the Alton purchase in terms that might have served as a definition of community of interest. The Alton was acquired "mainly for purpose of eliminating it as a factor, more or less, from the situation as a competitor in the South & Southwestern territory, and also through the personel [sic] of its management, to cement the various roads together."[8]

To accomplish this, Harriman wanted to put officers of the Union Pacific, Illinois Central, Wabash, Missouri Pacific, and Katy roads on the Alton board. Harriman dominated two of these companies, George Gould another two, and John D. Rockefeller the Katy. Harriman also suggested that the directors be chosen from the operating departments of the five roads. This bold departure from convention would, he thought, "tend to bring them into closer relations & enable them to adopt methods for saving much in expenses."

The idea was to make the Alton a sort of Switzerland in the complex power struggle between the Mississippi and Missouri rivers. For decades the Missouri River had served as a boundary between systems dominating territory east of it to Chicago and west to the Pacific coast. Harriman's own road, the Union Pacific, had never ventured east of the river because it interchanged traffic there with half a dozen roads to Chicago, and to acquire one of them for its own was to transform the other five into enemies.

For this reason there could be no Switzerlands in the community of interest. To favor one road meant hurting others, and every manager expected his road to be favored in the allocation of business. Even a rapidly growing traffic proved far more finite than the expectations of those who demanded part of the haul. Endless disputes arose that did much to undermine the goodwill painstakingly built up through cautious diplomacy.

Ultimately, however, the downfall of community of interest had less to do with these fights than with the inability of rail leaders to curb their own ambitions. During 1901 a new wave of merger mania swept the industry as the same men who had done so much to create a rational order through community of interest shattered it in a titanic struggle for supremacy and empire.

Once again E. H. Harriman served as the catalyst by trying first to acquire the Burlington and then gaining control of the Southern Pacific, at that time the largest transportation system in the world. When James J. Hill in league with J. P. Morgan snatched the Burlington from him, Harriman responded by trying to buy the Northern Pacific, which Hill and Morgan had used as a vehicle for acquiring the Burlington. In the spectacular fight that followed, peace was restored by creating a giant holding company called Northern Securities in which Hill, Harriman, and Morgan all had large interests. The formation of this company was to have fateful and far-reaching consequences for the rail industry.

But Harriman did not stop there. He also acquired half interest in a new line between Los Angeles and Salt Lake City, and bought a large interest in the powerful Atchison, Topeka & Santa Fe. By 1904 he had become the most powerful figure in the industry, but James J. Hill still dominated the northern transcontinental route, and George Gould launched a quixotic campaign to patch together the first unified system from ocean to ocean.

To casual observers these events seemed but a more virulent strain of community of interest. In fact they were its death rattle. The alliances among these men turned into bitter rivalries like those of an earlier generation but on a far grander scale. Unfortunately, their battles coincided with a growing public debate on the threat posed by large enterprises and the extent to which their power should be curbed by the government. This controversy lumped railroads together with other sectors in what soon became a wholesale political attack on the evils of bigness.

The turning point for railroads came earlier than for other sectors. In 1902 the government brought suit against the Northern Securities Company in what became the first attempt to apply the Sherman Antitrust Act to a rail merger. Two years later the Supreme Court upheld the government by a five to four vote and ordered Northern Securities dissolved. The major damage, however, went far beyond the individual roads to the future of the industry itself.[9]

The Northern Securities decision proved a turning point in several respects. It threw a damper on other merger plans in industrial as well as rail sectors. It also set in motion a chain of events that led to the forced separation of Harriman's Union Pacific–Southern Pacific merger. More important, it marked the demise of the last attempt at self-regulation through community of interest. In its place there soon followed comprehensive federal regulation that proved disastrous. For the next half century the railroads remained victims of wrong-headed public policies that pushed a large part of the industry toward extinction.

Some contemporary observers understood what was happening. In October 1905 the *Wall Street Journal* proclaimed flatly that " 'Community of Interest' is dead in the west." Those who applauded the growing power of the government over the carriers found themselves grappling with a persistent "railroad problem" for the next sixty years.[10]

The obvious question is, who or what killed the community of interest? It is misleading to blame a fatuous public or self-interested shippers or ambitious politicians for clamping the railroads into the strait jacket of federal regulation. While each of these groups bears a share of the blame, so do the railroads and the men who ran them. The harsh truth is that self-rule failed wretchedly because the rulers could not subordinate their own ambitions to the larger good. They were men of good will with the power to do great things, but they proved unequal to the challenge. In the end community of interest perished because there were too many interests and too little community among them.

No one realized this more than Harriman, the chief instigator of the clashes that brought on stricter federal rule. In 1907 he concluded his testimony before the Interstate Commerce Commission with words that serve as a fitting memorial for the era of community of interest:

I think the railroads themselves are more to blame than any other factor, for the condition that exists today, the antagonisms between the people and the legislatures and the railroads themselves. I think the management of the railroads themselves are more or less to blame than any other cause, and they had a right to agree and they had the right to get together, but they were always squabbling and never got together, and they lost the respect of the communities which they served.[11]

Replacement Technology: The Diesel as a Case Study

Here is another example of an invitation that prompted me to explore a new realm of ideas. Originally given at the Society for the History of Technology Conference in October 1989 and published later in Railroad History, *this piece developed in one format a pattern of the social impact of technology as a possible model for other examples. The case study approach came naturally to me from my experience at the Harvard Business School. What excited me most about this subject was the way it allowed me to develop my strong interest in the role of technology in American life.*

While it is a truism that technology is a catalyst for social change, little attention has been given to the role and repercussions of "replacement" technologies. By this term I mean a technology so superior that it does not merely improve earlier devices but supersedes them entirely. In the process it also brings sweeping changes to the context in which the technology is used. By its nature the influence of replacement technology spreads rapidly in ways that are neither intended nor predictable.

History is replete with examples of replacement technology ranging from the triumph of gunpowder over the bow and arrow to that of the transistor over the vacuum tube. This paper will discuss one most appropriate to the setting of this session: the advent of the diesel locomotive as a substitute for steam power. It will explore how the diesel, in rendering steam power extinct, also introduced changes that reshaped the world of both the railroad and the railroader.

Unfinished Business

The diesel locomotive revolutionized the way railroads performed their work; reconfigured the physical landscape of railroads; redefined the role of labor in this most traditional of industries; transformed the structure of labor relations; and consigned to the realm of nostalgia an entire subculture rooted in a shared passion for that dominant symbol of nineteenth-century America, the steam locomotive. What is more remarkable, this entire process took place in only about twenty years despite the intrusion of a major war.

Of course, the diesel engine did more than transform railway power. It had a similar effect on ships, trucks, buses, cars, and airplanes. But these were relatively new modes of transport except for ships, which followed a pattern of change comparable to that of railroads if not as striking in its totality.

In essence the diesel is an internal-combustion engine that converts liquid fuel into mechanical power with far greater efficiency and economy than a steam engine. Its German inventor, Rudolf Diesel, obtained his first patents and published his epochal book on the subject in 1893. The first commercial diesel engine was produced five years later in Germany and arrived in this country the same year. Like the early versions of the steam engine, these were strictly for stationary service.[1]

The man who brought the diesel to America was brewer Adolphus Busch, who spent considerable time in Germany and counted among his close friends Baron von Krupp of the Krupp Iron Works. So enthusiastic was Krupp about the potential of the new engine that Busch obtained from Diesel the American and Canadian rights, organized a new company, and built the first diesel constructed in America for use in his brewery. He stayed with the project, joining with the Swiss Sultzer brothers in 1911 to form a new firm, Busch-Sultzer.[2]

Despite the need to solve major technical problems, the use of diesel engines spread rapidly. Fittingly enough, one American pioneer turned out to be the Corliss Engine Works, described in 1902 as the largest in the world. In 1876 Corliss had given visitors to the American Centennial Exhibition in Philadelphia a breathtaking symbol of the new industrial era in the form of a mammoth steam engine that produced enough power to run 8,000 machines scattered over thirteen acres of exhibit hall. A quarter of a century later, the company renowned for its steam engines offered the new century a preview of coming attractions by running its entire operation for the first time without steam, using only diesel engines.[3]

Replacement Technology

In December 1903 an ad splashed across the *Wall Street Journal* heralded the diesel as the "Death Knell of the Steam Engine." By then a variety of applications had been tried. Busch used his engine to power 600 electric lights. Swift and Company, the American Locomotive Company, and William Cramp & Sons, the Philadelphia shipbuilders, all tested diesel engines with favorable results. In 1904 Kiev boasted the world's first diesel-electric power plant. By 1910 both German and English firms had developed diesel submarine engines, and war on the high seas would never be the same again. During the next decade the most important applications were in marine engines, with the first diesel-powered passenger liner appearing in 1921. The railroad industry was interested but slow to grasp the potential value of diesel engines.[4]

The reasons were not hard to find. Railroads were the oldest, largest, and most traditional industry in the nation. They had an enormous capital investment in the steam locomotive as well as in the shop facilities, tools, and skilled labor force needed to maintain it. Many roads also owned coal mines that provided them cheap fuel, and railroaders harbored a deep passion for the steam locomotive that cannot be quantified. It was no accident that the engineer, the man at the throttle, stood atop the pecking order of railroad labor, or that one reached this exalted post only after many years of paying dues in the ranks.

But the rail industry was in the throes of far-reaching changes. Since the late 1890s profits had depended on the ability to carry a high-volume traffic at low rates, which placed a steep premium on efficiency. The steam locomotive in all its many varieties—which reflected the wide range of climates, terrains, and uses to which it was put—had been steadily enlarged, improved, and redesigned to fit specific needs, but by the 1920s it was fast approaching the outer limit of its inherent capacities.[5]

By coincidence railroads also found themselves after 1920 facing for the first time serious competition from other modes of transport— notably automobiles, trucks, buses, airplanes, barges, and pipelines. The era of rail supremacy came to an abrupt end well before the Great Depression devastated the industry as other modes swept away much of the short-haul passenger and high-value freight traffic as well as such bulk cargoes as oil and grain. To make matters worse, the new competition struck the industry just when increased government regulation made it impossible for the railroads to respond effectively in the traditional areas of competition, rates and service.

Confronted by a growing crisis in the industry, rail leaders searched diligently for new ways to improve efficiency, cut costs, and provide more flexible service. The diesel engine struck the more enlightened of them as a possibility for accomplishing all three goals. In 1926 the Union Pacific Railroad, which had been monitoring progress on the diesel for years, sent its chief mechanical officer, A. H. Fetters, to Europe. W. Averell Harriman, whose father had created the modern Union Pacific, was an international banker with extensive contacts on the continent. He arranged for Fetters to visit the factories of every major firm doing research on diesels.[6]

Fetters was well suited to the task. He had designed all the company's steam locomotives in recent years, and in his youth he had worked on the pioneering self-propelled McKeen rail cars, for which he had done extensive work on fuels. His report provides a revealing insight into the state of the diesel art as of December 1926. Two key problems remained unsolved: no practical way had been found for transmitting the power of the constant-speed diesel engine to the varying-speed torque requirements of a locomotive, and no version of the engine had managed to reduce its weight without sacrificing the reliability and horsepower needed for traction use.[7]

Engineers were testing six different approaches to the variable speed problem. Of them Fetters considered electric transmission the only one suited to the high horsepower needs of locomotives. It was reliable, flexible, had high starting torque, was capable of higher turning speeds, relieved the engine from sudden shock loads, and handled all speeds and loads efficiently. Moreover, the technology of electric transmission was well known in 1926. Fetters saw that the Europeans were ahead of the Americans, but most of their work was in experimental units of modest horsepower for industrial use. Since European trains ran lighter loads over less distance, they needed less power.[8]

Since the appearance of the first experimental direct-drive locomotive in 1913, European firms had produced 38 diesel locomotives in sizes ranging up to 1,000 horsepower. By contrast, American companies had turned out 34 diesels since 1924, all but two of them built by American Locomotive Company and two associated firms, Ingersoll-Rand and General Electric. Fetters concluded that the Europeans were still engaged in experimental work along many lines while the Americans had settled on electric transmissions as standard and were hurrying toward commercial production.

Replacement Technology

But serious obstacles remained. No existing diesel engine was compact enough to fit the clearance requirements on American tracks, let alone haul trains. Nor was the use of multiple units deemed practical. The cost of diesels per horsepower was nearly double that of steam locomotives, but the return was impressive. "So many minds are working on the problem of perfecting the Diesel locomotive," concluded Fetters, "that it would be unwise at the present time to make a positive statement that the field of the Diesel locomotive may not in the future, broaden out beyond its present limitations, even so far as to general main line operations."[9]

In this statement Fetters proved a prophet. By 1934 the position of the railroads had changed so radically that some leading lines, notably the Union Pacific and the Burlington, were all but hounding developers to perfect diesel locomotives capable of handling trains at high speeds. The depression cut savagely into rail traffic and intensified the drain of what was left to competing modes. While cutting costs and laying off men, the stronger roads also searched for ways to take the initiative in reclaiming lost business. In this campaign the diesel emerged as a key element in the attempt to remake the image of the railroads.

To understand the revolution that loomed on the horizon in the 1930s, a brief comparison of the two types is useful. The steam locomotive could not be easily started or stopped but had first to get up a head of steam. Even then its speed was difficult to regulate smoothly. It could run only fifty or a hundred miles without stopping for fuel and water, thereby slowing schedules. On grades it could not use full speed efficiently and often required "helper" engines, which meant more expense and delay. Heavy engines were hard on rails, especially curves, and required costly maintenance. The shopwork on steam locomotives was intensive, difficult, and time-consuming. Most new parts had to be custom-made in the shop.

The diesel offered striking improvements in every area. It started and stopped on command, and could maintain whatever speed was needed for peak efficiency. It required no stops for water and could run five or six hundred miles between fuelings. Low axle headings, uniform wheel torques, and lack of "pounding" made diesels easier on rail and allowed them to take curves at faster speeds. On grades full power was available at any track speed, and units could be doubled to increase power without the use of helpers. Many functions such as oiling, which had been done manually on steam power, were performed automatically.[10]

The diesel could handle heavier trains at higher average speeds, thereby improving schedules as well as increasing loads. At terminals it turned around quickly, required far less servicing, used standardized parts, and was far more flexible in deployment. It was less sensitive to adverse weather and offered striking gains in thermal efficiency and fuel economy. Technical advances during the 1920s raised the thermal efficiency of steam locomotives from about 5 percent to 10 percent. Impressive as this achievement was, it paled before the 33 to 40 percent level of the diesel. "For all the romance that surrounds it," wrote one authority, "the steam locomotive was a relatively primitive form of converter with a very low efficiency."[11]

There are three distinct types of locomotive service: switching, passenger, and freight. Each has its own special needs, and the diesel far outstripped the steam locomotive in every case. Switchers work in yards making up trains; they must be light, versatile, flexible, reliable, and economical. Predictably, the diesel made its first inroad in switching, where its high traction at low speeds, fuel economy, easy maneuverability, low maintenance, and ability to remain constantly on line gave it an enormous edge over steam switchers. By 1936 there were 195 diesel switchers already at work in American and Canadian yards.[12]

Passenger service placed a premium on speed and required powerful engines capable of making long runs safely at high speeds. The elimination of stops for water and fuel by itself improved schedules greatly, but during the 1930s the diesel engine became part of a bold effort to lure the traveling public back to railroads. Other technologies were enlisted as well. Rapid growth in the automobile and aviation industries spurred the development of aluminum and steel alloys that could radically lighten passenger cars without reducing their strength. Aircraft builders had developed techniques for welding lightweight metals to endure great stress.

Borrowing heavily from these advances, the Union Pacific and Burlington roads launched intensive efforts to develop an entirely new type of passenger train. The result was the legendary streamliner, which succeeded in knocking an entire day off the schedule between Chicago and the Pacific coast. After inaugural runs in 1934, the new type of train spread rapidly to other companies, thanks in part to the development by General Motors of a new two-cycle diesel engine with alloys light enough for a train. In this age of commercial aviation we easily forget that the

Replacement Technology

streamliner became the travel sensation of the prewar years and was widely regarded as the wave of the future.[13]

As larger diesels moved successfully into passenger service, attention turned to the development of freight units. In February 1941 the Santa Fe garnered headlines by sending a giant 5,400-horsepower engine from Chicago to Los Angeles on the first mainline freight run made by a diesel-powered train. A team of technicians as well as reporters monitored the maiden voyage, which demonstrated the diesel's superiority in unmistakable terms. Steam locomotives making this trip required no less than 35 stops for water and/or fuel and nine changes of engine. The monster diesel breezed the entire distance with only five stops for fuel.[14]

Despite the shortages and demands caused by World War II, the diesel revolution swept irresistibly forward after 1946. By the mid-1950s nearly all major railroads had replaced their mainline steam fleets with diesel power. In 1941 there were 41,911 steam locomotives and only 1,517 diesels in service of all kinds throughout the nation. Twenty years later, when John F. Kennedy was inaugurated, there were 30,123 diesels in service compared to a mere 210 steam locomotives.[15]

A funny thing happened to the iron horse on its way to the future: it was no longer iron or a horse snorting fire and steam. Today the steam locomotive in America has become an artifact found only in museums or showcases where, on special occasions, the last survivors of the breed are trotted out for ceremonial runs to roars of approval from overflow crowds of devotees who worship the iron horse with a religious fervor and fanaticism normally associated with Civil War buffs and converts to Herbalife.

The speed with which this revolution occurred is remarkable given the amount of capital involved, the demands made on the decision-making process of railroad companies, the radical departure from tradition required for this most traditional of industries, and the other far-reaching changes set in motion by the conversion to diesels. This broader revolution can only be outlined here.

The diesel revamped the physical landscape of the modern railroad. Water and coaling stations vanished along with such support services as ash handling, water treatment and storage, boiler washing, and many helper engine facilities. Ashes, cinders, soot, and smoke disappeared from the roadway, terminals, and clothing. The roundhouse gave way to the pass-through facility. Shops became more technical, less cluttered, and cleaner places; they also required less equipment and fewer people to maintain units that used standard instead of custom-built parts.

The effect of the diesel on the labor force was even more drastic than on the landscape. To understand its impact, one must remember that railroaders inhabited a closed world of their own making. They shared traditions, practices, peculiarities, and even a language that separated them from others. Like all members of a closed society, they were prisoners of custom. Moreover, true railroaders did not include everyone who worked for railroads but embraced only those in the operating, mechanical, and maintenance of way departments.[16]

Decades of experience had forged the pattern of railroaders' lives and honed their relationships into a pecking order that also served as an apprentice system. Engineers and conductors sat atop this order, their prerogatives protected by union agreements that, in the quip of one writer, exceeded the French Civil Code in size. Firemen served as apprentice engineers and brakemen as fledgling conductors, making them together the Big Four of railway labor. Below them in rank were the dispatchers, who manipulated trains and equipment like chess pieces on a vast, complex board. The shopmen occupied the next rungs, and below them the maintenance of way crewmen.

The skills acquired by railroaders on the job bound their possessors together and were guarded as jealously as the craft of a medieval guild. For railroaders, as for medieval craftsmen, job security mattered more than anything else. The ranks of railroaders tended to be tight and self-selecting, with newcomers often coming from the families of veterans. A man could become an engineer or conductor only by starting at the bottom and serving his time in the ranks. Promotion was strictly by seniority, creating a hierarchy of age as well as service.[17]

The coming of the diesel revealed with ruthless clarity how completely the railroaders' world was tied to steam power. Never mind that diesels represented a quantum leap in efficiency and economy; most engineers eyed them as alien beasts. "They missed the feel of the throttle," observed one officer. "They were insecure." Gradually, however, the enginemen came to like the cleaner, quieter, steadier ride. On passenger runs they soon discarded the traditional overalls in favor of suits or sport coats. The once grimy engineer looked like another civilian at the office.[18]

Shopmen reacted more vehemently. "I felt like I was a steam engine expert," said Frank Acord, who was a master mechanic when

Replacement Technology

the diesels first arrived. "I knew my business, but I get up one morning and . . . I don't know what it is. I have to learn from scratch." Acord called Charlie Spicka, a shop superintendent for the Union Pacific Railroad "the greatest steam engine man that ever walked the earth." He was present the day Spicka saw the first diesels invade his domain. "It was," mourned Acord, "like they shot him." Spicka glared at the alien beast and roared, "You're not bringing those street cars in my shop."[19]

But they did, in growing numbers. When some of the shopmen refused to touch the diesels, officers like Acord had to tell them, "either you're gonna or you're not going to be here." It was not a happy task; as Acord admitted, "I was about as popular as a dose of clap." Men who regarded themselves as craftsmen found their skills obsolete. Where the shops had built everything for steam power, they merely bought them for diesels. "You become a parts exchanger," emphasized Acord. "Very, very seldom do you build anything for a diesel."[20]

Experience soon produced a new old saying in the shops: on a steam locomotive it took five minutes to find a problem and five hours to fix it; on a diesel it took five hours to find the problem and five minutes to fix it. The key was to keep the engines as clean as possible and set the timing right. The timing was done by the numbers; if you followed the book, you always got good results. But following the book was not the craftsman's way.[21]

In addition to restructuring the shop work force, the diesel put the design people out of the engine business and shifted them to rolling stock. Boilermakers and steamfitters were rendered extinct, as was the entire water service. As Cottrell has noted, "The elimination of the water service wiped out some apprentice programs that used to produce skilled workers required by railroad operations. It destroyed a source of skilled labor indoctrinated in railroad union subculture."[22]

Firemen also became dinosaurs and would have been swept away by the wrecking ball of progress had they not taken refuge in the strength of their union. Their struggle to survive drew national attention to the railroads for thirty years, and remains one of the most dismal sagas of labor history. Unfortunately, it did much to shape the tenor and tone of labor relations in the industry for four decades.

The power of the unions rested in the complex work rules that governed their relations with management. Those regulating pay originated at a time when a full day's pay was defined as twelve hours or a hundred miles traveled, after which train and engine men had to be paid extra. The Adamson Act in 1916 reduced the twelve hours to eight but left the hundred miles intact. A passenger train might make a hundred miles in two hours while a freight train took eight or more hours, which is why engineers coveted the passenger runs.[23]

Obviously the diesel rendered this rule even more obsolete than it had already become. A fast train averaging sixty miles an hour could travel 480 miles in eight hours, but the work rules required either that the engineer be paid for 4.8 days' work or that crews be changed five times during the run. The diesel eliminated many stops for water, fuel, inspections, oiling, and other needs, but companies ended up having to maintain some of them for crew changes.

Not surprisingly, a bitter fight erupted over the extent of management's right to change work rules. Nowhere did it take more revealing form than in the struggle of the firemen, which lasted from 1937 until well into the 1960s. The earliest precedent for engines running without firemen was not the diesel but gasoline-powered rail motor cars, which had run since the 1900s. The early diesel switchers also operated without firemen from 1925 to 1937 for the same reason: none were needed.

Once the streamliner made its debut, however, the Brotherhood of Locomotive Firemen and Enginemen awoke to the danger and demanded that firemen be included with the crews even though they had no clear function to perform. The first roads to confront this issue were the streamliner pioneers, the Union Pacific and the Burlington. Both reluctantly caved in to the demand for two main reasons: it affected so few trains at the time, and they feared that having only one man in the cab of such fast trains might make the public uneasy. When the carriers agreed in March 1937 to put a fireman on every diesel, this requirement covered only nine trains besides switchers.[24]

From this agreement sprang a precedent that proved disastrous for the railroads and unions alike. It marked the beginning of a vicious cycle: the more unions pressed for higher wages and shorter hours, the more productivity dropped, driving the carriers to seek new ways of cutting the work force through technological innovation. The unions countered by demanding new rules or preserving old ones that blunted the impact of new technology. In effect they tried to protect job security at the expense of the efficiency so urgently needed if the industry was to survive in the postwar world. The result was a pattern of labor relations shaped by negativism and myopia.

The cycle took off with the agreement of 1937. Two years later the

Replacement Technology

union launched a campaign for a second fireman on every diesel. The enginemen had already demanded a second engineer, and had also succeeded in preserving the eight hours or a hundred miles rule. A presidential board rejected both demands in May 1943, but four years later the firemen renewed their fight. When another fact-finding board ruled against them, the firemen went out on strike.[25]

Through the 1950s an endless seesaw of negotiations, punctuated by strikes and slowdowns, dogged the industry. In 1956 the carriers took the initiative by notifying the enginemen and firemen that in the future they would regard the use of firemen on diesels as optional. This unilateral attempt to change the work rules triggered a desperate seven-year struggle that culminated in 1963 with victory for the railroads. Since the original 1937 agreement, four fact-finding boards and a presidential commission had studied the request for an extra firemen. All had found no need for one firemen on diesels, let alone justification for two.[26]

After twenty-six years of struggle the Supreme Court in March 1963 upheld the carriers' right to change work rules. It took another year of legal battles to eliminate firemen and campaign against full-crew laws in five states. Still the union fought on, seeking reversal of the decisions and large wage hikes. As late as 1968 the Supreme Court sustained the right of states to enforce full-crew laws. Strikes and strife over everything from rules to wages to job protection stalked the industry's relations with other unions as well.[27]

Through the 1960s railroad labor relations bore an unhappy similarity to the growing Vietnam fiasco. It became a war of attrition costly to both sides and perpetuated by a mad-hatter logic all its own. Neither side could find a way out of the old traps that had landed them there in the first place. Half a century of conflict had not produced a single constructive approach on either side for dealing with the real problems that plagued the industry and threatened the very existence of railroaders. Having floundered early into a mutually destructive relationship, they simply continued a ritual that made as much sense as bleeding a hemophiliac.

Meanwhile the number of employees declined as rapidly as profit margins in the industry. In 1920 the industry hit a peak of nearly 2.1 million employees; this number dwindled steadily to just over a million in 1940 and 577,000 in 1970. Those who remained belonged to a new breed. As the diesel demonstrated, the insular world of the railroader could not survive the inroads of new technologies and techniques. The elite world of the engineer, for example, opened up to a wide variety of outsiders, including women, who would never have had a chance at such work under the old system.[28]

In other areas, too, different and usually younger people invaded the once exclusive domain of grizzled railroaders. The communications and computer revolutions forced carriers to import technicians from outside because no one on the railroad understood anything beyond the telegraph. Officers who had once held college graduates in contempt began actively to recruit them, and to establish management training programs so that old dogs might learn enough new tricks to stay productive.

"The supreme law of the Republic of Technology," wrote Daniel Boorstin, "is convergence, the tendency for everything to become more like everything else." Certainly this homogenizing tendency can be seen in the diesel and the larger experience of the rail industry itself. By 1970 railroads had begun to resemble other sectors in their zeal for modernization and improved efficiency through the latest gadgetry. The once exclusive world of railroaders both shrank and opened up to outsiders, thereby changing it forever. While railroad people may still be a breed apart, they are much more like workers in other fields than their rough and ready predecessors.[29]

Nostalgia being what it is, we tend to think first of the romance and individual flavor that was lost rather than recall how primitive or cumbersome the old ways often were. But like so many things, even nostalgia ain't what it used to be. The modern railroad, like the diesel, may be a duller, less colorful, more technical piece of goods, but it gets far more work done at far less cost than anything that came before it. If it did not, there might well not have been railroads around today.

High-Speed Trains: America's Lost Opportunity

This paper also opened up a new realm of investigation for me. In June 1990 the Stockholm School of Economics sponsored an international conference on "High Speed Trains, Entrepreneurship, and Society." I was invited as one of the American presenters on a subject where considerably more progress had been made in other parts of the world than in the United States. My research confirmed just how far behind Europe and Japan we were in this field. The paper was later published with other proceedings under the title *High Speed Trains: Fast Tracks to the Future*.

As is inevitable with so current a topic, events have outrun some parts of this article. The American projects continue to languish, and some have been abandoned altogether. The only glimmer of hope has been Amtrak's decision to complete the long-delayed electrification of the Boston–New York line and run a version of the Swedish X-2000 train on it. I continue to believe that high-speed trains make good sense for selected parts of the United States despite their high cost, and I remain disappointed that more has not been done to develop them.

For a brief time in the 1930s the United States held center stage in the development of high-speed trains. This supremacy survived World War II only by default and faded fast over the following decades until today the United States ranks far behind other nations in the field. The intriguing question is why this decline occurred. How did the nation with the largest and most highly developed rail system in the world lose this clear superiority?

This complex story can be told only in outline here. It begins properly with some of the factors that separate the American rail experience from that of most other nations. To serve a growing population expanding rapidly over a large continent, most early American roads were built hastily and flimsily. The object was to create not a few good lines but many adequate ones to serve its sprawling domain. By 1900 the United States had 1,224 operating railroads with 192,556 miles of track, yet her industrial economy had undergone such spectacular growth that it threatened to overwhelm this huge system.[1]

Shortly before 1900 the Age of Construction gave way to the Age of Reconstruction as Americans literally rebuilt their major rail arteries from the ground up. The entrepreneurs who undertook this gigantic task, led by the redoubtable E. H. Harriman, understood the domino effect wrought by railroad technology—namely, that one major improvement could not be attempted without undertaking several others at the same time. Bigger payloads required more powerful engines and larger cars, which in turn demanded heavier rails, more ballast, reduced grades and curvature, stronger bridges, improved signals, more durable ties, and an upgrading of other facilities.[2]

The staggering cost of this transformation was made possible by a flood of traffic that poured onto the rail system after 1898 and a capital market that cheerfully absorbed one enormous issue of new securities after another. It is important to remember that most American roads were originally built with private and or state funds. The national government played little part beyond offering land grants and providing loans in the form of bonds for the first transcontinental railroad completed in 1869. Even this modest role soon faded; the Age of Reconstruction was underwritten entirely by the private sector.[3]

Thus did the American experience produce not a cooperative partnership to develop this largest and most vital industry but an adversarial relationship between business and government. Between 1900 and 1916 a public clamor arose to curb the immense power accumulating in the hands of corporations and the entrepreneurs and bankers who controlled them. The result was a flood of legislation that put in the place the regulatory apparatus that still characterizes the American system.[4]

The railroads had always been under intense public scrutiny and were subject early to regulation by the states. With the passage of the Interstate Commerce Act in 1887, they became the first industry to be regulated by the federal government. While the scope of this regulation was weak at first, it was greatly extended during the 1900s. During World War I the rail system was nationalized briefly, then returned to private ownership under a new regulatory framework imposed by the Transportation Act of 1920.[5]

The events of this crucial period left a deep and lasting imprint on the destiny of American railroads in the twentieth century. They imposed a strait jacket of regulation that transformed the carriers into a captive industry unable to control either its pricing or its major costs such as labor. Unable to compete by offering lower rates, roads could only outdo competitors by providing better service. Yet even here they were limited in their scope of action and subject to regulatory strictures that left little room for initiative or innovation.

The timing of this change could not have been worse. The railroads came under severe restraints just when they were in urgent need of working capital to continue their modernization. Rising costs combined with strict regulation of rates slashed the return on capital enough to make many if not most roads unprofitable and unable to float new security issues. If that were not enough, the Act of 1920 bound the railroads in regulatory knots just as they were falling victim to a technological revolution.

For seventy years railroads had dominated the transport industry because no new forms had risen to challenge them. After 1920, however, the automobile, truck, bus, and airplane appeared on the scene, while older forms like water transport and pipelines were reinvigorated. A vicious contest for traffic arose among modes of transport competing less with each other than with other modes. The depression intensified this struggle as all sides vied for their share of a dwindling business.[6]

In these clashes the railroads found it impossible to compete against newer, more flexible modes unshackled by regulation. Many major systems tried to redefine themselves as transportation companies by adding truck, bus, and even air service, but every attempt at innovation ran up against the same barrier of whether regulation would permit it. One area offering a loophole around regulation was technology itself. Despite the limited capital resources at their disposal, the railroads never ceased trying to improve their efficiency and upgrade their facilities. It was one such effort that produced America's shining hour in the realm of high-speed trains.

By the 1930s automobiles and buses had already swept away much of the railroad's short-haul passenger business, but airplanes had yet to make inroads on the long-haul traffic. Although passenger travel was the smallest and least profitable area of railroad business, it had an important marquee value to both shippers and the public, whose contact with the carriers was as travelers. Unable to hold their short-haul business against the automobile, the railroads undertook a bold campaign to preserve their long-haul business by developing a new form of high-speed train.

Known popularly as the streamliner, the new train borrowed its technology from rival modes. Advances in two critical areas made it possible to conceive this new mode of travel: improvements in the internal combustion engine (most notably the diesel) and research in aerodynamics and lightweight metal alloys spurred by the rise of aviation. Two railroads, the Union Pacific and the Chicago, Burlington & Quincy, pioneered in this work and separately unveiled the first streamliners in the spring of 1934.[7]

Except for riding on rails, the new trains departed entirely from tradition. The revolutionary new diesel engine, by eliminating stops for fuel and water, could go twelve times the distance of a conventional train using coal. The sleek metallic cars cut both weight and wind resistance. The trains had new braking systems, sealed windows, climate control, improved lighting, adjustable seats with attached trays, and a host of other innovations. Even the crockery used modern materials that reduced its weight by more than half. The design and decor were striking, like nothing ever seen in a passenger train.

The streamliners went into service on long-haul routes, where they showed to the best advantage. Prior to May 1934 no locomotive had ever traveled more than 775 miles nonstop. That month the Burlington's *Zephyr* raced from Denver to Chicago, 1,017 miles, in little over thirteen hours or half the usual schedule time, reaching a top speed of nearly 113 miles per hour. As more companies ordered new trains, the setting of new speed records became old hat by 1936. The Union Pacific models cut a full day off travel time between Chicago and the West Coast, making the trip in $39^3/_4$ hours.[8]

Public response to the streamliners surpassed all expectations. Nearly 700,000 people lined up to inspect the Union Pacific and Burlington trains in the cities where they were put on display. Thousands more gathered alongside tracks to watch them whizz by. The streamliner aroused wild enthusiasm not only because it offered fast, luxurious travel but because it was a dazzling blend of old and familiar associations with futuristic technology. Where the airplane was something new out of the blue, the streamliner was stunningly new in a familiar setting where the leap of progress from its predecessors could be measured by one's own experience. The streamliner was not merely fast, though speed was one of its prime appeals. In this first age of chic it was sleek, glamorous, and thoroughly modern.[9]

For an old and stodgy industry like the railroad, these were potent selling points. A funny thing had happened on the way to the future: the iron horse was no longer iron or a horse. The hot breath of steam and the galloping surge of power that had always been a part of the romance of railroading had been put on the road to extinction. With these first high-speed trains the railroads made their greatest break ever with the past.

In retrospect the development of the streamliner seems a remarkable act of faith. During the throes of the Great Depression, when railroads were starved for capital no less than business, many of them risked large investments in an area of traffic that had always been the least profitable (in fact unprofitable) for them. While there were plenty of people willing and eager to ride the new trains, the carriers were not responding to any pent-up demand. Why then did they sink money so desperately needed elsewhere into an area that promised little return?

The answer boils down to two related factors: image and regulation. The railroads were prisoners of the regulatory system, which put them at the mercy of politics. For this reason their public image mattered greatly, and most of the public knew the carriers as travelers rather than as shippers. One provision of the Transportation Act of 1920 forbade roads from dropping passenger service on any route without approval from the Interstate Commerce Commission. This obliged carriers to continue passenger operations on routes that ran heavy deficits. Most attempts to abandon service encountered stiff resistance and took much time.[10]

Although streamliners might be a losing proposition financially—a question still hotly debated—they were important as a public relations device to boost the railroads' image. Given a choice, most companies would have preferred to go out of the passenger business altogether, but the law did not permit this option. The alternative was to spruce up passenger travel and try to make at least the long-haul service pay for itself.

By 1940 most major systems had installed streamliners and improved their passenger service in other ways. Public response remained enthusiastic and patronage high. While many problems still plagued the industry, the passenger puzzle seemed well on the road to solution. Then came World War II, which rendered a devastating blow to railroads in general and the passenger service in particular.

Here was another turn of events that no one could have foreseen. The crushing demands of war ran railroad plant and equipment into the ground. Wartime scarcity of labor and materials severely curtailed maintenance. The shiny new streamliners simply wore themselves out hauling record numbers of passengers and troops. At the same time, the war spurred technical developments in aviation that gave rise to radically improved passenger air service after the war. Full employment coupled with consumer shortages raised savings to record levels, creating a pent-up consumer demand that fueled a postwar boom in the automobile industry.[11]

In 1946 the rail industry confronted a situation riddled with irony. It emerged from the war fattened by the huge load of business but physically exhausted and in need of huge capital outlays for improvements. To rebuild its passenger fleet meant starting almost from scratch with another giant investment in new equipment. Most major systems undertook this task even though they were aware of swimming against the tide of events. They invested in new equipment because they saw no alternative. If the ICC would not let them get out of the passenger business, they had to do what they could to attract customers to their trains.

Unfortunately, the postwar environment could not have been worse for their efforts. The economy soared into a prolonged upward climb, keeping employment and consumer spending high. Automobile sales climbed to record heights as the American love affair with cars turned into a raging passion. As housing starts reached unprecedented levels, suburbs sprang up like mushrooms and with them new highway systems. On one side the railroads surrendered the last remnants of short-haul passenger business; on the other, they saw the long-haul business relentlessly whittled away by a growing fleet of new jet airplanes.[12]

By 1960 it was obvious to even the most incorrigible optimist that the railroads' massive postwar investment in new passenger equipment had been in vain. If the industry had been operating in a neutral environment, it might have taken the initiative to redefine its passenger mission in some positive manner and redirect its energies to capturing the traffic most available to it by developing new equipment and marketing tactics. Instead it remained bound by an archaic regulatory system that had dulled initiative and created a pervasive atmosphere of negativism.

Far from developing new approaches to the passenger traffic, therefore, the railroads looked to get out of the business altogether. Instead of seeking positive and imaginative ways to stimulate the carriers in this field, public policy continued to hold the roads prisoner to unprofitable routes and to play the same old game the same old way. The result was a downward spiral into financial disaster that swept once proud systems into bankruptcy or mergers with other lines. The shocking collapse of the Penn Central, an ill-fated amalgam of what had once been the two proudest and most powerful railroads in the nation, finally spurred a long overdue shift in public policy.[13]

A series of legislative enactments, culminating with the Staggers Act of 1980, gave the railroads a freedom of action they had not possessed in decades. For passenger service the key act was the formation in 1971 of a federal corporation called Amtrak to take over the passenger service. This was a historic moment in the rail industry: after 130 years of service the private carriers abandoned the passenger business to a government agency. The American rail industry became a collection of freight carriers with no interest in any other aspect of the business.

This evolution of function, along with the story behind it, explains how and why the United States not only fell rapidly from its leadership role in rail service but also lost interest in maintaining its primacy in the passenger field. The history of Amtrak has been one of constant struggle for survival, which makes all the more remarkable the achievements it has managed in twenty years. Moreover, it occupies the anomalous position of being a public corporation serving a field where innovation and funding has traditionally come from the private sector.

Where, then, does high-speed rail travel in the United States stand now? Ironically, rail passenger service seems to have come full circle. The American passion for the automobile has begun to turn sour in the fumes and traffic jams of freeways choked with traffic. Despite rapid expansion, the highway system has never managed to keep pace with the explosion of cars pouring onto it, and the need to refurbish this infrastructure grows at an alarming rate. Air travel too finds itself snarled in a form of gridlock that has made flying increasingly hectic and obnoxious.

This deteriorating state of travel has breathed some new life into high-speed trains in recent years. In 1956 the much heralded "Aerotrain," an American lightweight train built by General Motors, made its debut on the Pennsylvania Railroad and later the Union Pacific. Despite high hopes, the new train flopped. Nearly a decade later, as part of an attempt to revive the bankrupt New York, New Haven & Hartford Railroad, federal support was given for a high-speed experiment called the Turbotrain. Unfortunately, the prototype was rushed into revenue service too quickly and proved a failure.[14]

The fall of the New Haven in 1960 made it difficult for the government to ignore the commuter problem in the congested Northeast Corridor. In 1965 Congress passed the High Speed Ground Transportation Act, which contained three major provisions. It funded research and development on high-speed ground transportation of all types, authorized work on a demonstration project that spurred creation of both the Turbotrain and the Metroliner, and launched the planning process for what ultimately became the Northeast Corridor Improvement Project.[15]

Two years later a new cabinet position, the Department of Transportation, was created, and under it a new agency called the Federal Railroad Administration. The FRA took charge of research for high-speed trains and oversaw development of the Turbotrain. From its efforts evolved the Northeast Corridor project, a high-profile attempt to develop a modern rail transportation system in the most crowded area of the country. If successful, the project could serve as a model for similar efforts elsewhere.[16]

Between 1976 and 1986 the government poured $2.3 billion into the Corridor project. Most of the money was used to rehabilitate the line while coping with as many as a thousand train movements a day. Apart from this remedial work, some funds went to developing a new train called the Metroliner for high-speed service on the run between Boston and Washington. Despite heroic efforts, the Corridor project produced only half a loaf. The Metroliner went into service only between New York and Washington at 125 miles an hour, leaving the New York–Boston run with conventional service. Today the Metroliner remains the only high-speed train in actual service in the United States.[17]

Why was the Corridor project left uncompleted? The reason was primarily financial. In the end the government balked at tackling two expensive obstacles: reducing curvature on the Boston route to permit high-speed runs and electrifying the line from New Haven to Boston. The route from Washington to New Haven had been electrified as early as 1933, just before the advent of diesel power scuttled a growing movement toward conversion to electric lines. Although part of the original plan, electrification was dropped because of its cost. Today a traveler on the New York–Boston route still sits for ten or fifteen minutes in New Haven while the railroad shifts from diesel to electric power or vice versa.[18]

Here too irony abounds. In 1900 the United States was the world leader in electrified roads; as late as 1930 it owned 20 percent of the world's total. After World War II, when Europe had to rebuild its railroads, the decision was made to electrify. By contrast, American roads pursued a policy begun around 1937 of investing heavily in oil-powered diesels. That choice, however rational at the time, has come back to haunt us in an age where both oil and labor costs have gone through the ceiling. It also cost us a potential power source for new high-speed trains.[19]

One solution to this dilemma would be the creation of an entirely new technology. The work of two American scientists on one form of magnetic levitation helped prompt the FRA, which was underwriting research on linear induction motors, to produce a scale model demonstration of maglev as well, but the latter project was terminated in 1976. From this episode arose the half truth that Americans originated maglev only to see others develop it. "The Japanese and Germans took the ideas and theories of our scientists and turned them into working machines," complained Senator Harry Reid of Nevada. "We have the pride of authorship, but no longer the pride of ownership."[20]

This sort of grumbling over wounded national pride permeates much of the current American discussion over developing high-speed trains, but in truth the United States has only itself to blame for falling so far behind. Apart from the Metroliner, there is today no high-speed American train in service or even under testing. One knowledgeable authority believes that we are seven to ten years behind in developing high-speed technology.[21]

The final irony is that all the live projects in the realm of high-speed trains today are being promoted by private interests with some help from individual states. Except for the incomplete Corridor project, the federal government has at every critical juncture ducked responsibility for developing a coherent transportation system. Ours is a government that traditionally does not lead but rather responds to crisis. Transportation policy has provided a glaring example of this truth.

None of the current projects have reached construction stage, and all rely on foreign technology. Two of them are in Florida, one of the fastest-growing states. After six years of study, a consortium of interests was preparing to award a franchise in 1991 for a high-speed electrified railroad using a modified version of the Swedish X-2 train that will ultimately connect Tampa, Orlando, and Miami, a distance of about 300 miles. A second group hopes to construct a high-profile maglev line from the Orlando airport to a spot near several entertainment centers. Although this line will be only 14 miles long, it hopes to attain speeds of 250 miles an hour. The technology here will be a German Transrapid model, the financing largely Japanese.[22]

Another consortium has for some years been working with the states of Nevada and California to design and build a high-speed line from Las Vegas to the Los Angeles area. No decision has yet been made on whether to use maglev or some form of TGV system, and no franchise has yet been awarded. It is hoped that this will be done by 1991. In Texas a state agency has been formed to solicit proposals for a high-speed line to link the "Texas Triangle" cities of Houston, Dallas, and Fort Worth. The leading contenders here are the German ICE and the French TGV systems. This project is still in the feasibility study stage.

Two other projects deserve brief mention for the contrast they offer. The state of Ohio has taken the first steps toward feasibility studies for a high-speed line connecting Cleveland, Cincinnati, and Columbus. On the other hand, Pennsylvania has withdrawn funding from its state agency on high-speed transportation, thereby dashing hopes of building a high-speed line between Philadelphia and Pittsburgh. However, there is activity of a related sort in Pittsburgh, where the Carnegie-Mellon group that has long been involved in maglev research wants to bring together a collection of firms to create an industrial center capable of producing maglev technology.[23]

This brief survey constitutes the sum of American work in high-speed trains. It is not an impressive record. While the FRA has provided seed money for feasibility studies and is completing a study on the commercial viability of maglev in the United States, the federal government continues to dawdle. On May 2, 1990, a forum was held in Washington to explore ways of using federal money for research to help private industry develop an operational maglev system with technology designed and manufactured in the United States. On the other hand, an attempt to make bonds used for high-speed rail projects exempt from federal taxes, which was deemed critical to financing them, was rebuffed by Congress.[24]

In a curious way Americans have gone back to their roots in dealing with high-speed railroads. Although many analysts insist that federal aid is crucial, especially in the areas of research and development, we are relying on private entrepreneurs with some modest help from individual states. This approach worked well 150 years ago; whether it will be successful in today's very different world remains to be seen.

The Unfinished Business of American Railroad History

It is at once an axiom and a paradox for historians that the more we do, the more remains to be done. The more we learn about a subject, the less we really know about it. For every question answered a dozen more spring up, defying our efforts to contain them like the splinters from the broom of the Sorcerer's Apprentice.

If there is any subject that bears out the truth of this observation it is railroad history. Whole warehouses could be filled with the books written about railroads, yet our knowledge of the subject and our understanding of its many aspects have not advanced nearly as far as this bulk of materials would lead one to believe. A surprising number of gaps remain, questions unanswered and in some cases unasked. The nature of the railroad's role in American life remains misunderstood in many ways despite (some might say because of) all that has been written on the subject.

These gaps exist even at the most basic levels. For all that has been written about individual railroads, a surprising number of major lines lack good histories. Eastern roads have been especially neglected; neither the Pennsylvania, the New York Central, nor the Erie has a good modern study of its history.[1] Moreover, some recent studies of other roads, such as Burke Davis, *The Southern Railway*, qualify more as missed opportunities than as useful histories.[2] The Middle Atlantic, Midwest, and Southwest regions have fewer decent company histories than the South, West, and Northwest, but no section boasts a full roster of roads that have been treated in detail. Regional studies of quality are lacking for most of the nation.[3]

Biographies of major rail figures are also few in number and even more so in quality. The most glaring hole is the lack of a major biography of Cornelius Vanderbilt, who has been largely ignored since Wheaton Lane's study in 1942.[4] Surprisingly little has been done on the progenitors of the mighty Pennsylvania Railroad—J. Edgar Thomson, Thomas A. Scott, George B. Roberts, and A. J. Cassatt—or William Vanderbilt, John W. Garrett and his son Robert of the Baltimore & Ohio, Marvin Hughitt of the Chicago & Northwestern, or dozens of other key figures, let alone their lieutenants.[5] While several books have depicted the colorful saga of the Big Four (Collis P. Huntington, Leland Stanford, Mark Hopkins, Charles Crocker) in California, not one of them has a biography worthy of his contribution to railroad history.[6]

Beyond these obvious gaps lie whole stretches of untouched but fertile possibilities. Railroad labor history has received scant attention despite its importance not only to the industry but to the labor movement itself. Apart from recent studies by Walter Licht and Shelton Stromquist, few historians have looked closely at the railroad unions or the sociology of work on the railroads.[7] It is hard to imagine a richer lode of possibilities for scholars than that offered by railroad towns, the changing ethnic composition of rail workers, the elaborate hierarchy within the rail unions, the traditions that developed within railroad occupations, and a variety of related topics.

The institutional and managerial history of railroads has barely been touched in detail. Alfred D. Chandler, Jr., pointed the way in his magisterial *The Visible Hand* to a wealth of topics, such as accounting, pricing, the creation of organizational structures to fit the unique challenge of managing so far-flung an enterprise, and the evolving of systems to move goods.[8] Scholars have begun to probe these topics, but much more needs to be done.⁹ The gaps in twentieth-century railroad history are even more glaring. Little has been done to examine the railroad response to new modes of competition, new technologies such as the diesel engine, and efforts to redefine their function in an economy where outside forces radically changed their traditional roles and position.¹⁰

Nor has the social and cultural history of railroads been much explored. Apart from studies like Leo Marx's classic *The Machine in the Garden*, James A. Ward's *Railroads and the Character of America, 1820–1887*, and John R. Stilgoe's *Metropolitan Corridor*, few scholars have undertaken to place the railroad in the broader context of American life even though it reorganized that life during the nineteenth century.¹¹ There is an urgent need for more studies of critical periods like Albro Martin's *Enterprise Denied*, and works that place technical developments in a broader context like George Rogers Taylor and Irene D. Neu's *The American Railway Network, 1861–1890*.¹²

These are but a few of the gaps that comprise the unfinished business of American railroad history. What is lacking most in that history is not knowledge but understanding. Young scholars who shy away from the study of railroads because they want to sign onto some hotter topic or because railroads have been done to death, might want to reconsider their options. There is more to be learned about railroads and still more to be grasped from their experience.

The most obvious gap, and in many respects the most surprising, is the lack of a definitive or comprehensive general history of American railroads. How could the most important and influential industry of the first era of American industrialization lack interpretive overviews or comprehensive studies? To say that the subject is too large and complex is to beg the question when nations and whole civilizations receive sophisticated analyses and multivolume coverage. To say that the railroad has been upstaged by other subjects in recent times does not explain why no one produced anything like a definitive general history during the years when the railroad held center stage in American transportation.

If the general literature on railroads could fill a warehouse or two, the general histories could fit snugly in a drawer. John F. Stover's little volume, *American Railroads* (1961) had the field to itself until the recent appearance of Albro Martin's *Railroads Triumphant* (1992).¹³ Where Stover's survey is more descriptive than analytical, Martin's study is defiantly and joyously interpretive, a labor of love by a scholar who obviously

The Unfinished Business of American Railroad History

loves railroads. Flawed though it may be by a lack of documentation and a penchant for digression, Martin's book is the closest thing we have to an interpretive history of the American railroad experience. No other modern writer can match his grasp of so many aspects of railroad history, its social impact no less than its technical and managerial aspects.

Scholars have in recent years labeled some of Martin's work as "biased," by which I presume is meant that it has a point of view not to the liking of those who consider their own point of view "unbiased" or "balanced." This charge is, of course, the classic red herring of academia in that it offers the offended scholar a convenient way to ignore the argument behind the "biased" point of view. In our quest for "objectivity" we sometimes forget that it is entirely possible for someone holding even an extreme point of view to be right about a subject. I raise this point because it may help explain why so few people have attempted a comprehensive overview of railroad history.

To a degree beyond that of most other fields, railroad history has been a prisoner of its constituencies and partisans. Its story has been a controversial one from the first, locking detractors and defenders in fierce debate over almost every aspect of its being. So central was the railroad to its era that few people managed to view it with something other than a loving or a jaundiced eye. Those who worked in the industry developed a clan loyalty to their trade. Shippers cursed the railroad as an engine of evil holding them in its greedy clutches, while managers, speculators, and politicians alike saw it as a wondrous vehicle for propelling them to fame and fortune.

One constituency alone has filled a warehouse with its collected works on railroads. While several fields of history have amateur enthusiasts, none can approach the sheer volume of books, pamphlets, and articles produced by rail fans or buffs. The vast bulk of this work is devoted to minute descriptions of power, rolling stock, obscure short lines, and technical subjects. Much valuable information can be gleaned from these works, which are often the product of expertise as well as labors of love. But few address the larger questions of railroad history or place their topic in broader contexts. Railroad history is more than the sum of its stuff, and a literature produced by devotees is not likely to offer a searching examination or critical overview of the field.

Scholars have fared little better in searching out the high ground of detached judgment. The first generation of professional historians and economists happened to emerge at a time when the railroad had already become a highly charged political issue. Like most citizens, they found it difficult to avoid taking sides on matters relating not only to their expertise but to their views on public affairs as well. Those who tried to examine the issues objectively got caught in the political crossfire. Scholars who defended the railroads were dismissed as paid hirelings or harebrained theorists; those who attacked the carriers earned applause from the public and often censure from other quarters of the business community.

One of the first thoughtful students of railroad problems, Charles Francis Adams, Jr., managed to work both sides of the street. Early in his career Adams coauthored with his brother Henry the popular *Chapters of Erie*, which fixed the legend of Jay Gould, Jim Fisk, and Daniel Drew in the public mind.[14] A severe critic of what he deemed railroad rapacity, Adams found himself in 1884 the president of the Union Pacific Railroad and a spokesman for the industry he had roasted earlier. For all his good intentions, Adams foundered badly in his new role and was ousted by none other than Gould in 1890.[15]

The dual roles of critic and advocate overshadowed Adams's most enduring contribution to our understanding of railroads. In 1878 he published a slim volume called *Railroads: Their Origin and Problems* that contained a wealth of insights into what had already become a controversial subject. His influence on other railroad men ran deep. One of them, General Edward Porter Alexander, produced a valuable little volume of his own in 1887.[16] The views of both men are still worth reading today. In their own time they should have become an integral part of the public discourse over railroads. As the debate grew more shrill, however, Adams and Alexander were dismissed as mouthpieces for the industry along with other thoughtful rail officers like A. B. Stickney and E. H. Harriman. James J. Hill had more luck selling his message to the public, but not even his popularity could make his message the medium for a rational debate over railroad policy.[17]

The strange case of William Z. Ripley provides an even more revealing example of how warped and personal the debate became. Albro Martin has described Ripley as "the nation's leading 'expert' on railroad economics at the time, whose ignorance of the realities of his subject helped him poison the springs of public understanding for two generations."[18] This harsh judgment contains more than a modicum of truth. Well before Matthew Josephson's *The Robber Barons* imprinted the stock image of railroad villains, Ripley painted similar caricatures of some of the great railroad entrepreneurs in his *Railroads: Finance and Organization* and other books.[19]

The Ropes Professor of Economics at Harvard, Ripley had through his extensive writings established himself as a foremost authority on the railroad. He had served as expert agent on transportation for the United States Industrial Commission in 1900–1901 and investigated the relations between the anthracite coal industry and the railroads. His railroad volumes had a sweep of expertise that concealed some patchy research and a willingness to accept the conventional wisdom on subjects where that wisdom had little more than sensational newspaper accounts behind it.

One such episode involved a controversial set of transactions surrounding the Chicago & Alton Railroad when it fell under the domination of E. H. Harriman. In his book Ripley made the Alton a showcase for all the abuses and depredations of a generation of railroad operators, and labeled Harriman a "conspirator" who "crippled" the Alton with his "piratical" and "fraudulent" tactics.[20]

This approach outraged George Kennan, a noted traveler, writer, and authority on Russia, who had been engaged by Mary Harriman to write a biography of her husband.[21] With her encouragement, Kennan produced a detailed rebuttal of Ripley's version but could not get his article accepted by *Outlook*, in which he had often published before. The reason was clear: former President Theodore Roosevelt had long been associated with the magazine, and any piece defending Harriman would reflect on Roosevelt, his former friend who became a bitter antagonist. "I would strongly advise against referring to the controversy with Mr. Roosevelt," Lawrence Abbott of *Outlook* told Kennan pointedly. "It would be awkward for us to take that up."[22]

The article appeared instead in the *North American Review* of January 1916 and drew a prompt response from Ripley.[23] "I have received the interesting and presumably rather expensive defense of Harriman which you have permitted to appear over your name," he wrote Kennan haughtily. "The substance of it interests me not at all. You have too evidently marred a well-deserved literary reputation for money." After three more paragraphs of labored contempt, Ripley suggested, "Why not write Harriman's life by emphasizing the good work and passing over his crimes lightly. You can't whitewash them. Forget them."[24]

Kennan suppressed his indignation and dismissed the letter as ill-mannered, but Ripley was only warming to his task. He sent letters to railroad manager Samuel Felton and Wall Street lawyer Roberts Walker, who had worked for Harriman, seeking information on the Alton episode; both men passed copies along to Kennan. A month later Walker warned him that the professor was still "pretty well wrought up by your article and has also been prodded to reply to it by the Interstate Commerce Commission and by a very eminent gentleman at Oyster Bay."[25]

Kennan understood what had happened. The distinguished professor had been caught with his scholarly pants down. In his magisterial sweep he had seized on the notorious Alton case without looking at it closely, and had been challenged by someone Ripley deemed a mere amateur, a journalist. He then made a bad situation worse by sending *North American Review* a rejoinder that showed more venom than good sense. In a shockingly unprofessional performance Ripley resorted to ad hominem attacks, appeals to authority ("It takes years to master these affairs," he sneered privately to Kennan), innuendoes, digressions, vague generalizations, irrelevancies, and mishandled evidence. He ridiculed one source used by Kennan as a "third-rate hack" while ignoring the full list of other creditable references. Never did he engage Kennan's main points or refute his arguments.[26]

On the first page of his reply Ripley poured out this breathless indictment of Harriman:

> [Harriman] was a dominant factor in the inner circles of the greatest banking institutions. The vast resources of the New York life insurance companies were at his disposition. Ramifications of his political power, Federal and State, extended to every quarter of the land. State and even national conventions took his orders. Members of Congress did his bidding. Laws were enacted at his will. Only two men ever dared to block his path. The late J. P. Morgan stood between him and the possession of the Northern Pacific Railroad in 1901; and Theodore Roosevelt thwarted his purpose to become an absolute dictator of the transportation affairs of the United States.

Ripley also included a letter from Roosevelt, who alluded to the piece written by "a Mr. George Kennan" as if he had not known the author for years. Roosevelt dismissed the whole of Kennan's argument and for his pains drew an article from Kennan entitled "The Psychology of Mr.

Roosevelt." Kennan also responded to Ripley, shredding what little substance there was in his argument.[27]

Ironically, it was Kennan the "amateur" who proved more scholarly in this clash and Ripley the scholar who sounded more journalistic and amateurish. Kennan may have been a hired gun, as Ripley never tired of emphasizing, but he did his homework well and, unlike Ripley, took care to consult the participants in the episode. By any measure, Ripley and Roosevelt got the worst of the exchange, and both soon retreated in silence.[28]

The issue here is not who was right or wrong on the Alton question, which is a far more complex episode than earlier accounts depicted. It is rather the tenor of the discourse, which never acquired the faintest tone of objectivity. Although Kennan tried to present a scholarly restatement of the Alton episode, he was a partisan seeking to make the best case for Harriman. This approach could not help but step on some very sensitive toes, with results that quickly buried the quest for truth beneath a mound of personal acrimony.

From the first the controversial nature of the railroad encouraged scholars to view it less in its own right than through the lens of some pet economic, political, or social theory that explained its behavior in some broader context. The result was a curious literature that too often resembled a cake of self-interest coated with a thin icing of idealism proclaiming the railroad to be an engine of material progress or a menace to the free enterprise system. About the only thing all sides agreed on was the importance of its role in American life.

Labor strife, for example, has often been depicted as a clash between the downtrodden workers and the heartless railroad corporations that used their power to crush revolts. Hardly anyone has examined the economic issues involved, preferring instead the easier road that, in Albro Martin's trenchant phrase, allowed "the men to win the moral argument by default."[29] The upheavals of 1877, for example, have yet to receive a good interpretive treatment.[30] In recent times the debate on railroad labor has been impaled on the twin traumas of job loss through mechanization and the gross inefficiencies wrought by featherbedding.

So too with most of what has been written about the agrarian revolts of the late nineteenth century. Few Americans complained more about railroad rates, service, and influence than farmers. Their views on these issues were no less partisan than those of the railroad apologists, yet scholars have tended to accept the farmers' complaints without testing the truth of them—preferring once again the moral high ground to economic analysis. Fred A. Shannon, for example, stated flatly that "local rates were often outrageous," and condemned the "monopolistic practices of the railroads, which often took the last cent of profit out of a crop, thus retarding commercial agricultural ventures and forcing self sufficing practices, such as the burning of corn in the western Prairies."[31]

What did Shannon mean by an outrageous rate? He offers no analysis of costs and shows no indication that he knows or cares what factors underlay local or through rates. His general indictment proceeds along two broad lines: (1) the rates were outrageous because farmers could not afford to pay them, and (2) the railroads gouged farmers at every turn with rates, land holdings, elevators, grading of crops, and such practices as jacking up rates at harvest time to maximize return. There may be truth in some or all of these charges, but there is also another side to the story in every instance. That other side rarely got told except by partisans of that side, who tended naturally to dismiss the farmer's point of view.

The point is not who was right or wrong in these debates, but rather that few historians have tried to get past the debate to the issues themselves. It seems never to have occurred to Shannon or some other historians of agriculture that the structure of rail rates was a complex matter involving far more than the company's desire to gouge its customers or the farmer's need for cheap transportation. Nor did Shannon seem to realize that there is no necessary correlation between the legitimate cost of a service and the ability of a given customer to pay for it. It is possible that both sides had justice on their side in any given dispute, but the dialogue between them (if any) was not about truth. It was more about power.

One striking undertone seems to pervade the literature of strife between the railroads and their critics during the period before World War I. The real (and sometimes stated) complaint of farmers and other shippers was fueled less by rates or other alleged abuses than by the fact that, like it or not, they were dependent on the railroad for access to market. The railroad was at once their best friend and worst enemy in the business arena. This duality left them feeling helpless and made a rational, objective discourse on most issues difficult if not impossible.

As I have argued elsewhere, the debate over the railroad and its impact went wrong early because of widespread confusion over what the railroad was and a wholesale failure to grasp its unique elements.[32] Every issue from rates to costs to competition to construction to marketing deteriorated into arcane debates that veered ever farther from the underlying realities. This was hardly surprising. The railroad was so new and revolutionary a technology that its impact on the American scene could not help but overwhelm people's ability to analyze its disparate components and their effects.

Nothing attested more to the centrality of railroads in American life than the speed with which they aroused deep public concern about the power they wielded over individual shippers, the economic destiny of communities, local governments, state legislatures, Congress, and federal agencies. As the debate over the railroad's role grew more intense, it could not help but color the vision of those seeking to understand the issues involved.[33]

Similar forces shaped and warped the literature on our greatest national trauma, the Civil War, and the parallels between the two historiographies are instructive. For decades the literature on the coming of the war and its causes came largely from participants in those events and was fiercely partisan, justifying actions on one side and condemning them on the other.[34] Here, as with the railroad, timing played an important role: the first generation of professionally trained American scholars happened also to belong to the first generation of Americans who had not participated in the war or its coming.

As might be expected, these younger historians took a more detached view of events, but they could not escape the influence of so long and rancorous a debate. In their zeal to rise above the partisan bickering, they cast the national tragedy as a morality play in which both sides upheld their principles earnestly, no one was blamed, and the real winner was American nationalism, which emerged from the ordeal sealed in blood and more cohesive than ever. The point here is not to argue the correctness of this interpretation but to emphasize how it reflected more the world of the late nineteenth century than that of the Civil War era, and how, even in recast form, it remained a perspective shaped by the earlier partisan viewpoints it tried to resolve.

Later generations of scholars tried to avoid this trap by shifting the ground of discussion, but each one triggered its own controversies with roots that reached deep into the bitter divisions of their own era. Whatever the merits of their arguments, it is hard to escape the sense that the economic nationalists who portrayed the triumph of an industrial society over an agrarian one, or the revisionists who kindled a fierce debate over whether the Civil War could or should have been avoided, were speaking more to the issues of their own time than to the crisis of Union.

All this may seem like another example of how each age writes its own history (or, more precisely, writes its history over), but more is involved. Present experiences can illuminate past events, but only if those past events are viewed in their own context on their own terms. Too often scholars use the past as a vehicle to support a theory of their own rather than attempt the difficult task of entering that past world to glimpse it as much as possible through its own eyes. To understand the crisis of the Union, for example, we need to grasp not what secession means to us but rather what exactly it meant to those grappling with it.

More recently scholars have taken the literature in another direction by churning out specialized studies that have fragmented the broader issues and made them more complex and ambiguous than ever. The modern version of an overview is less a synthesis than a compendium in which virtually no point of view is left out. The tyranny of the footnote and of specialization has turned the genre of interpretive history into a historiographical survey in which the writer dare not omit reference to any relevant work lest reviewers pounce on the omission as evidence of a glaring ignorance of the literature.[35]

"Nothing left out" history may be more neutral and politically correct, but it is too often unintelligible. An overview without a point of view has little value, as does history that says only what we want to hear. Historiography may prove how well a scholar can use a library, but it does not inform us about the subject matter itself. And, lest we forget, this kind of history will comprise our signature for later generations, who will view it as more a reflection of our own times than of the age it discusses.

Railroad history has followed a comparable pattern.[36] Its clash of partisans lasted longer than a generation because, unlike the Civil War, the battle did not have a clear and clean termination. The long and bitter fight over regulation fueled the debate for years and left little middle ground between friends and foes of the railroad. The great railroad entrepreneurs suffered the same fate, cast as they were in the bookend caricatures of Robber Barons and Industrial Statesmen with little attention paid to what they actually did or why they did it.

Like his peers in Civil War history, Alfred D. Chandler, Jr., tried to shift the debate away from the old battlegrounds by focusing on the role played by the railroad in the evolution of organizational structure, management, and other aspects of American business.[37] The impact of his pioneering work in what he termed the "managerial revolution in American business" can scarcely be overestimated. In analyzing the pivotal role of the railroad in this process, Chandler created a new and compelling synthesis of how the American railroad system developed and the ways in which it served as a model for other industries.

Unlike the Civil War historians, Chandler managed to step outside the old partisan debates without stirring them up in new form. He accomplished this by paying little attention to the historical debate over such issues as regulation, rates, merger and monopoly, and concentrating instead on the elements of these issues most useful to his approach. This tactic enabled him to rise above the old divisions, but it also limited him to telling only part of the railroad's story. His work cast a long and enduring shadow over a major aspect of railroad history, but it does not comprise a general history of the railroad.[38]

Recent work in railroad history has suffered from the same fragmentation wrought by specialization that is typical of other historical fields. But there is one crucial difference. Other fields of study have often been shaped by broad overviews or themes that in recent times were challenged or demolished by a multiplicity of views.[39] Railroad history has never had a clear central theme or overview for new information and insights to demolish.

One reason for this situation may be the narrow source base on which so much railroad history has been written. There are archives bulging with primary materials on American railroads, but only a few of them have been tapped. Probably the most used—I am tempted to say overused—resource has been the papers of the Burlington Railroad at the Newberry Library. This rich collection provided the source materials for Richard C. Overton's masterful history of the Burlington as well as dozens of other studies.[40]

Scholars have flocked to this collection because it is large, varied, and well organized. This tendency has made the Burlington collection almost too much of a good thing. No rail managers are quoted more often than John Murray Forbes, Charles E. Perkins, and other Burlington officials. Their views were important but by no means definitive, and certainly not the whole story. Yet they have come to dominate the discourse on railroads among American scholars, who have relied on what amounts to a skewed source base on railroad topics. Meanwhile, the large and fertile Illinois Central collection at Newberry has gone virtually unused, while large collections from the Pennsylvania, Union Pacific, Baltimore & Ohio, Great Northern, Northern Pacific, Erie, and other major roads have scarcely been tapped.

"The history of the Chicago, Burlington, and Quincy railroad makes it a representative case study of the making of a managerial workforce," declared Olivier Zunz.[41] But what makes the Burlington representative? Forbes, Perkins, and others are often praised for making the Burlington one of the better managed and more efficient roads in the nation. If that is true, and I think it is, then it hardly qualifies as typical. For that matter, how do we even know what constitutes a representative case study when so few examples have been looked at in detail?

The universe of railroad management might be far more diverse than is generally known, similar in some obvious ways but surprisingly varied in others. One line of debate among railroad men centered around the differences between the division and the department forms of organization, but no one has examined that discussion closely or compared the organizational structures of several major roads or tried to correlate those structures with geographical regions or other factors.[42]

Two other factors help explain the lack of a central theme. Surprisingly few historians or writers have attempted to grasp all sides of the railroad's role and thereby cast off the blinders of partisanship. Nor have many people, partisans or historians, then or later, grasped how far removed the realities of the railroad were from the assumptions and generalizations made about it.

As budding specialists in change, Americans learned early that the easiest way to absorb the impact of revolutionary new technologies was to give them familiar names and images. Thus it was that the railroad became known as the "iron horse" and the automobile as the "horseless carriage." It was no less natural to apply other familiar concepts to the railroad where, to conventional wisdom, they seemed to fit very well.

But in fact they did not. Competition among railroads differed radically from other known forms of competition. So did the figuring of costs and the making of rates. The railroad required new methods of raising capital, a new kind of corporation to make this possible, and a new type of organization to manage the unprecedented nature of its operations. It needed a new concept of labor relations, of accounting, of determining routes and construction methods, of scheduling and coordinating the movement of trains, and of communicating within a far-flung organization and over long distances through remote regions.

The natural impulse was to do these things in old ways, but smart practitioners soon learned that they had to adopt or improvise new methods. The result was a steadily widening gap between the "insiders" of the industry, who understood these differences, and "outsiders" who did not. For example, observers and historians alike criticized American roads, especially in the South and West, for being flimsily built and meandering compared to British and the better New England roads. This approach was scorned as shoddy construction and a prime exhibit of financial chicanery, a vintage American scam in which the shell of a railroad was thrown up to reap profits through a variety of manipulative tactics.[43]

No doubt some roads deserved this criticism, but there is another side to the story. In those regions beyond New England it made good sense to construct railroads on the cheap rather than build them for the ages. The object was to secure transportation for thinly populated areas to facilitate settlement and develop business. Few areas of the West and South could afford a well-built railroad or provide enough business to sustain one, and few promoters had the capital or the inclination to build one until the business was there. Moreover, the rapid advance of technology made building for the ages a risky gamble, especially in regions where the distances to be covered dwarfed those of England or New England and the topography posed formidable engineering challenges.

Similarly, the explosive growth of rail mileage after 1880 is often viewed as a bubble of excess that was finally pricked by the depression of 1893–1897. Apart from some wasteful duplication of routes, however, this orgy of expansion laid rails into virtually every isolated corner of the country, creating the largest and most far-flung rail network on the globe. It is true that the depression forced a dramatic reorganization of this network, but to emphasize that point is to overlook a more important one. Once the depression lifted, a flood of new business poured down on the rail system that struggled to handle it all. This crush of traffic forced the brightest and boldest railroad managers, led by E. H. Harriman, to update the American rail network with massive reconstruction programs.

In essence, then, the American rail network was built during the 1880s and rebuilt during the 1900s. The first phase pushed lines into regions starved for transportation connections, sometimes overfeeding them; the second phase turned those scrawny original lines into much more solid systems physically and organizationally at a time when enough traffic had developed to support them. Regardless of who made or lost fortunes in the process, this pattern fit the needs of the nation during each of these periods. It created the transportation infrastructure that made possible the production and marketing revolutions between 1880 and 1910.[44] To say that the whole process should have proceeded more rationally or carefully is to miss the whole point about how an open system promotes economic development.

The lessons insiders learned about how the realities of railroading differed from past experience rarely filtered down to outsiders. The public knew the Iron Horse only by the service it provided and judged its performance by their own experience in similar matters. Here was yet another area in which the railroad set a precedent for the coming industrial society; as the nation's first big business it was the first to create the dual constituencies we call insiders and outsiders. Other institutions, most obviously the military, had constituencies that could be defined this way, but in the business sector it scarcely existed except perhaps on a much smaller scale among bankers.

I don't mean to suggest that all insiders were informed and all outsiders ignorant. Some railroad officers never grasped the basic realities of their business or lost touch with them over time. Many continued the wrong-headed pursuit of their goals, paving the road to that familiar destination with the best of intentions. The more savvy among them, however, learned well the lessons taught them, often by harsh experience. Many tried to impart these lessons to others in the industry only to meet a surprising degree of resistance and even hostility.

By the late nineteenth century another problem had surfaced: the railroad industry had long since begun to ossify its practices by wrapping them in the mantle of tradition. Past success had its usual effect of convincing people that they had found the magic formula to guide their actions even though conditions were changing rapidly around them. Men at every level of the business learned what to do and how to do it on the basis of how it had always been done. This was no less true of management than of labor, where the seniority system took hold. Once tradition infused the industry, insiders had as much trouble dealing with a changing world as outsiders did in comprehending what the industry was all about.

This distinction between insiders and outsiders mattered greatly because of the railroad's distinctive role as a private industry operating as a public carrier. There were other examples of this, such as water carriers, but none played so dominant a role in so many areas of American life. Railroads found themselves exposed to constant political pressure and entanglement in a body of law that was wholly unprepared to deal with the novel conditions wrought by their presence.[45] The Union Pacific Railroad carried this confusion to a new level by being a private corporation with a federal rather than state charter, thus subjecting it directly to the whims of Congress. This arrangement blighted three decades of its history.[46]

It exaggerates little to say that the anomaly of a private industry operating on so vast a scale as a public service did much to hamper understanding of both the railroad and its relationship to other constituencies. In the political arena the railroad became, as did Standard Oil, a symbol wrapped in a set of controversial issues. This confusion distorted the realities behind many issues that were already unfathomable to outsiders because of their complexity, and made the railroad a convenient target for discontent from several quarters.

Long before 1901, when Frank Norris gave the nation its favorite image of the railroad as the "Octopus," the carriers were flayed as corporate ogres trampling on the rights of a helpless public. Newspapers delighted in parading before the public every morsel of scandal or outrage associated with railroads, and they had plenty of wares to display: the notorious Erie wars of the 1860s; the Hepburn hearings from which the mangled "The public be damned!" outburst of William H. Vanderbilt was extracted; the bizarre and thoroughly misunderstood Credit Mobilier scandal;[47] the obeisance of the Pennsylvania legislature to the Pennsylvania Railroad and of legislatures elsewhere to powerful carriers in their state; the ferocious rate wars; the stunning, often outrageous maneuvers of men like Jay Gould; and the lurid accounts of people crushed or roasted to death in railway accidents, to name but a few.

This unrelenting stream of negative publicity could not help but jade public attitudes toward the railroads, and rarely was it countered by positive accounts. The issue here is not whether the railroads deserved this publicity or who was to blame; it is rather to indicate how difficult it was for anyone to view the railroads through detached eyes when so much of the information about them reaching the public was loaded on one side or the other. In this environment it was easy for earnest reformers and ambitious politicians alike to depict the clash in simplistic terms as one between the railroads and the public.

But who was the public? One of the convenient fictions of American politics is the way in which crusades against wrongs real or imagined are waged on behalf of a public interest that claims no stake in the contest other than the desire for justice and equity. While there is obviously a public interest in controversial issues, it does not follow that there is a public *presence* in the contest over them, or that those claiming to represent the public are in fact the voice of the people rather than a chorus of other special interests. In practice many of the fights perceived as pitting the public against some public enemy were in fact clashes between opposing special interests in which one party managed to position itself as the *vox populi*.[48]

So it was with many of the railroads' battles. The point again is not who was right or wrong on any given issue but rather who was fighting whom. The railroads were unabashedly a special interest, but so was the "public" that opposed them. As I have argued elsewhere, it consisted not of disinterested citizens but of individuals, firms, interest groups, rival lines, speculators, opportunists, politicians, and whole communities, each one seeking some advantage in the form of contracts, jobs, payoffs, lower rates, rebates, services, branch or spur lines, or profits from the rise or fall of security prices, to name but a few of the possibilities.[49]

In many cases the driving force behind the attack on railroads was an assortment of shippers, whether tightly organized like the industrialists who wrung rebates from roads or loosely affiliated like some farm groups. To view farmers as the voice of an oppressed public rather than as an interest group seeking better terms misses the point of what the conflict was about. The reality of the struggle was that Standard Oil got better rail rates than farmers or even other oil firms because it had more power and could exert more leverage, but this should not obscure the fact that all of them wanted the same thing from the railroad.

The railroad made an inviting target because it wielded so much power, actual and potential. It was the queen on the chessboard of economic development, capable of making or breaking the destiny of communities as well as firms and individuals. The most enlightened or disinterested policy on a railroad's part (and it was seldom accused of either one) could not have satisfied the whole range of interests clamoring for its favors. Decisions that pleased one group usually disappointed others, who did not hesitate to blame their misfortunes on the railroad's greed and malevolence. Farmers attributed their distress to high rates and unfair classification policies, businessmen to rebates or other discriminatory practices that gave rivals an edge. Towns left off the main line denounced the railroad for consigning them to economic stagnation, while those on the line demanded favorable rates to foster their growth at the expense of rival communities.

From these fights arose a double standard inherent in the confusion over the role of large corporations in American life. It was perfectly natural for individuals to advance their own self-interest, but when a railroad acted in its own interest it was gouging the public or harming those whose self-interest suffered from the action. The heart of the matter was power: the behavior of both was comparable, but the power wielded by corporations was disproportionate to that wielded by individuals. Such an imbalance in power could be redressed either by creating organizations with comparable power to fight the railroads or by enlisting the political power of government.

Both approaches were tried with striking success. Shippers, farmers, and other interests organized into effective pressure groups that enabled them to rectify the imbalance of power with the railroads. The main battles were fought in the political arena, where the size and strength of the railroads proved as much a liability as an asset. Like giant beasts, railroads were subject to attacks from all sides by foes too numerous and too quick to be repelled effectively.

In addition to the federal government, which did not enter the fray until the Interstate Commerce Act of 1887, the railroads had to contend with state legislatures (from which most roads derived their charters), county courthouses, municipal governments, town councils, and local authorities. To transact business the carriers had to deal with congressmen, legislators, governors, federal and state officials, judges, aldermen, mayors, sheriffs, editors, bankers, merchants, and a host of others. For every favor the railroad sought, a dozen were demanded of it in return: payment, passes, privileges, investments, securities, contracts, agencies, jobs, political contributions, bribes. In courts, where every road appeared often, the carriers had to defend many more suits than they brought, before juries notoriously unsympathetic to the railroad's position.

Ultimately politics was a self-defeating exercise for railroads. Most never wanted to be in the political arena but could find no way to stay out of it. The railroad was a mutation in a society unprepared for it or the changes it wrought. It ran afoul of the law because little in the law applied clearly to much of what it did. Law is by nature rooted in tradition and slow to adapt to change. When change comes in ever larger dimensions at ever increasing speed, social and legal dislocation can hardly be avoided. The railroad happened to be the unwilling pioneer of this process in American society, which entangled it in politics and subjected it to attack from many quarters.

But there is more to the story. A balanced history of the railroads will reveal that politics alone did not cause their downfall. In the end it was not only external attack but internal ineptness that brought on the fatal attack of regulation that made the railroads a captive industry in the twentieth century. The failure of rail leaders to keep up with changing times, and to unite in constructing their defense against attack and their strategy for the future, made outside intervention all but inevitable. The shortest history of railroads might be this one sentence: the railroads at the height of their success failed to solve their own problems, forcing government to intervene with solutions that did more harm than good.

Railroads lost their position of dominance in the twentieth century not because they shrank in importance but because other sectors and technologies rose to prominence with astonishing speed. For nearly a century the railroads virtually owned inland transportation and competed mostly against each other. After 1920, however, new modes of transport ended their suzerainty with stunning swiftness: automobiles, trucks, buses, airplanes, as well as rejuvenated pipeline and water service. The once powerful rail industry found itself on the defensive and scrambling to stay afloat in a new competitive environment.

Here is yet another pattern familiar to the twentieth century for which the railroad was pioneer. For much of the nineteenth century, railroads were the cutting edge of change and innovation. Their success and the power they wielded led the industry to grow complacent and hidebound. The carriers changed the world and then stood still while that changing world made them prisoners of their own traditions. The policies and strategies that drove them to success in one era led to their downfall in the next. In later years a similar fate would befall a variety of mighty companies, including Ford, A & P, Sears, General Motors, Wang, and IBM.

Once the railroads became a political football, an objective dialogue became nearly impossible even for later generations of scholars. Some retreated to studies of individual companies or specialized topics like freight rates, rolling stock, labor relations, or managerial strategy. A few tried to pour new wine into old bottles; Gabriel Kolko for one attempted a new slant on the regulatory conundrum that provoked more controversy than insight.[50] Others used new tools like econometrics to explore older topics with unconvincing results.[51] Outside academia, partisans continued their long tradition of sniping at each other. "Those responsible for private railway enterprise," observed Kent T. Healy delicately, "from its beginning have held a hostile position toward government regulation."[52]

In his astute article, "The Dark and Bloody Ground of Reconstruction Historiography," Bernard A. Weisberger observed that "there has been no synthesis ... in a good general history of Reconstruction.... The other failure of historians to deal adequately with Reconstruction is evident in textbooks, many of which play old tunes on worn keys."[53] The same holds true for the Dark and Bloody Ground of railroad history, and for many of the same reasons.

The railroads belong to a tainted era of our past in terms of our ability to view them objectively. This legacy of tainted dialogue, or sometimes monologue, is the unfinished business of railroad history. It remains a field in search of an overview that will serve not only as a broad interpretation but also as a perspective on all sides of a story that has seldom been free of distortions.

But the railroads also belong to our future. Despite all the shifts in transportation technology and the vicissitudes of their fortunes, the carriers continue to be a much larger part of our national transportation system than the public realizes. Like an entertainer who has not had a recent hit, railroads seem to have faded from the public consciousness and become an emblem of the past. Prior to Amtrak, the fact that railroads provided transportation for so many people helped keep them in the public mind. As freight haulers in recent years they have grown all but invisible to outsiders except when an accident thrusts them back into the headlines.

As the twenty-first century looms, the railroads are very much alive and for the most part well, even though what they do and how they do it has changed enormously. That too is a story that remains to be told. The problem, the unfinished business, is how to find a perspective that encompasses so large a subject without distorting it. A new generation of scholars has an opportunity to rectify one of the strangest mysteries in our cultural history: The golden age of railroads has come and gone, and we have yet to grasp fully what it meant to American civilization.

Notes

A Memoir by Way of Introduction

1. This collection includes all of my full-length work except for one major article, which was deemed too technical to include here. For this missing piece see Maury Klein and Kozo Yamamura, "The Growth Strategies of Southern Railroads, 1865–1893," *Business History Review*, vol. 41, no. 4 (Winter 1967), 358–77.

Patterns of Early American Railroad Development

1. Quoted in George R. Taylor and Irene D. Neu, *The American Railway Network, 1861–1890* (Cambridge, Mass., 1956), 5.
2. Albro Martin, *Railroads Triumphant* (New York, 1992) 17–18.
3. Ibid., 135.
4. Quoted in ibid., 18.
5. Arthur C. Cole, *The Irrepressible Conflict* (New York, 1934), 5.
6. Martin, 82.
7. J. Willard Hurst, *Law and the Conditions of Freedom in the Nineteenth Century United States* (Madison, Wisc., 1967), 39.

The Strategy of Southern Railroads

1. The standard work on restoration is Carl Russell Fish, *The Restoration of Southern Railroads* (Madison, Wis., 1919). An excellent insight into problems involved and solutions attempted can be garnered by reading the annual reports of the various companies. Sizable collections can be found at Baker Library, Harvard Graduate School of Business Administration, and at the Bureau of Railroad Economics, Washington, D.C.
2. These calculations are based on figures taken from Henry V. Poor, *Manual of the Railroads of the United States for 1894* (57 vols., New York, 1868–1924), xiv–xv. They include the states embraced within Groups IV and V of the Interstate Commerce Commission divisions with the exception of West Virginia. These ten states comprise the basis for this study. The index given in Column C represents the ratio of growth of southern railroads over that of the rest of the nation. Column A, the growth rate of southern railroads, serves as numerator. Column B, the denominator, is the growth rate for the rest of the nation. The equation thus used was $A/B = C$.
3. See *Railroad Gazette*, XIII, 586–87; *Railway World*, XXV, 762–63.
4. Alfred Marshall, *Principles of Economics* (London, 1920); Joseph Schumpeter, *The Theory of Economic Development* (Cambridge, Mass., 1961).
5. For more detail on the role of these roads, see my article on southern railway leaders, to be published in a forthcoming issue of *Business History Review*.
6. This conclusion is based upon a study of biographical data on eighty-eight prominent southern railroad men, a survey of boards of directors for the

period 1855–1875, and the testimony given in *Southern Railroads*, 40 Cong., 2 sess., House Reports, No. 3 (Washington, D.C., 1868), I, 1–130.
7. The origins and development of several major southern roads are traced in detail in U. B. Phillips, *A History of Transportation in the Eastern Cotton Belt to 1860* (New York, 1913); see also George R. Taylor, *The Transportation Revolution 1815–1861* (New York, 1951), Chap. v. The emphasis upon localization of traffic on antebellum and early postwar southern roads is succinctly illustrated in *id.* and Irene Neu, *The American Railway Network, 1861–1890* (Cambridge, Mass., 1956), 3–5, 41–48.
8. Julius Grodinsky, *Transcontinental Railway Strategy 1869–1893* (Philadelphia, 1962), 104–105.
9. A good example of such a threat can be found in the objections of President R. R. Cuyler of the Central of Georgia to the proposed building of a line from Macon to Brunswick. (Annual Report of the Central of Georgia Railroad & Banking Company, 1856, 52–55; 1857, 77–80; 1858, 104–107; 1860, 14–15.)
10. This reluctance to compete for through traffic is well illustrated in the Annual Report of the Seaboard & Roanoke Railroad, 1867, 14–15.
11. For a quantitative study substantiating this point, see Maury Klein and Kozo Yamamura, "The Growth Strategies of Southern Railroads, 1865–1893," *Business History Review*, XLI (Winter 1967), 358–77.
12. Schumpeter, *Theory of Economic Development*, 6.
13. Annual Report of the East Tennessee, Virginia, & Georgia Railroad, 1870, 14; Annual Report of the Central of Georgia, 1880, 7. Such alliances occasionally extended to river and coastal steamers. (See Annual Report of the Southwestern Railroad, 1868, 574.)
14. *Commercial and Financial Chronicle*, XXX, 384, 542; XXXIII, 357; *Railway World*, XXV, 980; XXVII, 1072.
15. *Commercial and Financial Chronicle*, XXXII, 121.
16. For background on the Green Line and the association, see William H. Joubert, *Southern Freight Rates in Transition* (Gainesville, Fla., 1949), Chap. 11; *Report of the Industrial Commission* (19 vols., Washington, D.C., 1900–1902), IX, 626–27; Taylor and Neu, *American Railway Network*, 71–74; Henry Hudson, "The Southern Railway and Steamship Association," *Quarterly Journal of Economics*, V (No. 4, 1891), 70–94. Good insight into the conditions that produced the association can be found in the Annual Report of the Central of Georgia, 1872, 15.
17. For typical reactions to such "invasions," see Annual Report of the East Tennessee, Virginia, & Georgia, 1873, 7–11; Annual Report of the Nashville & Chattanooga Railroad, 1870, 9; Annual Report of the Richmond & Danville Railroad, 1875, 324; Annual Report of the Central of Georgia, 1866, 308–309; *Commercial and Financial Chronicle*, XXIV, 466.
18. *Ibid.*, XX, 501. Laments over the loss of key connections are plentiful. (See *ibid.*, XXII, 180; XXXII, 576–77; Annual Report of the Raleigh & Gaston Railroad, 1873, 18; Annual Report of the Richmond & Danville, 1879, 204.)

19. The Annual Reports of the Louisville & Nashville Railroad, 1866–1873, nicely explain the early phase of its growth. (See also Ethel Armes, *The Story of Coal and Iron in Alabama* [Birmingham, 1910], 245–47.)
20. Annual Report of the Louisville & Nashville, 1873, 10.
21. *Ibid.*, 1880, 17–23. Virtually all this expansion came during Victor Newcomb's brief tenure as president, March 24–December 1, 1880.
22. Annual Report of the Richmond & Danville, 1873, 121–37.
23. Annual Report of the East Tennessee, Virginia, & Georgia, 1877, 7–13.
24. Annual Report of the Central of Georgia, 1873, 11–12. The Central's expansion is clearly outlined in the annual reports for the period 1866–1873.
25. For examples of such admissions, see Annual Report of the East Tennessee, Virginia, & Georgia, 1877, 12; Annual Report of the Richmond & Danville, 1874, 229; *Commercial and Financial Chronicle*, XIX, 118.
26. Annual Report of the Louisville & Nashville, 1880, 21.
27. *Ibid.*, 1877, 10–11.
28. Annual Report of the Central of Georgia, 1879, 7.
29. Unidentified clipping, Dec. 22, 1882, in William Raoul Scrapbooks, Emory University, III, 22–23; see also Annual Report of the Nashville & Chattanooga, 1870, 9.
30. Figures on the number and mileage of roads in default can be found in John F. Stover, *The Railroads of the South 1865–1900* (Chapel Hill, N.C., 1955), 123–25.
31. *Railroad Gazette*, XIII, 586–87.
32. A good example of rivals seeking a bankrupt road can be found in *Commercial and Financial Chronicle*, XXIX, 381, and Annual Report of the Central of Georgia, 1879, 7.
33. *Railroad Gazette*, X, 247–48; Augusta *Chronicle and Constitutionalist*, May 7, 1880.
34. See the Edward Porter Alexander papers, Southern Historical Collection, University of North Carolina, and the Savannah *Morning News and Evening Press*, July 1882–Jan. 1883; July 1886–Jan. 1887.
35. *Encyclopedia of Virginia Biography*, ed. L. G. Tyler (5 vols., New York, 1915), V. 701–702.
36. Joseph Nimmo, Jr., *First Annual Report on the Internal Commerce of the United States* (Washington, D.C., 1877), 59.
37. Annual Report of the Richmond & Danville, 1880, 413.
38. More detail on the new group of managers can be found in my forthcoming article on southern railway leaders.
39. These figures include lines directly and indirectly controlled and are based upon mileage figures in Poor, *Manual of Railroads* for 1878 and 1883.
40. *Railroad Gazette*, XIII, 586–87. A similar list in *Railway World*, XXV, 762–63, included the Georgia Pacific, a Danville subsidiary, the Erlanger roads, most of which were acquired by the East Tennessee in 1890, and the Baltimore & Ohio system, which abandoned its southern efforts by selling the Virginia Midland to the Danville in 1881.
41. Stover, *Southern Railroads*, 225–26.

42. Annual Report of the Central of Georgia, 1881, 9–10; Annual Report of the Louisville & Nashville, 1881, 11.
43. Annual Report of the Richmond & Danville, 1881, 501–502.
44. Annual Report of the Richmond & West Point Terminal Railway and Warehouse Company, Mar. 23, 1887, *passim; Railroad Gazette*, XX, 705.
45. Specific examples of the consolidation process and figures for the rate of new construction can be found in Stover, *Southern Railroads*, Chap. IX.
46. Annual Reports of the Norfolk & Western Railroad, 1883–92, *passim; Commercial and Financial Chronicle*, XXXIX, 87.
47. *Ibid.*, XXXV, 430.
48. Annual Report of the Richmond Terminal, 1890, 12; for other examples, see *Commercial and Financial Chronicle*, XXXIX, 86–87.
49. Annual Report of the Louisville & Nashville, 1887, 20.
50. Annual Report of the Richmond Terminal, 1887, 7.
51. *Railroad Gazette*, XVII, 96.
52. Annual Report of the East Tennessee, Virginia, & Georgia, 1888, 22–26; *Commercial and Financial Chronicle*, XXXIII, 357; *Railway World*, XXV, 980; *Railroad Gazette*, XIII, 577.
53. A copy of the agreement dated August 1, 1885, can be found at the Bureau of Railroad Economics; for other alliances, see *Commercial and Financial Chronicle*, XLV, 853; XLVI, 828; *Railroad Gazette*, XV, 677; *Railway World*, XXVII, 1072.
54. For one example, by no means unique, see the account of the Richmond Terminal in Stuart Daggett, *Railroad Reorganization* (Cambridge, Mass., 1908), Chap. V.
55. Annual Report of the Richmond Terminal, 1890, 4.
56. Annual Report of the Central of Georgia, 1888, 20; 1889, 8; 1892, 3; Annual Report of the Mobile & Ohio Railroad, 1888, 14.
57. Annual Report of the Central of Georgia, 1889, 9; 1891, 13.
58. Developments during the period 1890–1900 are treated in Stover, *Southern Railroads*, Chap. XII.
59. *New York Indicator*, June 7, 1893.
60. Stover, *Southern Railroads*, 188–89, analyzes dividend data. He notes that expansion proceeded at a record pace despite an "indifferent dividend record," but offers no explanation for it.
61. Another explanation might be found in comparative bond yields between southern and other roads, but considerable research needs to be done to establish any clear-cut relationship on this point.
62. Albert Fishlow, *American Railroads and the Transformation of the Ante-Bellum Economy* (Cambridge, Mass., 1965). Though dealing with a different time period, Fishlow's study suggests a valuable approach to the problem of social return in the postwar era.

Southern Railroad Leaders, 1865–1893

1. By the South, I mean here the following states east of the Mississippi and south of the Ohio rivers: Virginia, North Carolina, South Carolina, Georgia,

Alabama, Florida, Mississippi, Tennessee, Kentucky, and Louisiana. The railroads of these states comprise a homogeneous network that developed about the same time and faced similar problems. In general, the study applies most specifically to the roads north and east of Mobile and does not attempt to treat the complex relationships of Louisiana roads serving territories west of the Mississippi River.

    In writing this article I am deeply grateful for the generous advice and assistance given me by Professors James P. Baughman, Ralph W. Hidy, Arthur M. Johnson, Fritz Redlich and Kozo Yamamura. Financial assistance was provided by the Harvard Newcomen Society Fellowship in Business History.

2. John F. Stover, *The Railroads of the South 1865–1900* (Chapel Hill, 1955).
3. *Ibid.*, xiii–xviii.
4. *Ibid.*, 284. See also *ibid.*, 37–38, 129–34, 153–54, 206–209, 279–82.
5. Henry V. Poor, *Manual of Railroads* (New York, 1890), 399, 416. Calhoun had to claim Georgia residence because the Central's charter stipulated that 11 of the 13 directors must be Georgians and the board already had two New York men.
6. Poor, *Manual of the Railroads of the United States* (New York, 1882), 385, 393.
7. Poor, *Manual of Railroads* (New York, 1888), 639, 646.
8. Poor, *Manual of Railroads* (New York, 1889), 619, 687.
9. A curious example of hidden control arose in 1880 when Moses Taylor, the New York merchant and leading stockholder in the C. G., obtained control of a majority of shares in the Western & Atlantic Railroad lease. Since Taylor could not legally hold the majority he asked the C. G. to take it, but the company could not handle it either. For a time Taylor controlled the road but could not publicly exercise that control. See Edward C. Anderson Diary, January 5, 1880, Anderson Papers (Southern Historical Collection, University of North Carolina).
10. For this election, see the Edward Porter Alexander Papers (Southern Historical Collection), and the Savannah *Morning News* and *Evening Press*, July 1882–January 1883 and July 1886–January 1887. Complete proxy lists for the 1883 election can be found in the William G. Raoul Letterbooks, Raoul papers (Emory University Library), II.
11. The testimony given by various southern railroad presidents in "Southern Railroads," *House Reports*, 40 Cong., 2 Sess., No. 3, I, 1–130, makes this pattern of local control abundantly clear. For more specific examples of stock distribution, see the stockholder lists in the annual reports of the C. G. 1869–81 and the W. & W. in 1867–68. See also the list of R. & D. stockholders for 1869 in the Virginia State Library, Richmond. The L. & N. provides an example of a large block of stock being owned by the city of Louisville. See *Commercial and Financial Chronicle*, XXIX (July 12, 1879), 41. For the Georgia Railroad see *Railway World*, XXIV (May 22, 1880), 482.
12. See the figures in Poor, *Manual of the Railroads of the United States* (New York, 1874), xxviii–xxix.
13. There would seem to be evidence that the two groups analyzed here may be considered as "coevals" as described by Fritz Redlich in his *History of American*

Business Leaders (Ann Arbor, 1940), I, 23–30. Certainly the analysis given here suggests that the members of each group perceived their problems and responded to them in quite similar fashion. In this vein it is interesting to note that the youngest of the group, Robinson, proved the most adaptable and enduring in his role as president.

14. See the summaries in Albert Fishlow, *American Railroads and the Transformation of the Ante-bellum Economy* (Cambridge, 1965), 8–9, 269–88, and George R. Taylor and Irene D. Neu, *The American Railway Network 1861–1890* (Cambridge, 1956), 3–5. Excellent detailed accounts of the origins and development of several major southern roads can be found in U. B. Phillips, *A History of Transportation in the Eastern Cotton Belt to 1860* (New York, 1913).
15. To cite some examples: King was deeply involved in cotton manufacturing in Augusta; H. D. Newcomb was a Louisville merchant; and Cole, Stevenson, and Wilson all had extensive mining and real estate interests in Tennessee.
16. *Proceedings of the Stockholders of the Raleigh & Gaston Railroad Company at their 21st Annual Meeting* (Raleigh, 1871), 12. Similar examples abound in the reports of other roads, and the language used suggests the bitterness of the contest for business.
17. This continuity of management is made clear by a survey of boards of directors for the period 1855–70 and by the testimony given in "Southern Railroads," *House Reports,* 40 Cong., 2 Sess., No. 3, I, *passim.*
18. For more precise definition of this term see Arthur M. Johnson and Barry E. Supple, *Boston Capitalists and Western Railroads* (Cambridge, 1967), 8–10, 181–91, 333–46.
19. For the roads included in this study, the testimony in "Southern Railroads" lists the following approximate proportions of state ownership: R. & D. 60 percent; S. & R. 60 percent; A. M. & O. 60 percent; A. & G. 33 percent; E. T. & G. (half the consolidated E. T. V. & G.) 33 percent. According to Howard D. Dozier, *A History of the Atlantic Coast Line Railroad* (Cambridge, 1920), 57–59, the state owned 40 percent of the W. & W.'s stock. The city of Louisville and counties along the right of way held about 26 percent of the L. & N.'s stock. See *Chronicle,* XXIX (July 12, 1879), 41.
20. See the *Annual Reports of the President and Directors, and the Chief Engineer and Superintendent of the Wilmington & Weldon Railroad Company* (Wilmington, 1868), 6–7.
21. *25th Annual Report of the Richmond & Danville Railroad Company* (Richmond, 1872), 10–11.
22. *The Second Annual Report of the Officers to the Stockholders of the East Tenn., Va. & Geo. R. R. Co.* (Knoxville, 1871), 9.
23. *Wilmington & Weldon Report,* 5.
24. Use of the terms "natural law" and "nature" occurs frequently in annual reports. See for example *19th Annual Report of the President and Directors to the Stockholders of the Seaboard & Roanoke Railroad Company* (Norfolk, 1867), 14–15; *The First Annual Report of the Officers to the Stockholders of the East Tenn., Va. & Geo. R. R. Co.* (Knoxville, 1870), 14–15; *26th Annual Report of the Richmond & Danville Railroad Company* (Richmond, 1873), 123, 126.

25. Bridgers, Buford, Guthrie, King, Mahone, Screven, and Standiford all had direct political experience, and of course every road counted influential political figures among its directors, stockholders, and general counsel. An interesting report analyzing the attitude of each member of the Georgia senate toward the C. G. can be found in the W. W. Gordon Papers (Southern Historical Collection). For specific examples of political activity by Buford, Mahone, and Robinson see Nelson M. Blake, *William Mahone of Virginia* (Richmond, 1935), chaps. 4–5.
26. *1st Annual Report of the President and Directors of the Atlantic, Mississippi & Ohio Railroad Company* (Lynchburg, 1872), 12.
27. The standard work on restoration is Carl R. Fish, "The Restoration of the Southern Railroads," *University of Wisconsin Studies in the Social Sciences and History* (Madison, 1919), No. 2. A good insight into the scope and nature of the problems involved can be gained by reading the annual reports of individual companies. Sizeable collections of these can be found in Baker Library, Harvard Graduate School of Business Administration, and at the Bureau of Railroad Economics, Washington, D.C. To cite one example, Wadley estimated the cost of restoring the C. G. at around $2,000,000. See "Southern Railroads," I, 40.
28. A conspicuous exception to the pattern of restoration is the L. & N. Since it suffered no appreciable war damage and possessed strong, aggressive management, it remained a chronological step ahead of the other roads in its development. The pattern of its leadership, however, closely parallels the other roads.
29. *Supplemental Report of the President and Directors of the Central Railroad and Banking Company of Georgia* (Savannah, 1866), 288–89, and *38th Report of the President and Directors of the Central Railroad and Banking Company of Georgia* (Savannah, 1874), 95, 99, 103.
30. C. C. Hall (ed.), *Baltimore: Its History and People* (3 vols., New York, 1912), III, 165–69; New York *Times*, March 31, 1901.
31. *Chronicle*, XIV (March 23, 1872), 386 and XXIII (December 9, 1876), 576; Fairfax Harrison, *A History of the Legal Development of the Southern Railway Company* (Washington, 1901), 93–94.
32. A list of S.R.S.C. stockholders in 1872 can be found in *Proceedings of the Stockholders Convention in the Memphis & Charleston Railroad Company, January 17–19, 1872* (Memphis, 1872), 6. H. B. Plant was listed as a resident of Georgia in the stockholder's list and had in fact lived in the South for some time, but he was a native of Connecticut. For details of the Pennsylvania's involvement see George H. Burgess and Miles C. Kennedy, *Centennial History of the Pennsylvania Railroad Company* (Philadelphia, 1949), 279–81.
33. The B. & O. had moved south by acquiring control of the Orange, Alexandria & Manassas Railroad. See Harrison, *Southern Railway Company*, 471.
34. Blake, *Mahone*, chaps. 4–5.
35. *East Tenn., Va. & Geo. Report 1870*.
36. *27th Annual Report of the Richmond & Danville Railroad Company* (Richmond, 1874), 227.

37. The most clearly articulated expression of this attitude can be found in the statements by Presidents R. R. Cuyler and Wadley opposing the construction of a line from Macon to Brunswick. See the C. G. annual reports for 1856–60, 1866, 1869, and 1872. The acute lack of interconnections and gauge integration described in Taylor and Neu, *American Railway Network*, 41–48, illustrates well the desire to localize traffic at the terminal cities.
38. Examples of such laments are plentiful. See *Seaboard & Roanoke Report 1867*, 17; *Wilmington & Weldon Report 1868*, 19; *Annual Report of the President and Directors of the Louisville & Nashville Railroad Company* (Louisville, 1867), 10–11. For a statement on the L. & N.'s growing awareness of the importance of through traffic around 1871 see Ethel Armes, *The Story of Coal and Iron in Alabama* (Birmingham, 1910), 145–46.
39. Nearly any southern railroad report will illustrate this point. See *The Fourth Annual Report of the Officers to the Stockholders of the East Tenn., Va. & Geo. R. R. Co.* (Knoxville, 1873), 7–8; *37th Report of the President and Directors of the Central Railroad and Banking Company of Georgia* (Savannah, 1872), 7–8; *Chronicle*, XXII (May 13, 1876), 469.
40. For details of expansion policies see the reports of the various companies for the period 1868–78.
41. *Railroad Gazette*, XVI (October 17, 1884), 757.
42. *Annual Report of the President and Directors of the Louisville & Nashville Railroad Company* (Louisville, 1880), 21–22.
43. Henry Plant constitutes a basic exception to much of the following description. A native of Connecticut, he moved south in 1853 and went into the express business. He remained during the war, formed the Southern Express Company and gradually drifted into railroads. Enchanted with the commercial possibilities of Florida, he devoted much of his energy to developing that state. Adapting quickly to the changing economic environment, he combined with other financiers to form the Plant Investment Company, a holding company in southern railroads, in 1882.
44. Interesting and suggestive sketches of several of these men can be found in Henry Clews, *Twenty-Eight Years in Wall Street* (New York, 1888), chap. 50.
45. These figures are taken from Poor, *Manual of Railroads* (New York, 1893), xv.
46. These figures are drawn from Poor, *Manual of the Railroads of the United States* (New York, 1878), 452–53, 473–74, *Manual of the Railroads of the United States* (New York, 1883), 536, and *Manual of Railroads* (New York, 1884), 491.
47. For a good contemporary description of these consolidations see *Railroad Gazette*, XIII (October 21, 1881), 586–87.
48. The Morgan reorganization plan for the Richmond Terminal indicated clearly how worn down three major systems, the R. & D., E. T. V. & G., and C. G., had become by 1893. Copies of the plan can be found in Baker Library and the Bureau of Railroad Economics.
49. The most satisfactory account of the Terminal is Stuart Daggett, *Railroad Reorganization* (Cambridge, 1908), chap. 5.
50. W. W. Gordon to John H. Inman, October 28, 1889, Gordon Papers (Southern Historical Collection).

51. For definition of this term see Jan Kimenta and Jeffrey Williamson, "Determinants of Investment Behavior: United States Railroads 1872–1941," *Review of Economics and Statistics*, XLVIII (May 1966), 172–81.

The Overland Route

1. Diary of Arthur Ferguson, July 21, 1868, Union Pacific Collection, Nebraska State Historical Society, Lincoln. Hereafter cited as UP.
2. Lucius Beebe, *The Overland Limited* (San Diego, 1963), 9.
3. These figures are in Charles E. Ames, *Pioneering the Union Pacific*, (New York, 1969), 4–6.
4. Samuel B. Reed to his wife, April 5 and April 15, 1864, UP. These letters are not the originals but a typescript compilation of extracts made by Levi O. Leonard.
5. Ibid., April 19, April 28, May 3, and May 8, 1864, UP; Peter Dey to Reed, April 25, 1864, and to William C. Durant, April 28, 1864, both in Levi O. Leonard Collection, University of Iowa Library, Ames. Hereafter cited as LL.
6. Reed to his wife, May 21, 1864, UP.
7. Ibid., May 21 and May 26, 1864, UP.
8. Ibid., June 7 and June 12, 1864, UP.
9. Ibid., June 12, June 18, June 25, June 29, July 24, August 2, August 15, August 17, and September 18, 1864, UP.
10. Ferguson diary, 5A-R, 156–63; Henry C. Parry, "Letters from the Frontier— 1867," *Annals of Wyoming* (October 1958), 30:129.
11. Parry, "Letters," 136–37.
12. Dodge Autobiography, 647–48, 698–700, Grenville M. Dodge papers, Iowa State Department of Archives and History, Des Moines.
13. Ibid., 648–49.
14. Ibid., 648–57, 698–703. Some incidents from the desert march are in Parry, "Letters," 140–41.
15. Ibid., 702.
16. Ibid., 657, 660–64, 697–98, 702–3.
17. Ibid., 664–67.
18. Evans to Durant, June 9, 1868, LL.; Jack Casement to his wife, August 1, 1868, Casement Papers, American Heritage Center, University of Wyoming, Laramie.
19. The description of Benton is drawn from Emmett D. Chisum, "Boom Towns on the Union Pacific: Laramie, Benton and Bear River City," *Annals of Wyoming* (Spring 1981), 53:2–13.
20. Colfax to Dodge, July 16, 1868, Dodge Papers, Iowa State Department of Archives and History, Des Moines; Snyder to Dodge, August 26, 1868, Dodge Papers; Jack Casement to his wife, August 17, 1868, Casement Papers; James Hall et al. to Jack Casement, August 18, 1868, Casement Papers; Dodge Autobiography, 796–97.
21. New York *Tribune*, August 12 and October 8, 1868; Evans to Dodge, July 30, 1868, Dodge Papers.

22. George F. Mayer to Fred Hodges, September 6, 1869, UP; C. G. Hammond to Oliver Ames, July 19, 1869, UP.
23. Paul Rigdon, "Historical Catalogue" (Omaha, 1951), 1595–98, UP. This in-house compilation of historical material on the Union Pacific Railroad is an invaluable source.
24. Mitchell Wilson, *American Science and Invention* (New York, 1954), 224; Dee Brown, *Hear That Lonesome Whistle Blow* (New York, 1977), 141.
25. Rigdon, "Historical Catalogue," 1044–48; Pullman to A. N. Towne, August 4, 1870, UP.
26. Hammond to C. P. Huntington, April 1, 1870, Collis P. Huntington Papers, microfilm edition, copy at University of Iowa Library. Hereafter cited as CPH.
27. Crocker to Huntington, February 15 and May 10, 1870, CPH; Hopkins to Huntington, June 8, 1870, CPH.
28. Hopkins to Huntington, June 8, 1870, CPH.
29. New York *Tribune*, May 15, 1869.
30. Ibid., May 6, 1870; New York *Times*, July 17 and July 18, 1868; New York *Herald*, July 18, 1869, July 3, 1870; Omaha *Republican*, October 6, 1869, January 19, 1870; Brown, *Lonesome Whistle*, 136–44.
31. *The Union Pacific Magazine* (March 1922), 1:51.

In Search of Jay Gould

1. John A. Garraty, *The Nature of Biography*, (New York, 1957), 6.
2. These interpretations of the late nineteenth century and the figures regarded as its central characters are so familiar that extensive citation of the literature hardly seems necessary. A few of the standard works are Matthew Josephson, *The Robber Barons: The Great American Capitalists 1860–1901* (New York, 1934); Vernon L. Parrington, *The Beginnings of Critical Realism in America* (New York, 1930); Ray Ginger, *Age of Excess* (New York, 1965); Robert H. Wiebe, *The Search for Order: 1877–1920* (New York, 1967); Thomas C. Cochran and William Miller, *The Age of Enterprise* (New York, 1942); Louis Hacker, *Triumph of American Capitalism* (New York, 1940); Alfred D. Chandler, Jr., *Strategy and Structure* (Cambridge, Mass., 1962); and *The Visible Hand* (Cambridge, Mass., 1977); Allan Nevins, *John D. Rockefeller: The Heroic Age of American Enterprise* (New York, 1941); and Jonathan R.T. Hughes, *The Vital Few* (Boston, 1966).

    One interesting insight into changing views of the era appears in H. Wayne Morgan, ed., *The Gilded Age: A Reappraisal* (Syracuse, 1963). This collection of interpretive essays appeared first in 1963 and then in a revised, enlarged edition in 1970. For the 1963 edition John Tipple contributed an essay entitled "The Robber Baron in the Gilded Age: Entrepreneur or Iconoclast?" In the 1970 edition this same essay, with little more than stylistic changes, bore the title, "Big Businessmen and a New Economy."
3. Henry Clews, *Fifty Years in Wall Street* (New York, 1908), 119.
4. Quoted in Richard O'Connor, *Gould's Millions* (New York, 1962), 191. Contemporary editorials abound with similar sentiments. To cite but one

example, the New York *Times,* April 13, 1873, declared that "The work of reform is but half done when the insidious poison of an influence like that of JAY GOULD can be detected in politics, in finance, in society, and when people claiming to be respectable are not ashamed of being associated with a man such as he." See also New York *Herald,* April 3, 1888. Bennett's *Herald* habitually referred to Gould not by name but simply as "The Corsair."

5. Quoted in Julius Grodinsky, *Jay Gould: His Business Career 1867–1892* (Philadelphia, 1957), 418.
6. New York *Herald,* May 22, 1886.
7. Charles Francis Adams, Jr., and Henry Adams, *Chapters of Erie* (Ithaca, 1966), 104–106. This is a paperback reprint of the original 1886 edition.
8. Grodinsky, *Jay Gould*; Lucius F. Ellsworth, "Jay Gould and the Leather Industry; Success or Failure?" in Allen L. Dickes, ed., *Proceedings of the Business History Conference* (Texas Christian University, 1973).
9. John A. Garraty, *The New Commonwealth 1887–1890* (New York, 1968), 13.
10. John M. Blum, Bruce Catton, *et al., The National Experience: A History of the United States Since 1865* (New York, 1968), Second Edition, 440.
11. Josephson, *Robber Barons,* 192–193. Josephson entitled his chapter on Gould "Mephistopheles," a characterization frequently applied to him. For an early usage of it see New York *Times,* April 15, 1873.
12. Cochran and Miller, *Age of Enterprise,* 147. This conclusion is at best exaggerated. Twice in his career, in 1878 and 1884, Gould badly misgauged the market and suffered heavy, almost fatal, losses. The crisis of 1884, which seriously undermined his already frail constitution, led Grodinsky to conclude that "As a stock-market trader he must be classed as a failure." Grodinsky, *Jay Gould,* 514. Even one of Gould's contemporary biographers noted that "his principal success, it must be remembered, was in operations outside of the street." Henry D. Northrop. *Life and Achievements of Jay Gould* (Philadelphia, 1892), 178–179. On one occasion Gould himself said in an interview that " 'I go into almost everything' that promises a return.... Unfortunately I do not always succeed. I have been in a score, a hundred speculations, from which almost as soon as I was in I would gladly have withdrawn." New York *Herald,* February 28, 1881.
13. *Ibid.,* 148.
14. Gustavus Myers, *History of the Great American Fortunes* (New York, 1936), 398. This is the Modern Library edition.
15. Gould's niece, Alice Northrop Snow, after listing all the vices her uncle eschewed, concluded that "it would be entirely accurate to say that Jay Gould never abused his limited physique, except in one way—overwork." Alice Northrop Snow, *The Story of Helen Gould* (New York, 1943), 80.
16. Actress Clara Morris recalled once meeting Gould backstage at the theatre and receiving not the usual proposition but words of comfort, encouragement, and an offer of help if she encountered trouble: "I thought of the gentle voice, the piercing eyes that had grown so kind, the friendly promise.... I am forced to believe Mr. Jay Gould was perfectly honest and

sincere in his offer of assistance." Clara Morris, *Life on the Stage* (New York, 1901), 305.
17. In a letter to his former teacher Gould, then sixteen, wrote, "I think I have learned one thing this (past) winter from actual observation . . . that happiness consists not so much in indulgence as in self-denial." Quoted in Snow, *Helen Gould*, 80. On this point Alice Snow probably has the last word: "It has often been repeated that Jay Gould was a man who took little pleasure in life. . . . The truth was that he derived unlimited pleasure, satisfaction, from many things, but that his enjoyment was deep, contemplative, appreciative in quality; quiet rather than the reverse." *Ibid.*, 116.
18. Gould was clearly fascinated by the legend of Atalanta, since he gave the name to both his yacht and private railway car. Atalanta was the virgin huntress who promised to marry the first man who could defeat her in a foot race. She lost finally to Hippomenes, who distracted her by dropping three golden apples given him by Aphrodite.
19. New York *Times*, December 8, 1892. See also New York *Times*, December 3, 1892 and Northrop, *Life and Achievements of Jay Gould*, 285.
20. Quoted in Murat Halstead and J. Frank Beale, Jr., *Life of Jay Gould: How He Made His Millions* (New York, 1892), 171–172.
21. New York *Times*, December 8, 1892; also quoted in *ibid.*, 182–183.
22. New York *Times*, December 3, 1892. See also Sage's remarks in *ibid.*, July 1, 1887.
23. See the account by Morosini, Gould's most trusted employee, in Northrop, *Life and Achievements of Jay Gould*, 271, for a typical example of Gould's secretiveness.
24. New-York *Times*, December 25, 1872.
25. *Bradstreet*, March 29, 1884, 200.
26. Philadelphia *North American*, December 21, 1881. See also New York *Times*, February 19, 1875, April 14, 1877, and January 14, 1881. The latter editorial complained that "all that is necessary to make a fertile soil for damaging rumors in Wallstreet is to prepare the ground by the free use of JAY GOULD'S name. . . . There is a sinister power in JAY GOULD'S reputation which is as unrivaled as it is unenviable."
27. It must be emphasized again that not all speculators followed Gould in a straight line. Many took his pronouncements as a cue to go in the opposite direction, knowing full well Gould's tendency to conceal his true objective. This added dimension of second guessing compounds the ambiguities surrounding his trading career.
28. Joseph Frazier Wall, *Andrew Carnegie* (New York, 1970); Albro Martin, *James J. Hill and the Opening of the Northwest* (New York, 1976).
29. See Gould's testimony in *Report of the Committee of the Senate upon the Relations between Labor and Capital*, Senate Hearings, 41 Cong., vol. 28 (Washington, 1885), I, 1062–1066. For other Gould testimony before committees see "Labor Troubles in the South and West," *House Reports*, 49 Cong., 2d Sess., 1886 (Serial 2502), No. 4174, Pt. 1, 28–72; "U.S. Pacific Railway Commission," *Senate Executive Documents*, 50 Cong., 1st Sess., 1887 (Serial 2505), No.

51, 446–592; "Investigation into the Causes of the Gold Panic," *House Reports*, 41 Cong., 2d Sess., 1870 (Serial 1436), No. 31, 131–168; New York State Assembly, "Select Committee to Investigate the Erie Railroad," *Assembly Documents*, 1873, No. 98, 545–570.

30. For nearly two decades the New York *Times*, Gould's most severe critic, printed articles and editorials denouncing his growing control over the media. At various times he was credited with dominating the New York *Tribune*, New York *Evening Express*, New York *Sun*, Denver's *Rocky Mountain News*, and several other papers. In 1881 the *Times* accused him of trying to gain control over four of the seven papers in the Associated Press and railed against his budding monopoly in transportation (railroads and elevated railways) and communications (newspapers, telegraph). See for example, New York *Times*, December 25, 1872; July 23, 1878; February 11 and February 23, 1881, July 1, 1886, and March 23, 1891. The Adamses' essays on the 1868 fight between the forces of Gould and Vanderbilt for the Erie, first published in installments at the time, were collected in *Chapters of Erie and Other Essays* (New York, 1886).

31. A careful reading of Grodinsky's study of Gould's career confirms this point again and again.

32. Grodinsky, *Jay Gould*, 480. One reporter, describing how Gould used interviews for his own purpose, observed that "He did not impress one as speaking the truth.... The public heard from him only when he, not the public, would profit by the utterance." See the full account quoted in Northrop, *Life and Achievements of Jay Gould*, 314–316.

33. Halstead and Beale, *Life of Jay Gould;* Northrop, *Life and Achievements of Jay Gould;* Trumbull White, *The Wizard of Wall Street*, (New York, 1892).

34. Halstead was a well-known political reporter, famous for his election coverage, and editor of the Cincinnati *Commercial Gazette*. "Offered the editorship of the Brooklyn *Standard-Union* in 1890, Halstead disposed of the *Commercial Gazette* and entered a new field at sixty-one years of age. But he was not as successful in Brooklyn as he had been in Cincinnati, and after a few years he retired to devote himself to free-lance work and hackwriting." Frank Luther Mott, *American Journalism: A History: 1690–1960* (New York, 1962), 459–460. This is the third edition.

35. Marquis Boni DeCastellane, *How I Discovered America* (New York, 1924).

36. Twain to William Dean Howells, April 2–13, 1899, in Henry Nash Smith and William M. Gibson, eds., *Mark Twain—Howells Letters* (Cambridge, Mass., 1960), II, 692.

37. Celeste Andrews Seton, *Helen Gould Was My Mother-in-Law* (New York, 1953); Snow, *Story of Helen Gould*.

38. Much of this affection, and the close ties between the Northrops and the Goulds, stemmed from the fact that Gould undertook to support his sister's family after her husband failed in business and committed suicide. He educated the children, followed their progress closely, and provided for their every want even to the extent of building a school for Ida Northrop, Alice's sister, to operate. Alice Snow's book documents in detail

Gould's devotion to family and his close attention to the affairs of every member.

39. Clews, *Fifty Years in Wall Street*, 620–658 and *passim*; Edward W. Bok, *The Americanization of Edward Bok* (New York, 1920), 68–76; Adams and Adams, *Chapters of Erie*, *passim*; Alexander D. Noyes, *Forty Years of American Finance* (New York, 1909), 63. See also "The Great Imbroglio," *Atlantic Monthly* (July 1868), 111–121, and Henry Demarest Lloyd, "The Political Economy of Seventy-Three Million Dollars," *Atlantic Monthly* (July 1882), 69–81.
40. Robert I. Warshaw, *Jay Gould: The Story of a Fortune* (New York, 1928), 183.
41. O'Connor, *Gould's Millions;* Edwin P. Hoyt, *The Goulds* (New York, 1969).
42. For some of these briefer accounts see Josephson, *Robber Barons*, 192–215 and *passim;* Myers, *History of the Great American Fortunes*, 395–446, 478–503; Meade Minnigerode, *Certain Rich Men* (Freeport, N.Y., 1970), reprint of 1927 edition, 135–187. All these works portray Gould in highly unflattering terms as a prime specimen of the genus *Baronus Robberae*.
43. Grodinsky, *Jay Gould*, 7.
44. The difference in figures stems of course from the use of multiple citations in some footnotes. All multiple citations were broken down and tabulated by *type* of reference rather than number of references. Thus, if a footnote contained three citations, all of them newspapers, it was tallied as one newspaper citation. But if a footnote referred to a newspaper, a journal, and a private letter, it was counted as a citation in each of these categories. As a rule of thumb, newspapers were defined as dailies; all other publications were classified under journals or periodicals.
45. There is abundant testimony on this point. Alice Snow said of Gould, "He had always done his best to learn everything there was to learn as he went along; to master scrupulously every last detail; to perform each step as perfectly as it was in him to perform it." Snow, *Story of Helen Gould*, 83–84. See also the comments of E. Ellery Anderson and Chauncey M. DePew quoted in Northrop, *Life and Achievements of Jay Gould*, 249–253, 463, 467. For a detailed description of Gould touring one of his railroad systems see New York *Times*, April 27, 1887.
46. Grodinsky, *Jay Gould*, 112.
47. *Public*, April 15, 1880, quoted in *ibid.*, 162. It was widely rumored that Gould was saved from disaster only when the operators seeking to ruin him went too far and outraged Russell Sage, who lent Gould $2,000,000 to ride out the crisis. See New York *Times*, November 20, 1881, and Philadelphia *Press*, December 3, 1892.
48. Grodinsky, *Jay Gould*, 165.
49. Even in his favorite enterprises Gould seldom held more than a minority interest. Grodinsky observed that "The greater part of his empire, even at the peak of his influence in 1881, was kept together by minority holdings, and occasionally by no holdings at all." *Ibid.*, 321.
50. *Ibid.*, 353–354.
51. On Gould's ability to think big, Alice Snow offers a revealing comment: "It

was one of Uncle Jay's life characteristics that he seemed actually to prefer a large, apparently impossible problem to a small and easier one." On another occasion she recalls overhearing Gould say to Cyrus Field and John Terry during a business conference at Lyndhurst, "The procedure, gentlemen! The procedure! That is always the important thing. We need not hesitate about dimensions." Snow, *Story of Helen Gould*, 94, 155.
52. For some typical reactions see New York *Times*, October 18, 1885, and December 1, 1885. An editorial in the December 1 issue dismissed Gould's declaration with the sneering remark that "Mr. JAY GOULD has made as many last appearances as any actress on the boards."
53. Grodinsky, *Jay Gould*, 498–499. Gould was quoted as saying, "I am out of the street, and nothing whatever could induce me to go back into it." New York *Tribune*, July 5, 1886. Similar statements appeared regularly during the next six years.
54. Alice Snow provides several revealing glimpses of an exhausted and haggard Gould during the last decade of his life. In describing his youthful days as a clerk in a country store she captured the pattern he followed until his stamina broke down: "Jay Gould found that the work in the store took up almost his entire day. Also it was much more of a drain on his limited vitality than he had anticipated; two obstacles which he promptly attacked by steeling himself to sleep even less and work even more, as hard as he knew how in spite of fatigue—which is to say, again, by strength of will." Snow, *Story of Helen Gould*, 68.
55. For a good example of one such trip see New York *Times*, July 28, August 2, August 5, and August 29, 1888. This same trip to Saratoga is described in *ibid.*, 166–168.
56. Grodinsky, *Jay Gould*, 476. By contrast White, *Wizard of Wall Street*, 152, concluded that "Nothing Mr. Gould did in his life so arrayed public sentiment against him as his creation of the telegraphic monopoly."
57. Referring to the late 1880s, Grodinsky wrote: "When rate wars had produced their baneful effects upon railroad earnings and finances in the West, it was Gould who for the first time in his career assumed leadership in an effort to stabilize rates and maintain values. It was a unique position for a man who in the popular eye had for so many years been considered a railroad wrecker. He was now to come forth in a new role—that of railroad stabilizer." *Ibid.*, 554–555.
58. *Ibid.*, 561.
59. See *ibid.*, 86. Grodinsky observed trenchantly that "A Gould road in the Southwest was a byword for poor *service*." *Ibid.*, 599. The same judgment may be applied to his other roads as well.
60. *Ibid.*, 608. In summarizing Gould's influence Grodinsky notes that "The record building construction in 1879–81 and in 1886–87 were in part the consequence of competitive fears inspired by the Gould policies. Gould was in this sense a public servant. The building program in the eighties of the Atchison, the Union Pacific, the Burlington, the Rock Island, the

Northwestern, and the St. Paul, reflected to a considerable degree adjustments to his rate-cutting, business disturbing policies." *Ibid.*, 598. For a comprehensive account, see also Grodinsky's *Transcontinental Railway Strategy, 1869–1893* (Philadelphia, 1962).
61. *Ibid.*, 610.
62. Of one early episode Alice Snow wrote, "If the manner in which this fifteen-year-old boy next proceeded to extricate himself from his difficulties, with a profit for good measure, reads too much like a page from Horatio Alger, that cannot be helped." Snow, *Story of Helen Gould*, 74.
63. Henry Clews observed that "of all the self-made men of Wall Street he [Gould] had probably the most difficulty in making the first thousand dollars of the amazing pile which he now controls." Clews, *Fifty Years in Wall Street*, 620.
64. Unlike many "self-made" men, Gould never deceived himself into making a virtue of his childhood hardships. On one occasion he was quoted as saying. "Do you know that my father's poverty was never worth a single thousand dollars to me?" New York *Times*, December 3, 1892.
65. Perkins to John Murray Forbes, November 19, 1879, quoted in Grodinsky, *Jay Gould*, 232.
66. See for example the incidents recounted in Halstead and Beale, *Life of Jay Gould*, 179–182. Grodinsky, *Jay Gould*, 196, observed that "In assuming control, Gould took pains to select a proper managerial leadership. This was one of Gould's strong points. He was usually careful to select just the right man for the right job and to keep that man only as long as necessary to do that job." See also *ibid.*, 421.
67. After his health began to fail, so did his self-control. For the most publicized of Gould's breakdowns see New York *Times*, October 1, 1892, and December 3, 1892.
68. Grodinsky, *Jay Gould*, 300, 450. Northrop commented that "It is probable that no man in this or any other country has ever been a party to so many lawsuits as Gould." *Life and Achievements of Jay Gould*, 48.
69. Gould's attitude toward the law bears a striking resemblance to that of Frank Cowperwood in Theodore Dreiser, *The Financier* (New York, 1912), 291. This is the Signet Classic paperback edition.
70. Grodinsky, *Jay Gould*, 448, cites one classic instance of this misappraisal: "Gould's stroke in acquiring the Western Union in 1881, far from being accepted as a masterpiece of corporate strategy, was almost universally regarded as a serious blunder."
71. Gould was once quoted as explaining his success by saying "There isn't any secret. . . . I avoid bad luck by being patient. Whenever I am obliged to get into a fight I always wait and let the other fellow get tired first." New York *Times*, December 3, 1892.
72. "He became invested with a sinister distinction as the most coldblooded corruptionist, spoliator, and financial pirate of his time; and so thoroughly did he earn this reputation that to the end of his days it confronted him at every step, and survived to become the standing reproach and terror of his descendants. For nearly a half century the very name of Jay Gould was a

persisting jeer and byword, an object of popular contumely and hatred, the signification of every foul and base crime by which greed triumphs." Myers, *History of the Great American Fortunes*, 397.

73. Warshaw, *Jay Gould: The Story of a Fortune*, 122. See also New York *Times*, January 14, 1881.

74. See for example the New York *Times*, February 19, 1875, April 4, April 5, April 12, and April 14, 1877, and February 23, 1881.

75. For this episode see Northrop, *Life and Achievements of Jay Gould*, 142–143; O'Connor, *Gould's Millions*, 252–254; New York *Herald*, March 30, April 1–3, 1888; New York *Sun*, April 1 and April 3, 1888; New York *Times*, April 2, 1888. Bennett was also a business rival to Gould, having invested in a telegraph company engaged in a fight with Western Union. Of Gould's usual aloofness from controversy Alice Snow wrote: "What contributed, probably more than anything else, to some public acceptance of even the most far-fetched allegations was my uncle's obstinate and absolute refusal to make reply either by word or in print. He would neither defend himself nor attack his attackers. He would neither affirm nor deny—anything." Snow, *Story of Helen Gould*, 185.

76. See the amusing episodes in New York *Times*, August 8, 1873; Halstead and Beale, *Life of Jay Gould*, 290–292; Northrop, *Life and Achievements of Jay Gould*, 298–316.

77. W. A. Swanberg, in his *Jim Fisk: The Career of an Improbable Rascal* (New York, 1959), 170, wrote: "Possibly in part because of this almost unanimous rejection of Fisk by the elite, the less privileged classes were inclined to view him with forgiveness and even fondness. Obviously he was a rascal, but he was the *honestest* rascal in sight." See also the comments of General Francis Barlow in Northrop, *Life and Achievements of Jay Gould*, 78–79, and the comparison of Gould with Chauncey M. Depew in their handling of reporters in Snow, *Story of Helen Gould*, 184–185.

78. "Uncle Jay's attitude toward the press and its personnel was strictly passive, a mixture of aloofness and disgust." Snow, *Story of Helen Gould*, 182.

79. Northrop, *Life and Achievements of Jay Gould*, 338. For some of Gould's charitable acts and their repercussions see *ibid.*, 330; Halstead and Beale, *Life of Jay Gould*, 217–218; Snow, *Story of Helen Gould*, 173, 179–181; New York *Times*, September 6 and September 13, 1879, January 22, 1880, March 9 and 10, 1892. In 1890, when Gould bought some land between two churches and donated it to them, the *Times* ran the story under the head "GOULD SOOTHES HIS CONSCIENCE." New York *Times*, July 8, 1890.

80. Halstead and Beale, *Life of Jay Gould*, 189.

81. Northrop, *Life and Achievements of Jay Gould*, 314. See also *ibid.*, 306.

82. New York *Herald*, February 28, 1881.

83. Gould's wealth and reputation naturally made him and his family a prime target for cranks, blackmailers, and would-be assassins. For the last decade or so of his life he lived in constant dread of assailants. He kept a personal bodyguard, never walked the streets alone, and obtained the loyal services of a New York police inspector, Thomas Byrnes, whom he rewarded with stock

market tips. At Lyndhurst, Gould maintained an elaborate security system of guards, dogs, alarms, and telephones. For some examples see Halstead and Beale, *Life of Jay Gould*, 63–66, 195–201; Northrop, *Life and Achievements of Jay Gould*, 208, 230–232, 288–297; Snow, *Story of Helen Gould*, 144–148, 186–187; New York *Times*, May 7, 1891.

84. See, for example, Morris, *Life on the Stage*, 304–305; Halstead and Beale, *Life of Jay Gould*, 211–212, 290–292, 295; O'Connor, *Gould's Millions*, 244. To cite one example: "He was too intelligent to hate and too unsympathetic to love very strongly. He produced the impression of extreme intellectuality; indeed, leaving out the affectionate element, he was feminine in nature, with marked intuitive perceptions." White, *Wizard of Wall Street*, 216–217. See also *ibid.*, 20.

85. Quoted in White, *Wizard of Wall Street*, 218–219.

86. Numerous observers confirm Gould's zest for business combat. Alice Snow concluded that her uncle "did thoroughly enjoy business, and, in particular, the opportunity to fight and overcome great obstacles. . . . I shall always believe that with Uncle Jay money was secondary to his intense desire to win, his burning will to succeed, in life, in business. . . ." *Story of Helen Gould*, 117.

87. New York *Times*, December 8, 1884. Northrop stated simply that "Physically Mr. Gould was not a courageous man." *Life and Achievements of Jay Gould*, 208. See also White, *Wizard of Wall Street*, 217.

88. *Ibid.*, December 3, 1892.

89. For this episode see New York *Times*, April 30, May 1, May 11, and May 13, 1873, and White, *Wizard of Wall Street*, 179–180.

90. Clews, *Fifty Years in Wall Street*, 232–233.

91. *Ibid.*; White, *Wizard of Wall Street*, 170–173. The New York *Times*, August 3, 1877, editorialized, "That a man who represents at least a hundred million dollars . . . should have been soundly walloped seemed too good to be true. As the news spread, there was a general feeling of regret—that the walloping had been so private. . . . If reprisals like this are to be countenanced, Mr. JAY GOULD will be hung by the nape of the neck and pummeled by indignant stock operators from January to December."

92. Clews, *Fifty Years in Wall Street*, 233–235. Keene, like other of Gould's foes, returned to haunt the little financier later. For some episodes of violent threats against Gould see *ibid.*, 198–200; Halstead and Beale, *Life of Jay Gould*, 295–296; Myers, *History of the Great American Fortunes*, 420n., 427; O'Connor, *Gould's Millions*, 167, 214–218, 239–240.

93. New York *Tribune*, December 3, 1892. White, *Wizard of Wall Street*, 218, agreed that "His triumphs were, for the most part, over men who would have ruined him if he had not ruined them."

94. "After all," Gould told a reporter, "what does any man, however rich he may be, get in this world except his board and his clothes and a place to live?" New York *Times*, March 7, 1887.

95. Quoted in Halstead and Beale, *Life of Jay Gould*, 218.

96. Alice Snow seems on solid ground in her appraisal of Gould's religious habits: "I am quite aware of the oft-repeated statement that Jay Gould was an

unreligious man.... I know that characterization to have been totally untrue. It is a fact that he was not a strong denominationalist...." *Story of Helen Gould*, 143.
97. Even the hostile *Times* editorialized that "we really know nothing about Mr. GOULD's creed, for he has never posed as a religious man. We do not like Mr. GOULD. We do not think he is a good man to have around. But it is much to his credit that he is wholly free from hypocrisy in the matter of religion." New York *Times*, August 8, 1883. See also *ibid.*, March 9 and March 10, 1892.
98. Dreiser, *The Financier*, 291–292.
99. See, for example, Louis Galambos, "The Emerging Organizational Synthesis in Modern American History," *Business History Review*, 44 (Autumn 1970), 279–290.
100. Peter G. Filene, "An Obituary for 'The Progressive Movement,' " *American Quarterly*, 22 (Spring 1970), 20–34.

The Man Who Saved the Railroads

1. Robert L. Frey (ed.), *Railroads in the Nineteenth Century, The Encyclopedia of American Business History and Biography* (1988), 72.
2. Frank Vanderlip, *From Farm Boy to Financier* (New York, 1935), 144.
3. Computed from *Historical Statistics of the United States, Colonial Times to 1970*, part 2, 1114.
4. All data taken from Maury Klein, *Union Pacific: The Rebirth, 1894–1969* (New York, 1989), 56–59.
5. Klein, *Union Pacific*, 65.
6. W. L. Park, "Personal Recollections of Mr. Harriman in Connection with the Union Pacific," 29, copy in my possession; Klein, *Union Pacific*, 59–62.
7. Klein, *Union Pacific*, 168.
8. Quoted by George Kennan from unfinished Batson manuscript. Copy in my possession.
9. Quoted in Klein, *Union Pacific*, 125.
10. Ibid., 132–33.
11. Edwin Lefevre, "Harriman," *American Magazine* (June 1907), 64:129–30.

Competition and Regulation

1. Given the voluminous literature on railroads, it is remarkable how few general works treat the subject, let alone interpret it in broad terms. John F. Stover, *American Railroads* (Chicago, Ill., 1961) and *The Life and Decline of the American Railroad* (New York, 1970) are descriptive and largely repetitive of each other. Stewart H. Holbrook, *The Story of the American Railroads* (Garden City, N.Y., 1953) is a popular history. The most useful volumes remain Alfred D. Chandler, Jr., *The Railroads: The Nation's First Big Business* (New York, 1965), and the same author's broad synthesis in *The Visible Hand: The Managerial Revolution in American Business* (Cambridge, Mass., 1977), 122–87.

2. For a useful discussion of why historians have been so slow to treat railroad history intelligently and comprehensively, see Albro Martin, "Light at the End of a Very Long Tunnel: The Railroads and the Historians," *Railroad History* (Autumn 1986): 15–33.
3. E. Porter Alexander, *Railway Practice* (New York, 1887), 6.
4. I am aware that competition existed in many areas between railroads and water carriers. The point here is that the most influential and decisive form of competition was between rival rail lines rather than intermodal competition.
5. Charles Francis Adams, Jr., *Railroads: Their Origin and Problems* (New York, 1888), 85, 185; "Transportation Developments in the United States," *Proceedings of the Academy of Political Science* 17 (Jan. 1937): 73–74.
6. The literature on costs and pricing is extensive but diffuse. See, for example, Albert Fink's pioneering "Cost of Railroad Transportation" [extract from the Annual Report of the Louisville & Nashville Railroad] (Louisville, Ky., 1875); Emory R. Johnson and Thurman W. Van Metre, *Principles of Railroad Transportation* (New York, 1920), 337–51; Harry Gunnison Brown, *Transportation Rates and Their Regulation* (New York, 1921); Eliot Jones, *Principles of Railway Transportation* (New York, 1924), 71–90; Owen Ely, *Railway Rates and Cost of Service* (Boston, Mass., 1924); Winthrop Daniels, *The Price of Transportation Service* (New York, 1932); James C. Nelson, *Railroad Transportation and Public Policy* (Washington, D.C., 1959), 327–73; U.S. Senate, *National Transportation Policy*, Sen. Report No. 445, 57th Cong., 1st Sess. (Washington, D.C., 1961), 385–424 [hereafter cited as Doyle Report]; John R. Meyer et al., *The Economics of Competition in the Transportation Industries* (Cambridge, Mass., 1960); Theodore E. Keeler, *Railroads, Freight, and Public Policy* (Washington, D.C., 1983), 43–61. Historically, the pricing of rail service has been based on value of service rather than its cost.
7. The literature on rates, the classification system, and discriminations is too enormous to cite here. Virtually every work cited in this article has something to say on these subjects. For some standard introductions see Jones, *Principles of Railway Transportation*, 71–180; Walter Chadwick Noyes, *American Railroad Rates* (Boston, Mass., 1905); Ely, *Railway Rates and Cost of Service*, 1–80; Emory R. Johnson and Grover G. Huebner, *Railroad Traffic and Rates* (New York, 1911) 1: 331–492; Doyle Report, 385–443.
8. The intensity of these early rate wars can best be appreciated by extensive browsing in such periodicals as the *Commercial and Financial Chronicle*, *Railroad Gazette*, *Financier* (later *Public*), and *Bradstreet's* for the 1870s and 1880s. Contemporary newspapers in New York and Chicago, as well as in other affected cities, also contain a wealth of detail on rate wars.
9. This conclusion is derived from reading thousands of pages of testimony scattered through state and federal hearings for the period 1870–1900. For two examples see the testimony in the proceedings cited in footnote 10.
10. A. B. Stickney, *The Railway Problem* (St. Paul, Minn., 1891), 69, 143, 219, 223–24. For examples of this view of rates, see the testimony in [Hepburn Committee], *Proceedings of the Special Committee on Railroads . . .* (New York, 1897)

and U.S. Senate, *Report of the Senate Select Committee on Interstate Commerce*(Washington, D.C., 1886).
11. For accounts of these wars and attempts to stop them see Maury Klein, *The Great Richmond Terminal* (Charlottesville, Va., 1970), *The Life and Legacy of Jay Gould* (Baltimore, Md., 1986), and *Union Pacific: The Birth, 1862–1893* (New York, 1987); Julius Grodinsky, *The Iowa Pool* (Chicago, Ill., 1950), and *Transcontinental Railway Strategy, 1869–1893* (Philadelphia, Pa., 1962). There is no satisfactory account of the eastern rate wars or the trunk line pool. For a brief discussion see Albro Martin, "The Troubled Subject of Railroad Regulation in the Gilded Age—a Reappraisal," *Journal of American History* 61 (Sept. 1974): 353–59.
12. Stickney, *Railway Problem*, 140; Alexander, *Railway Practice*, 59; Richard Hadley Waters, *Competition and Regulation* (Philadelphia, Pa., 1938), 97; Nelson, *Railroad Transportation*, 112; George W. Hilton, *The Transportation Act of 1958* (Bloomington, Ind., 1969), 4. For a survey of the literature on regulation see Thomas K. McCraw, "Regulation in America: A Review Article," *Business History Review* 49 (Summer 1975): 159–83.
13. Nelson, *Railroad Transportation*, 112; Thomas K. McCraw, *Prophets of Regulation* (Cambridge, Mass., 1984), 9.
14. McCraw, *Prophets of Regulation*, 10. The pooling issue and its alter ego, the long haul–short haul clause, are expertly discussed in Martin, "Troubled Subject of Railroad Regulation," 339–71.
15. Different aspects of this story are found in Albro Martin, *Enterprise Denied: Origins of the Decline of American Railroads, 1897–1917* (New York, 1971); Albro Martin, *James J. Hill and the Opening of the Northwest* (New York, 1976); George Kennan, *E. H. Harriman: A Biography*, 2 vols. (Boston, Mass., 1922); B. H. Meyer, *A History of the Northern Securities Case* (Madison, Wisc., 1906); Maury Klein, *Union Pacific: The Rebirth, 1894–1969* (New York, 1990).
16. The Northern Securities decisions are in 193 U.S. 197 and 197 U.S. 244. For the dissolution of the Union Pacific–Southern Pacific merger see *United States v. Union Pacific Railroad et al.*, 266 U.S. 61, 33 S. Ct. 53, and 57 L. Ed. 124.
17. Gabriel Kolko, *Railroads and Regulation* (Princeton, N.J., 1965), 74, 87; "Transportation Development in the United States," 68–69. Kolko's version of the "capture" thesis of regulation has been pretty thoroughly demolished. See, for example, Richard H. K. Vietor, "Businessmen and the Political Economy: The Railroad Rate Controversy of 1905," *Journal of American History* 64 (June 1977): 47–66, and McCraw, "Regulation in America," 164–66.
18. The best and most lucid account of the prewar struggle between the carriers, the ICC, and the government is Martin, *Enterprise Denied*. See also K. Austin Kerr, *American Railroad Politics, 1914–1920: Rates, Wages, and Efficiency* (Pittsburgh, Pa., 1968); Kolko, *Rates and Regulation;* I. L. Sharfman, *The Interstate Commerce Commission: A Study in Administrative Law and Procedure* (New York, 1931–37), 5 vols. For the wartime experience see Kerr's book and Walker D. Hines, *War History of American Railroads* (New Haven, Conn., 1928).

19. Ari Hoogenboom and Olive Hoogenboom, *A History of the ICC: From Panacea to Palliative* (New York, 1976), 105. The literature on the Transportation Act of 1920 is voluminous. A full description of the act is in Sharfman, *Interstate Commerce Commission*, 1: 177–244.
20. Details on the consolidation provisions of the 1920 act and their tortuous fate are in Sharfman, *Interstate Commerce Commission*, 3A: 385–501, and Hoogenboom and Hoogenboom, *ICC*, 105–10.
21. Quoted in Sharfman, *Interstate Commerce Commission*, 3A: 432–33, 461.
22. Quoted in ibid., 3A: 358–59. For details on these provisions see ibid., 3A: 327–85.
23. Quoted in ibid., 3A: 359.
24. This quest for diversity can be seen by glancing through issues of *Railway Age* for the interwar years. In 1926, for example, this trade journal began a section devoted to truck and bus activities undertaken by railroads. For the Union Pacific flirtation with air travel, see Klein, *Union Pacific*, 2: 320–26.
25. For the mood of the 1930s see Earl Latham, *The Politics of Rail Coordination, 1933–1936* (Cambridge, Mass., 1959).
26. These acts are summarized briefly in Keeler, *Railroads, Freight, and Public Policy*, 26–43.
27. Ibid., 136; *Railway Age*, 108: 851–54, 1043–45; 109: 371–73, 399–403; Keeler, *Railroads, Freight, and Public Policy*, 27.
28. Doyle Report, 152–84; Nelson, *Railroad Transportation and Public Policy*, 111–45; Association of Railway Executives, "Declaration of Policy Deemed Necessary to the Continuance of Adequate Transportation Service to the Public," 20 Nov. 1930, copy in possession of Union Pacific Corporation.
29. Nelson, *Railroad Transportation and Public Policy*, 3–110, 148–92; Doyle Report, 47–74.
30. For a pivotal work in this transition see Meyer, *Economics of Competition*.
31. Keeler, *Railroads, Freight, and Public Policy*, 147.
32. There has been another interesting trend in recent years toward the creation of short-line roads operating over the better routes of abandoned larger systems. See, for example, *Providence Journal*, 7 Nov. 1988.
33. Adams, *Railroads: Their Origin and Problems*, 203.

The Turning Point in American Railroad History

1. Maury Klein, *Union Pacific: The Birth, 1862–1893* (New York, 1987), 584.
2. Ibid., 585.
3. For these efforts see ibid., 586–600, 632–35, 648–51.
4. *Report of the Industrial Commission on Transportation*, House Report No. 178, 57 Cong., 1st Sess. (Washington, D.C., 1901), 9:770.
5. *Wall Street Journal*, Jan. 10, 1901.
6. Ibid., Apr. 5, 1901.
7. New York *Tribune*, Jan. 6, Jan. 7, Mar. 24, and Apr. 13, 1900; *Wall Street Journal*, Jan. 9 and Mar. 23, 1901.

8. E. H. Harriman to Stuyvesant Fish, Apr. 19, 1899, Stuyvesant Fish papers, Columbia University, New York City.
9. B. H. Meyer, *A History of the Northern Securities Case* (Madison, Wisc., 1906).
10. *Wall Street Journal*, Oct. 30, 1905; Albro Martin, *Enterprise Denied: Origins of the Decline of the American Railroad, 1897–1917* (New York, 1971).
11. *United States of America v. Union Pacific Railroad Company et al.*, U. S. Circuit Court for the district of Utah, docket no. 993, 2:805.

Replacement Technology

1. J. W. Anderson, *Diesel Engines* (New York, 1949), 4, 6; P. M. Heldt, *High-Speed Diesel Engines* (Nyack, N.Y., 1936), 1–3. Surprisingly little has been written in English about Diesel and his engine. See Donald E. Thomas, Jr., *Diesel: Technology and Society in Industrial Germany* (Tuscaloosa, Ala., 1987).
2. Charles E. Beck, "Historical Development of the Large Modern Diesel Engine in America," *The First Fifty Years of the Diesel Engine in America* (New York, 1949), 3–6.
3. Dee Brown, *The Year of the Century: 1876* (New York, 1966), 129–30; *Wall Street Journal*, May 17, 1902.
4. Ibid., May 17, 1902, Dec. 8, 1903; Thomas, *Diesel*, 206; Anderson, *Diesel Engines*, 6–7.
5. For a full description of the varieties of steam locomotives see Alfred W. Bruce, *The Steam Locomotive in America* (New York, 1952).
6. Carl Gray to C. B. Seger, Jan. 20, 1927, Union Pacific papers, New York files, Union Pacific Museum, Omaha. Hereafter cited as UPN.
7. *Railway Age*, 87:95–96, 98:364; A. H. Fetters, "The Diesel Locomotive," December 1926, 1–2, UPN.
8. Fetters, "Diesel Locomotive," 1–3.
9. Ibid., 6.
10. Anderson, *Diesel Engines*, 544–45; W. Fred Cottrell, *Technological Change and the Railroad Industry* (Lexington, Mass., 1970), 8–15.
11. Fetters, "The Diesel Locomotive," 5–6; Cottrell, *Technological Change and the Railroad Industry*, 11.
12. Anderson, *Diesel Engines*, 545; R. O. Brice (?) to W. A. Harriman, Apr. 17, 1936, UPN. Diesel switchers were available 24 hours a day compared to 16 for steam switchers. Since the latter had to get up a head of steam before working, they were kept fired up even when not active. By contrast, diesels could easily be shut off when not in use and be ready to go when turned on.
13. *Railway Age*, 98:364; Harold E. Ranks and William W. Kratville, *The Union Pacific Streamliners* (Omaha, 1974), 11–14; Alfred P. Sloan, Jr., to W. A. Harriman, Apr. 14, 1936, UPN; W. A. Harriman to Sloan, Apr. 17, 1936, UPN.
14. Chicago *Tribune*, February 2 and February 8, 1941; *Journal of Commerce*, February 6–8, 1941; *Wall Street Journal*, February 7, 1941. For a profile of the big diesel see *Collier's*, April 5, 1941, 12, 73–76.

15. *Historical Statistics of the United States, Colonial Times to 1970* (Washington, D.C., 1975), Part 1, 727–28.
16. True railroaders included enginemen, firemen, trainmen, dispatchers, telegraphers, superintendents, master mechanics, trainmasters, yardmasters, machinists, boilermakers, carmen, other shopmen, and part of the maintenance of way force. For more detail see W. Frederick Cottrell, *The Railroader* (Palo Alto, Cal., 1940), 4–35.
17. For a portrait of nineteenth-century railroaders see Walter Licht, *Working for the Railroad* (Princeton, N.J., 1983).
18. Interview with William J. Fox, Sept. 6, 1982, 15, 33–34. Fox, like the other officers cited here, worked for the Union Pacific Railroad.
19. Interview with Frank Accord, Nov. 8, 1984, 29–31, 40.
20. Ibid., 41–42.
21. Ibid., 33, 42.
22. Cottrell, *Technological Change and the Railroad Industry*, 128–29.
23. Ibid., 131. Put another way, a train or engineman completed a full day's work by covering either a hundred miles or putting in eight hours on the job.
24. "Background of Diesel Dispute," n.d., Union Pacific Collection, Nebraska State Department of Archives and History, Lincoln; James C. Nelson, *Railroad Transportation and Public Policy* (Washington, D.C., 1959), 273–74; Richard C. Overton, *Burlington Route* (Lincoln, Neb., 1965), 435–36; "Transcript of Proceedings of the National Labor Arbitration Board No. 282," September 25, 1963, Oregon Historical Society, Portland.
25. "Background of Diesel Dispute."
26. Nelson, *Railroad Transportation and Public Policy*, 274–75; *Annual Report of the Union Pacific Railroad*, 1963, 15, 1964, 14, 1965, 15. For details on the struggle see "Transcript of Proceedings of the National Labor Arbitration Board No. 282," September–October 1963.
27. *Annual Report of the Union Pacific Railroad*, 1965, 15, 1966, 15, 1967, 14, 1968, 14; *Journal of Commerce*, November 19, 1968; Cottrell, *Technological Change and the Railroad Industry*, 132–35.
28. *Historical Statistics*, 1:739–40.
29. Daniel J. Boorstin, *The Republic of Technology* (New York, 1978), 5.

High-Speed Trains

1. *Historical Statistics of the United States, Colonial Times to 1970* (Washington, D.C., 1975), Part 1, 728.
2. Harriman's role in this process is depicted in Maury Klein, *Union Pacific: The Rebirth, 1894–1969* (New York, 1990), 48–181. It will be expanded in my forthcoming biography of Harriman.
3. The complex, often adversarial relationship between private interests and the federal government in the building of the first transcontinental road is depicted in Maury Klein, *Union Pacific: The Birth, 1862–1893* (New York, 1987).
4. Maury Klein, "The Turning Point in American Railroad History," paper

given at Coloquio Internacional sobre Transporte e Industrializacion siglos XIX y XX, Madrid, January 1990; Albro Martin, *Enterprise Denied: Origins of the Decline of American Railroads, 1897–1917* (New York, 1971).

5. Maury Klein, "Competition and Regulation: The Railroad Model," article in forthcoming issue of *Business History Review* (Summer 1990), 64:2, 311–25; Ari and Olive Hoogenboom, *A History of the ICC: From Panacea to Palliative* (New York, 1976); Walker D. Hines, *War History of American Railroads* (New Haven, Conn., 1928).
6. For more detail see Klein, *Union Pacific: The Rebirth*, 258–78.
7. For details on each prototype see Klein, *Union Pacific: The Rebirth*, 295–308, and Richard C. Overton, *Burlington Route* (Lincoln, Neb., 1965), 393–406. The original versions had two major differences. The Burlington began with a diesel engine while the Union Pacific first used a Winton distillate engine before switching to a diesel. Where the Union Pacific's first cars were built of aluminum, the Burlington used stainless steel.
8. Overton, *Burlington Route*, 396–97, 400.
9. Klein, *Union Pacific: The Rebirth*, 307–8.
10. For the 1920 act see I. L. Sharfman, *The Interstate Commerce Commission: A Study in Administrative Law and Procedure* (New York, 1931–1937), 5 vols., 1:177–244.
11. Klein, *Union Pacific: The Rebirth*, 402–45.
12. For details on this loss of business see James C. Nelson, *Railroad Transportation and Public Policy* (Washington, D.C., 1959), and U. S. Senate, *National Transportation Policy*, Sen. Report No. 445, 57 Cong., 1st Sess. (Washington, D.C., 1961), 385–424. The latter is better known as the Doyle Report.
13. For the collapse of Penn Central see Stephen Salsbury, *No Way to Run a Railroad* (New York, 1982).
14. Klein, *Union Pacific: The Rebirth*, 487, 489; "Tax Exempt Bonds for High Speed Rail Projects," Hearing before the Committee on Finance, 100 Cong., 2d Sess., Sen. Hrg. 100-674, Mar. 24, 1988, 41–42.
15. Interview with Arrigo Mongini of the Federal Railroad Administration, May 29, 1990. I am grateful to Mr. Mongini for his cooperation in this project.
16. "Advanced Transportation Systems," Hearing before the Subcommittee on Surface Transportation, 100 Cong., 1st Sess., Sen. Hrg. 101-369, Oct. 17, 1989, 8.
17. "Advanced Transportation Systems," 8, 14, 34–35; "Tax Exempt Bonds," 41–42. The Corridor project involved track utilized by three freight and five commuter lines, some private and some public.
18. Transportation Research Board of the National Academy of Sciences, *Railroad Electrification: The Issues*, Special Report 180 (Washington, D.C., 1977), 6, 8.
19. Ibid., 13–15.
20. "Advanced Transportation Systems," 4, 8, 14–15; Mongini interview, May 29, 1990. This myth that Americans created maglev overlooks the pioneering work of Hermann Kemper in Germany during the 1930s and after.
21. Ibid., 26, 53.

22. Ibid., 37–38; "Tax Exempt Bonds," 42–45, 49–52, 80–82; Mongini interview, May 29, 1990.
23. Mongini interview, May 29, 1990.
24. Galen J. Reser to Senator Claiborne Pell, April 12, 1990. I am grateful to Todd G. Andrews of Senator Pell's office for providing me a copy of this letter and a press release on the forum. For the argument in favor of the bonds see the testimony in "Tax Exempt Bonds."

The Unfinished Business of American Railroad History

1. The best book on the Erie's history remains Edward H. Mott, *Between the Ocean and the Lakes: The Story of Erie* (New York, 1908).
2. Burke Davis, *The Southern Railway* (Chapel Hill, N.C., 1985).
3. The best of a thin lot in regional studies remains Edward C. Kirkland, *Men, Cities and Transportation* (Cambridge, Mass., 1948), 2 vols. See also John F. Stover, *Railroads of the South, 1865–1900* (Chapel Hill, N.C., 1955).
4. Wheaton J. Lane, *Commodore Vanderbilt: An Epic of the Steam Age* (New York, 1942).
5. James A. Ward, *J. Edgar Thomson: Master of the Pennsylvania* (Greenwood, Conn., 1980), has improved our understanding of that key figure, while Patricia Davis, *End of the Line: Alexander J. Cassatt and the Pennsylvania Railroad* (New York, 1978), has little to offer about either the man or the railroad.
6. The classic study is Oscar Lewis, *The Big Four* (New York, 1938). David Lavender, *The Great Persuader* (New York, 1970), is a helpful study of Collis P. Huntington but by no means definitive or complete.
7. Walter Licht, *Working for the Railroad* (Princeton, N.J., 1983); Shelton Stromquist, *A Generation of Boomers: The Pattern of Railroad Labor Conflict in the 19th Century* (Urbana, Ill., 1987). See also James H. Ducker, *Men of the Steel Rails* (Lincoln, Neb., 1983).
8. See Alfred D. Chandler, Jr., *The Visible Hand: The Managerial Revolution in American Business* (Cambridge, Mass., 1977). Another valuable and pioneering work is Thomas C. Cochran, *Railroad Leaders, 1845–1890: The Business Mind in Action* (Cambridge, Mass., 1953).
9. See for example Gregory L. Thompson, "Misused Product Costing in the American Railroad Industry: Southern Pacific Passenger Service between the Wars, *Business History Review* (Autumn 1989) 63:3, 510–54.
10. I have tried to deal with these questions as part of the broader context in my *Union Pacific: The Rebirth, 1894–1969* (New York, 1990). For one useful exception see Kent T. Healy, *Performance of the U.S. Railroads since World War II* (New York, 1985).
11. Leo Marx, *The Machine in the Garden* (New York, 1964); James A. Ward, *Railroads and the Character of America, 1820–1887* (Knoxville, Tenn., 1986), John R. Stilgoe, *Metropolitan Corridor: Railroads and the American Scene* (New Haven, Conn., 1983).
12. Albro Martin, *Enterprise Denied: Origins of the Decline of American Railroads,*

1877–1917 (New York, 1971); George Rogers Taylor and Irene D. Neu, *The American Railway Network, 1861–1890* (Cambridge, Mass., 1956).
13. John F. Stover, *American Railroads* (Chicago, 1961); Albro Martin, *Railroads Triumphant* (New York, 1992). Martin does include a useful, annotated bibliography. John F. Stover, *The Life and Decline of the American Railroad* (New York, 1970), is more anecdotal and adds little to his earlier work.
14. Charles Francis Adams, Jr., and Henry Adams, *Chapters of Erie and Other Essays* (New York, 1886).
15. For this story see Maury Klein, *Union Pacific: The Birth, 1862–1893* (New York, 1987), 461–631.
16. Charles Francis Adams, *Railroads: Their Origin and Problems* (New York, 1878); Edward Porter Alexander, *Railway Practice* (New York, 1887).
17. See Albro Martin, *James J. Hill and the Opening of the Northwest* (New York, 1976).
18. Martin, *Railroads Triumphant*, 407.
19. Matthew Josephson, *The Robber Barons* (New York, 1934); William Z. Ripley, *Railroads: Finance and Organization* (New York, 1915), and *Railroads: Rates and Regulations* (New York, 1912).
20. Ripley, *Railroads: Finance and Organization*, 77, 112, 262–67. This episode is treated in more detail in my forthcoming biography of Harriman.
21. This George Kennan should not be confused with George F. Kennan, who emerged as an authority on Soviet affairs during the 1940s. They are distantly related and often mistaken for each other because of their expertise on Russia. See George F. Kennan, *Memoirs 1925–1950* (New York, 1969).
22. Lawrence Abbott to George Kennan, November 8, 1915, materials housed at Arden Farms, Harriman, N.Y. Hereafter cited as AF.
23. The magazine version of the article was shortened. The original version was published privately as *The Chicago & Alton Case: A Misunderstood Transaction* (Garden City, N.Y., 1916).
24. Ripley to Kennan, January 19, 1916, AF.
25. Walker to Kennan, February 15, February 18, and February 28, 1916, AF. The copies of Ripley's letters are also at AF.
26. Ripley to Kennan, March 10, 1916, AF; William Z. Ripley, "Federal Financial Railway Regulation: The Alton as a Test Case," *North American Review* (April 1916), 203:538–52. The source Ripley denounced was Frank Spearman, a popular railroad writer.
27. Roosevelt's letter is in Ripley, "Federal Financial Railway Regulation," 548–51. Kennan's rejoinder and his piece on Roosevelt are both in George Kennan, *Misrepresentation in Railroad Affairs* (Garden City, N.Y., 1916).
28. Kennan went on to write a two-volume biography of Harriman. See George Kennan, *E. H. Harriman* (New York, 1922).
29. Martin, *Railroads Triumphant*, 412. See for example Donald L. McMurry, *The Great Burlington Strike of 1888: A Case History of Industrial Relations* (Cambridge, Mass., 1956), and the discussion of strikes against the Gould roads in Maury Klein, *The Life and Legend of Jay Gould* (Baltimore, 1986), 357–63. The

one study that has approached these issues from a fresh vantage point is Stromquist, *Generation of Boomers*. His work should serve as a point of departure for what needs to be done on a much broader scale.

30. Robert V. Bruce, *1877: Year of Violence* (Indianapolis, 1959), offers a graphic account of events but little insight into the broader issues or context. Stromquist, *Generation of Boomers*, provides a different slant on the strikes of 1877 but does not analyze the economic issues.
31. Fred A. Shannon, *The Farmer's Last Frontier: Agriculture, 1860–1897* (New York, 1945), 173, 301.
32. See the earlier article on "Competition and Regulation: The Railroad Model."
33. Consider, for example, this observation: "Railroads in the West received part of the federal land as a subsidy. The facts are confusing and have resulted in some interesting calculations on the actual amount given away. However, most historians have used their calculations chiefly to condemn the railroads." John T. Schlebecker, *Whereby We Thrive: A History of American Farming, 1607–1972* (Ames, Iowa, 1975).
34. For background on Civil War historiography see the still serviceable Thomas J. Pressly, *Americans Interpret Their Civil War* (New York, 1954).
35. By this I mean in part that it seems never to occur to critics that a writer omits references to certain works not from ignorance of them but because he or she simply doesn't think them worth mentioning.
36. One might suggest other fields that have similar if not comparable patterns, such as the debate over slavery and aspects of American foreign policy.
37. Chandler, *The Visible Hand*.
38. I do not mean to suggest that this is a flaw in Chandler's work. His study was never meant to be a general history of railroads.
39. See for example the seminal article by Peter G. Filene, "An Obituary for the Progressive Movement," *American Quarterly* (Spring 1970), 20–34.
40. Richard C. Overton, *Burlington Route* (New York, 1965). For examples of other studies see Arthur M. Johnson and Barry E. Supple, *Boston Capitalists and Western Railroads* (Cambridge, Mass., 1967), and John Lauritz Larson, *Bonds of Enterprise: John Murray Forbes and Western Development in America's Railway Age* (Cambridge, Mass., 1984).
41. Olivier Zunz, *Making America Corporate* (Chicago, 1990), 40. Zunz used the Burlington as his model for a variety of managerial and organizational growth patterns.
42. For a brief summary of this debate, including a quotation from Perkins, see Klein, *Union Pacific: The Rebirth*, 138. See also Ray Morris, *Railroad Adminstration* (New York, 1920), 46–89.
43. See for example Thomas C. Cochran and William Miller, *The Age of Enterprise* (New York, 1945), 130–35. "The crime of the railroad profiteers," concluded Cochran and Miller, ". . . was not that they, as great speculators, milked an army of little speculators either directly or through venal politicians. Their crime was that they built poor roads."
44. For these revolutions see Chandler, *Visible Hand*, passim.

45. See for example George H. Miller, *Railroads and the Granger Laws* (Madison, Wisc., 1971).
46. This story is told in Klein, *Union Pacific: The Birth*.
47. For an account of how grossly distorted the public version of the Credit Mobilier scandal was, and how it oversimplified extremely complex issues, see ibid., chapter 14.
48. As an example of this tendency one might look closely at the uproar over the free silver issue during the late 1880s and 1890s.
49. Ibid., 367–68.
50. Gabriel Kolko, *Railroads and Regulation, 1877–1916* (Princeton, N.J., 1965). Kolko's thesis that the railroads themselves were behind the movement for federal regulation has a grain of truth buried in a mound of chaff.
51. The classic examples here are Albert Fishlow, *Railroads and the Transformation of the Ante-Bellum Economy* (Cambridge, Mass., 1965), and Robert W. Fogel, *Railroads and American Economic Growth* (Baltimore, 1964). Neither has stood the test of time well, although Fishlow's work offers some useful insights. Fogel's once controversial study has been reduced to a curiosity piece with both its thesis and methodology dismantled by critics.
52. Kent T. Healy, *Performance of the U. S. Railroads since World War II* (New York, 1985).
53. Bernard A. Weisberger, "The Dark and Bloody Ground of Reconstruction Historiography," *Journal of Southern History* (November 1959), vol. 25:4, 434–35.

Bibliography of Articles and Papers

"Patterns of Early American Railroad Development," given at International Conference on the Comparative Effects of Early Railroad Development, Erlangen Zentralinstitut 06, Erlangen, Germany, January 1992. Published with other papers of conference in spring 1993.

"The Rise of the Iron Horse," *American History Illustrated* (June 1975), 4–10, 42–48.

"The Strategy of Southern Railroads," *American Historical Review*, 73:4 (April 1968), 1052–1068.

"Southern Railroad Leaders, 1865–1893: Identities and Ideologies," *Business History Review*, 42:3 (Autumn 1968), 288–310.

"The Overland Route: First Impressions," *Railroad History* (Autumn 1989), 16–34.

"In Search of Jay Gould," *Business History Review*, 52:2 (Summer 1978), 166–199.

"The Man Who Saved the Railroads," appeared in shortened version as "A Hell of a Way to Run a Railroad," *Audacity*, 1:1 (Fall 1992), 22–31.

"Competition and Regulation: The Railroad Model," original version as printed here given at Business History Conference, March 1988. Slightly edited version published in *Business History Review*, 64:2 (Summer 1990), 311–325.

"The Turning Point in American Railroad History," given at Coloquio Internacional sobre Transporte e Industrializacion siglos XIX y XX, Madrid, Spain, January 1990.

"Replacement Technology: The Diesel as a Case Study," *Railroad History* (Spring 1990), 109–120.

"High-Speed Trains: America's Lost Opportunity," given at Conference on High-Speed Trains, Entrepreneurship, and Society, Stockholm School of Economics, Stockholm, Sweden, June 1990. Reprinted in John Whitelegg, Staffan Hultén, and Torbjörn Flink (eds.), *High Speed Trains: Fast Track to the Future* (North Yorkshire, England, 1993), 66–77.

Index

Abbott, Lawrence, 171
Acord, Frank, 150–151
Adams, Charles Francis, Jr., 90, 91, 124, 126, 170
Adams, Henry, 18, 85, 90, 91, 170
Adamson Act of 1916, 152
Aerotrain, 162
agriculture, 15, 173–174
airplane transportation, 131, 132, 157–158, 160, 161
Alexander, Edward Porter, 2, 3, 4, 45, 50, 51, 123, 170
American Centennial Exhibition of 1876, 144
American Locomotive Company, 145, 146
American Railroads (Stover), 168
American Railway Network, 1861–1890 (Taylor and Neu), 168
Amtrak, 132, 161
Anderson, E. Ellery, 88
Associated Railways of Virginia and the Carolinas, 44
Atchison, Topeka & Santa Fe Railroad, 23, 111, 119, 140, 149
Atlantic, Mississippi & Ohio Railroad, 33, 38, 52, 60
Atlantic & Gulf Railroad, 33, 40, 52, 54
Atlantic Coast Line, 44, 65
automobiles, 131, 157, 158, 160, 161

Baldwin, C. C., 62, 66
Baltimore & Ohio Railroad, 21, 22, 43, 58, 118, 139, 167, 178
bankruptcies, 26, 39–40, 45, 111, 127, 136, 161
Barron, Clarence W., 92
Baughman, James P., 3
Beadle, J. H., 77

Beebe, Lucius, 70
Bennett, James Gordon, 102
Berry, John B., 116
Birmingham, Alabama, 15
Blackstone Canal, 9
Bok, Edward, 92
Boorstin, Daniel, 154
Boston & Albany Railroad, 21
Boston & Worcester Railroad, 9
Bowles, Samuel, 77
brakemen, 150
brand-name revolution, 16
Brewer, Thomas B., 4
Brice, Calvin S., 62, 63, 66
Bridgers, Robert R., 50, 53, 54, 56, 57, 62
bridges, 11, 25, 81, 116
Brotherhood of Locomotive Firemen and Enginemen, 152
Browne, Percy, 74
Buford, A. S., 40, 41, 53, 55, 58, 60
Burlington Railroad. *See* Chicago, Burlington & Quincy Railroad
bus service, 131, 157
Busch, Adolphus, 144, 145
Busch-Sultzer, 144

Cady, Alva B., 82
Calhoun, John C., 50
Calhoun, Patrick, 49, 50
California, 164
Callaway, Thomas H., 58
Carnegie, Andrew, 79, 90
Carnegie-Mellon University, 164
Carroll, Charles, 21
cartels, 126, 128–132
Casement, Jack, 76, 78
Cassatt, A. J., 167
Castellane, Marquis de, "Boni," 91–92

Index

cattle raising, 14
Central of Georgia Railroad, 22, 33, 45; elections of 1883 and 1887, 50–51; mileage, 42, 52, 65; and Richmond Terminal, 43, 66; and Wadley, 38, 57
Central Pacific Railroad, 14, 23, 28, 79–80
Chandler, Alfred D., Jr., 167, 177
Chapters of Erie (Adams and Adams), 90, 91, 170
Charlotte, Columbia & Augusta Railroad, 58
Chesapeake & Ohio Railroad, 36, 139
Chicago, Burlington & Quincy Railroad, 23, 119, 140, 147, 148, 152, 158, 177–178
Chicago, Ill., 10, 15, 22, 23
Chicago, Milwaukee & St. Paul Railroad, 23
Chicago, Rock Island & Pacific Railroad, 23
Chicago, St. Louis & New Orleans Railroad, 42
Chicago & Alton Railroad, 118, 139, 171–173
Chicago & Northwestern Railroad, 23, 167
Chisholm, Walter S., 49, 50
Cincinnati Southern Railroad, 36
cities and towns, 9, 11, 14, 15, 20, 27, 111
Civil War, 8, 12, 14, 175–176
Clark, Clarence H., 62
Clark, William A., 119
Clews, Henry, 92, 106
Clyde, William P., 62, 63, 66
coal, 11, 15, 74, 139, 145
Cochran, Thomas C., 85
Cole, Edwin W., 42, 53, 54
Colfax, Schuyler, 78
common carrier service obligations, 128–130, 132, 181
"community of interest," 127, 135, 138–142
competition, railroad: and cartelization (1920–1958), 128–132; intermodal, 130–132, 145, 157–158, 184; and regulation (1860–1920), 123–128; and restructuring/deregulation (1958–present), 132–134; Southern, 36, 43, 45, 59–60; transcontinental (1880s), 23–24
Congress, 12, 14
Connor, Washington, 88
consolidation, railroad, 25–26, 42–43, 128–129, 135, 137–138
continental divide, 74, 75
Contract and Finance Company, 28
Corliss Engine Works, 144
Cornell, Alonzo B., 88
Corning, Erastus, 10
cotton industry, 15
Cottrell, W. Frederick, 151
Cramp & Sons, 145
Credit Mobilier scandal, 28, 181
crewmen, 150
Crocker, Charles, 28, 80, 167

Dana, Charles, 78
Danville Railroad, 38, 40, 42, 43, 44
Davis, Burke, 167
deflation, 15
Department of Transportation, 162
Depression of 1893–97, 26, 45, 111, 112, 127, 135–136, 179
Diesel, Rudolf, 144
diesel locomotive, 143–154. *See also* streamliner train
Dillon, John F., 88
Dillon, Sidney, 88
dispatchers, 150
Dodge, Grenville M., 74–76
Dreiser, Theodore, 108, 109
Drew, Daniel, 28, 84, 170
Durant, Thomas C., 77–78

East Tennessee, Virginia & Georgia Railroad, 33, 36, 43, 52, 56, 60, 64, 65

220

Index

East Tennessee Railroad, 38, 42, 43, 44
economic development, 11, 12–13, 14–16, 99
education programs for workers, 120. *See also* management training programs
electric transmission, 146, 163
enginemen, 150, 153, 154
Enterprise Denied (Martin), 168
Erie Railroad, 22, 28, 94, 111, 118, 178, 181
Erlanger railroads, 36
Evans, James A., 75, 76

farmers, 15, 173–174
federal land grants, 10–11
Federal Railroad Administration, 162, 163, 164
federal regulation, 16, 17, 125–132 *passim*, 145, 156–157, 161, 181. *See also* Interstate Commerce Act; Interstate Commerce Commission; Transportation Act (by year)
Felton, Samuel M., Jr., 67, 172
Ferguson, Arthur, 69, 73
Fetters, A. H., 146–147
Filene, Peter G., 108–109
Fink, Henry, 67
firemen, 150, 151, 152–153
Fish, Stuyvesant, 113–114
Fishlow, Albert, 46–47
Fisk, Jim, 28, 87, 103, 170
Florida, 164
Forbes, John Murray, 178
4R Act of 1976, 132
French TGV train, 164

Garraty, John A., 83, 85
Garrett, John W., 167
Garrett, Robert, 167
General Electric, 146
General Motors, 148, 162
Georgia Pacific Railroad, 43
Georgia Railroad, 33, 40, 42, 52, 60
German ICE train, 164

German Transrapid train, 164
Gilded Age, The (Twain and Warner), 20
Gold Conspiracy of 1869, 94
gold rush, 70, 71
Gould, Anna, 91
Gould, Jay, 5, 28, 83–109, 118, 139, 140, 170, 181
Gould railroads, 26
grain traffic, 23
Granger roads, 23, 28
Great American Desert, 13, 68–69
Great Depression, 130, 131, 145, 147, 157, 159
Great Northern Railroad, 23, 115, 178
Great Plains, 13, 15
Green, Hetty, 51
Green, Norvin, 88
Green Line, 36
Grodinsky, Julius, 33–34, 85, 90, 91, 93–98, 100, 101
Guthrie, James, 37, 53, 54

Harriman, E. H., 5, 76, 112–121, 127, 136–142 *passim*, 156, 170, 180; and Alton case, 118, 139–140, 171–173; and Illinois Central Railroad, 112, 113–114; and Union Pacific Railroad, 114–120
Harriman, Mary, 171
Harriman, W. Averell, 146
Harriman railroads, 25
Healy, Kent T., 185
Hepburn Act of 1906, 29, 181
High Speed Ground Transportation Act of 1965, 162
high-speed trains, 155–165; streamliner, 148–149, 152, 157–160
Hill, James J., 90, 112, 115, 119, 140, 170
Hill railroads, 26
Hilton, George, 126
Hodges, Fred, 75

Index

holding companies, 3, 26–27, 57–58, 65, 119, 133, 140
Hollins, Harry B., 62
Homestead Act, 12
Hoogenboom, Ari and Olive, 128
Hopkins, Mark, 28, 80, 167
Hoyt, Edwin P., 93
Hughitt, Marvin, 167
Huidekoper, Frederick W., 67
Huntington, Collis P., 28, 67, 80, 88, 96, 100, 112, 118, 167
Hurst, J. Willard, 16

ICE train (Germany), 164
Illinois Central Railroad, 10–11, 22, 42, 112, 113–114, 139, 178
immigrants, 78–79
Indians, 14, 73, 81
Industrial Commission, United States, 171
industrial development, 14, 19, 20
Ingersoll, Robert G., 85
Ingersoll-Rand, 146
Inman, John H., 50, 62, 63, 66
Interstate Commerce Act of 1887, 29, 111, 125, 126, 131, 136, 156, 183, 185
Interstate Commerce Commission, 29, 127–130, 137, 141, 159, 172
iron and steel industry, 15

James, D. Willis, 57
Johnson, Arthur M., 3, 55
Josephson, Matthew, 85, 170–171

Kansas City, Pittsburg & Gulf Railroad, 118
Kansas Pacific Railroad, 96
Kantor, Harvey A., 5
Katy Railroad, 139
Keene, James R., 84, 106
Kennan, George, 171–173
Kentucky Central Railroad, 36
King, John P., 40, 53, 54, 60, 61
Knapp, Martin, 127

Kolko, Gabriel, 185
Krupp Iron Works, 144

labor unions, 20, 151–153, 167, 173
land grants, 10–11
Lane, Wheaton, 167
legal environment, 16–17
Licht, Walter, 167
Logan, Thomas M., 49, 50
Louisville & Nashville Railroad, 4, 22, 33, 40, 42, 43, 44, 52; expansion (1866–1880), 37–38, 60–61; financial problems (1880s), 64, 66

Maben, James C., 50
McAnerney, John, 50
McCraw, Thomas K., 126
McGhee, Charles M., 49, 50, 58
McGrath, William J., 40
Machine in the Garden, The (Marx), 168
McKeen rail cars, 146
Macon & Brunswick Railroad, 36
magnetic levitation (maglev), 163, 164–165
Mahone, William, 53, 54, 56, 58
mail order business, 15–16
management training programs, 154. *See also* education programs for workers
Manhattan Elevated Railway, 89, 94, 96
Mann-Elkins Act of 1910, 29
market mechanism, 133, 134
Marshall, Alfred, 32
Martin, Albro, 11, 15, 111, 168–169, 170, 173
Martin, Joseph J., 106
Marx, Leo, 168
meat-packing industry, 14, 15, 16
Memphis & Charleston Railroad, 38, 60
mergers, railroad, 10, 118–120, 127, 128, 140, 141, 161. *See also* consolidation
Metroliner, 162

Index

Metropolitan Corridor (Stilgoe), 168
Miller, William, 85
Minneapolis, 15
Mississippi River, 11, 12
Missouri Pacific Railroad, 89, 94, 139
Mobile & Ohio Railroad, 22, 45
monopoly power, 34, 124–125, 126, 127, 129–130, 132
Montgomery & Eufaula Railroad, 39
Montgomery Ward, 15
Morgan, J. P., 27, 98, 119, 140, 172
Morgan, Junius S., 57
Morgan railroads, 26
Mormons, 71, 72
Morosini, Giovanni P., 88
Motor Carrier Act of 1935, 131
Myers, Gustavus, 86

Nashville, Chattanooga & St. Louis Railroad, 33, 42, 52
National Banking Act, 12
national consciousness, 17
national markets, 15, 17
Nelson, James, 126
Neu, Irene D., 168
Nevada, 164
New Deal, 131
New York, New Haven & Hartford Railroad, 162
New York Central Railroad, 10, 22, 139
Newberry Library, 177, 178
Newcomb, H. D., 37, 39, 50, 53
Newcomb, H. Victor, 37–38, 39, 40, 42, 50
Newcomer, Benjamin F., 57, 58
Nimmo, Joseph, 41
Norfolk & Western Railroad, 33, 42, 43, 44, 65, 139
Norris, Frank, 21, 181
North American Review, 171, 172
North Carolina Railroad, 60
North-South transportation, 12
Northeast Corridor Improvement Project, 162–163

Northern Pacific Railroad, 23, 111, 119, 140, 172, 178
Northern Securities Company, 119, 120, 127, 140, 141
Norton, Eckstein, 43, 50, 62, 66
Noyes, Alexander D., 92

O'Connor, Richard, 93
Octopus, The (Norris), 21, 181
Ohio, 164
Outlook magazine, 171
Overton, Richard C., 4, 177

Pacific Railway Act of 1864, 12, 14, 71
Panic of 1873, 37, 39–40, 60
Panic of 1884, 96
Panic of 1893, 66. *See also* Depression of 1893–97
Penn Central Railroad, 161
Pennsylvania, 164
Pennsylvania group of railroads, 26
Pennsylvania Railroad, 9–10, 22, 38, 58, 60, 139, 162, 167, 178, 181
Perkins, Charles E., 96, 100, 136, 178
Philadelphia, Pa., 9–10, 144
Philadelphia & Reading Railroad, 111
Phillips, U. B., 48
Piedmont Air Line, 38
Plant, Henry B., 42, 62, 63
Plant System, 65
Platte River Valley, 71
pools, railroad, 26, 36, 126, 128, 136
Poor's *Manual of Railroads*, 49
Port Royal Railroad, 60
productivity, 15, 152
Progressive movement, 108–109
Promontory Point, Utah, 23, 76
Pulitzer, Joseph, 84
Pullman, George M., 79
Pullman Pacific Car Company, 79–80

rail car exchange, 24
rail gauge differential, 11, 24, 25
rail mileage, 8, 22, 25–26; 1850/1860, 10; 1850/1900, 110; 1860/1890, 13; 1860/1900/1920,

Index

rail mileage (*continued*)
21; 1893, 135; 1900, 156; 1916, 29; dominated by Gould, 96, 99; Illinois Central in 1856, 10–11; Louisville & Nashville in 1873/1880, 37; in the South, 23, 31, 42, 64, 65

rail motor cars, 146, 152

rail travel time, 10, 79, 117, 158

railroads: abuses, 27–29, 66, 111; biographies, 167; block signals, 116; branch lines/feeders/connectors, 10, 13, 59, 60; construction practices (regional differences), 13, 179; critics, 20–21, 27–28, 111, 124, 125, 140–141, 156, 181–183, 185; development (1830–1860, 8, 9–14; 1865–1890, 8, 12–17, 22–23, 111–112, 136, 179–180; *see also* Southern railroads); discriminatory practices, 27, 124–126; diversification, 130–131; financing, 13, 57, 64, 137, 138, 156; freight service, 25, 36, 44, 117, 132, 149; high-speed (*see also* streamliner train), 155–165; histories, 20, 21, 167–173, 177–178 (by Klein, 3, 4, 5; by Stover, 48–51); "insiders"/"outsiders," 179, 180, 181; integration, 11, 24–25; labor force, 150–154; local/outside control, 51, 54, 57, 58, 59, 61; local/through traffic, 79–80, 124–125, 174; modernization, 114–120, 136–137, 156, 157, 180; organizational structure, 16–17, 19–20, 177, 178–179; passenger service, 78–79, 132, 148–149, 157–158, 159–160, 161; profits/dividends, 35, 44, 46, 62, 64–65, 117–118, 153, 157; strikes, 29, 153; switchers, 148, 152; traffic control devices, 24, 25; traffic flow (regional shift), 9, 12, 22. *See also* competition; consolidation; mergers; pools; rates; regulation;
Southern railroads; transcontinental railroads

Railroads: Finance and Organization (Ripley), 171

Railroads: Their Origin and Problems (Adams), 170

Railroads and the Character of America, 1820–1887 (Ward), 168

Railroads Triumphant (Martin), 168–169

Raleigh & Gaston Railroad, 54

Raoul, William G., 40, 51

rates, railroad, 27, 28, 60, 99, 111, 124–126, 136, 137, 174, 181; short haul/long haul, 9, 10, 157–158

Rawlins, John A., 74

Red Desert, 74–75

Reed, Samuel B., 71–73

Reed-Bulwinkle Act of 1948, 131

refrigerator cars, 16

regulation, railroad: federal, 16, 17, 29, 30, 125–132 *passim*, 136, 137, 141, 145, 156–161 *passim*, 172, 181, 185; state, 16, 17, 29, 35, 111, 126, 136, 153

Reid, Harry, 163

Republican party, 12

Richmond, Virginia, 11

Richmond & Danville Railroad, 33, 52, 54, 55, 58, 65

Richmond Terminal (Richmond & West Point Terminal Railway & Warehouse Co.), 3, 4, 26–27, 43, 65, 66

Ripley, William Z., 170–173

Robber Barons, The (Josephson), 170–171

Roberts, George B., 167

Robinson, John M., 50, 53, 54, 62

Rock Island group, 26

Rockefeller, John D., 139

Roosevelt, Theodore, 120, 171, 172–173

rural merchandising, 15–16

224

Index

safety campaigns, 120
Sage, Russell, 88
St. Louis, 11
Salt Lake City, 72
Salt Lake Valley, 71, 72, 75
Sanford, E. J., 50
Santa Fe Railroad. *See* Atchison, Topeka & Santa Fe Railroad
Savannah, Florida & Western Railroad, 33, 42
Schiff, Jacob H., 118, 138
Schumpeter, Joseph, 32, 35
Scott, George S., 62
Scott, Thomas A., 97, 167
Screven, John, 40, 53, 54
sea travel from coast to coast, 13, 70
Seaboard Air Line, 44
Seaboard & Roanoke Railroad, 33, 52, 65
Sears, Roebuck, 16
Selma, Rome & Dalton Railroad, 38
Selover, A. A., 106
Shannon, Fred A., 174
Shepard, Helen Gould, 92
Sherman Antitrust Act, 127, 138, 141
Shoemaker, S. M., 58
shopmen, 150–151
slavery, 12
sleeper cars, 79, 80
Sloan, Samuel, 88
Smith, Henry N., 106
Smith, Milton H., 50, 67
Snow, Alice Northrop, 92
Snyder, Webster, 78
South, the: Southern Reconstruction politics, 23, 28, 36, 56; secession of 1860–1861, 12, 14. *See also* railroads
South and North Alabama Railroad, 37
South Carolina Railroad, 36, 40
Southern Pacific Railroad, 23, 118–120, 127, 140, 141
Southern railroads, 23, 25, 28, 31–47; interterritorial expansion (1880–1893), 41–47, 62–66; leaders and local development (1856–1880), 52–62; leaders and separation of financial/operational controls (1880–1893), 62–66; Northern dominance, 48–51; nuclei, 51–52; territorial expansion (1865–1880), 33–41, 59–62
Southern Railway, The (Davis), 167
Southern Railway and Steamship Association, 36, 61
Southern Railway Company, 27
Southern Railway Security Company, 57–58
Southwestern Railroad, 38, 60
Spencer, Samuel, 50, 67
Spicka, Charlie, 151
stage coach travel, 13, 70, 71–72
Staggers Act of 1980, 132, 161
standard time system, 25
Standiford, E. D., 37, 53
Stanford, Leland, 28, 97, 167
state regulation, 16, 17, 29, 35, 111, 126, 136, 153
state subsidies, 10
steam locomotive, 18–19, 147–148
steamboats, 11
steamships, 60
Stevenson, Vernon K., 50, 53, 54
Stickney, A. B., 125, 126, 170
Stilgoe, John R., 168
Stillman, James, 118
Stover, John F., 25, 48–51, 168
streamliner train, 148–149, 152, 155, 157–160
Stromquist, Shelton, 167
subsidies, 10
Sully, Alfred, 44–45
Supple, Barry E., 55
Supreme Court, 17, 127, 128, 141, 153
Swann, James, 50
Swedish X-2 train, 164
Swift and Company, 16, 145

Taylor, George Rogers, 168
Taylor, Moses, 57

225

Index

telegraph lines, 10, 14. *See also* Western Union
"Texas Triangle" cities, 164
TGV train (France), 164
Thomas, Samuel, 62, 63, 66
Thomson, J. Edgar, 167
3R Act of 1973, 132
time zones, 25
transcontinental railroads, 13, 28, 68–82; competition, 23–24; construction crews, 76; dangers, 80–81; excursionists, 77–78; "Hotel Train," 79–80; passenger service and fares, 78–79; porta-towns, 76–77; surveys, 14, 22, 69–76; trunk lines, 13, 22–23, 28
transcontinental travel, 13, 70
Transportation Act of 1920, 30, 128, 129, 130, 157, 159
Transportation Act of 1940, 131
Transportation Act of 1958, 132
Transrapid train (Germany), 164
truck service, 131, 132
Turbotrain, 162
Twain, Mark, 20, 92

Union Pacific Railroad, 5, 111, 131, 139–140, 162, 178, 181; and diesel locomotive, 146, 147; and Gould, 94, 96, 170; and Harriman, 114–120; "Hotel Train," 79–80; Oregon Short Line, 75, 118; and Southern Pacific, 118–120, 127, 141; streamliner, 148, 152, 158; transcontinental railroad, 14, 23, 68–82 *passim*

Vanderbilt, Cornelius, 28, 167
Vanderbilt, William H., 96, 100, 167, 181

Vanderbilt railroads, 26
Vanderlip, Frank A., 112
Virginia Midland, 43
Visible Hand, The (Chandler), 167

Wabash Railroad, 29, 94, 96, 139
Wadley, William M., 38, 39, 40, 50, 53, 54, 57, 60
Walker, Roberts, 172
Walters, W. T., 57, 58
Ward, James A., 168
Warner, Charles Dudley, 20
Warshaw, Robert I., 92–93, 102
water transport, 9, 11
Waters, Richard, 126
Webster, Daniel, 18
Weeks Committee, 132
Weisberger, Bernard A., 185
West, the, 12–14, 22
Western & Atlantic Railroad, 43
Western Union, 88, 89, 94, 96, 98, 106
Whitman, Walt, 18–19, 69
Wiley, Bell I., 2
Wilmington & Weldon Railroad, 33, 52, 55, 57
Wilson, Richard T., 50, 53, 56, 58
Wilson administration, 29
World War I, 29–30, 128, 157
World War II, 132, 160

X-2 train (Sweden), 164

Yamamura, Kozo, 3
Young, Brigham, 71, 72

Zunz, Olivier, 178